Diasporas and Foreign Direct Investment in China and India

This book offers a comparative and historical analysis of foreign direct investment (FDI) liberalization in China and India and explains how the return of these countries' diasporas affects such liberalization. It examines diasporic investment from Western FDIs and finds that diasporas, rather than Western nations, have fueled globalization in the two Asian giants. In China, diasporas contributed the lion's share of FDI inflows. In India, returned diasporas were bridges for, and initiators of, Western investment at home. Min Ye illustrates that diasporic entrepreneurs helped to build China into the world's manufacturing powerhouse and that Indian diasporas facilitated their homeland's success in software services development.

Min Ye is an assistant professor of international relations and the director of the East Asian Studies Program at Boston University. She has served as a visiting scholar and professor in China, Japan, South Korea, Singapore, and India and has given lectures at Fudan University, Zhejiang University, and the Chinese University of Broadcasting and Mass Media. Her publications include *The Making of Northeast Asia* (with Kent Calder, 2010) and various articles published in such journals as the *Journal of East Asian Studies, Modern China Studies*, and *China Public Affairs Quarterly*. In China, Ye also serves as a consultant on globalization for private and state-run companies and development of special zones in various localities.

Diasporas and Foreign Direct Investment in China and India

MIN YE
Boston University

CAMBRIDGE
UNIVERSITY PRESS

CAMBRIDGE
UNIVERSITY PRESS

32 Avenue of the Americas, New York, NY 10013-2473, USA

Cambridge University Press is part of the University of Cambridge.

It furthers the University's mission by disseminating knowledge in the pursuit of education, learning, and research at the highest international levels of excellence.

www.cambridge.org
Information on this title: www.cambridge.org/9781107054196

First published 2014

Printed in the United States of America

A catalog record for this publication is available from the British Library.

Library of Congress Cataloging in Publication Data
Ye, Min, 1975–
Diasporas and foreign direct investment in China and India / Min Ye.
pages cm
ISBN 978-1-107-05419-6 (hardback)
1. Investments, Foreign – China. 2. Investments, Foreign – India. I. Title.
HG5782.Y425 2014
332.67′30951–dc23 2013048109

ISBN 978-1-107-05419-6 Hardback

To my parents

Ye Jianxin and Xia Aiyu

for the lives they live and the life they gave me

Contents

Illustrations

MAPS

FIGURES

TABLES

Abbreviations

ACMA	Automotive Component Manufacturers Association of India
AIEI	Association of Indian Engineering Industry
AMC	American Motors Company
ASSOCHAM	Associated Chambers of Commerce and Industry of India
BJP	Bharatiya Janata Party
BOP	Balance of payments
BPO	Business process outsourcing
CASI	Center for Advanced Study of India
CCP	Chinese Communist Party
CII	Confederation of Indian Industry
CKD	Completely knocked down
CNAIC	China National Automobile Industry Corporation
CPE	Comparative political economy
DOE	India's Department of Electronics
EEPC	Engineering Export Promotion Council
EHTP	Electronics hardware technology parks
EPZ	Export processing zones
FAW	China's First Auto Works
FDI	Foreign direct investment
FERA	Foreign Exchange Regulations Act
FICCI	Federation of Indian Chambers of Commerce and Industry
FIF	Foreign-invested firm
GIC	General Insurance Corporation
GM	General Motors
HCL	Hindustan Computers Ltd.
HK	Hong Kong
HKSE	Hong Kong Stock Exchange
IFC	International Finance Corporation
IMF	International Monetary Fund

IO	International organization
IPE	International political economy
IPO	Initial public offering
IT	Information technology
JV	Joint venture
LIC	Life Insurance Corporation
MEI	Ministry of the Electronics Industry
MNC	Multinational corporations
MOFTEC	Ministry of Foreign Trade and Economic Cooperation
MOU	Memorandum of understanding
MRTP	Monopolies/istic and Restrictive Trade Practices Act
NASSCOM	National Association of Software and Services Companies
NRI	Nonresident Indian
OCC	Open coastal city
PMO	Prime Minister's Office
PRC	People's Republic of China
QR	Qualitative restriction system
RSS	Rashtriya Swayamsevak Sangh
SEZ	Special economic zone
SIAM	Society of Indian Automobile Manufacturers
SJM	Swadeshi Jagran Manch
SKD	Semi–knocked down
SNT	Social network theory
SOE	State-owned enterprises
SSI	Small-scale industry
STP	Software technology park
TCS	Tata Consultancy Services
UNCTAD	United Nations Conference on Trade and Development
UNESCAP	United Nations Economic and Social Commission in Asia and the Pacific
WTO	World Trade Organization

Preface

Confucius once said, "*Fumu zai, bu yuanxing*" [When parents are alive, do not travel afar]. Generation after generation of Chinese, however, have gone to all corners of the world to seek better lives. They left, but they kept strong emotional and social ties to their homeland, and they returned to contribute to homeland development. Indians also have emigrated to many places to better their livelihood. In various historical junctures, those who left returned to play critical parts in forging a modern India. The transformation of the economies of China and India from socialism to capitalism, from isolationism to globalism, from backwaters of the globe to the world's engines of growth, has drawn on immigrant networks, with the Chinese entrepreneurial diasporas returning to shape liberal foreign direct investment (FDI) policies and Indian professional diasporas coming back to create policies that have resulted in the enormous divergence in the two giants' economic transitions – one heavily reliant on FDI, the other domestic industry-centric.

Diasporas' developmental impact is most effective when domestic politics is open to their influence. When China initiated economic reform, the government made remarkable efforts to build ties to the diaspora, provided incentives for their return, and availed opportunity for their success in their homeland. India's reformist leaders likewise placed diaspora professionals at key positions of apex economic agencies. Diasporas are most developmental if they possess advanced ideas, technology, and resources. The Chinese diaspora entrepreneurs occupied key manufacturing niches in the global market. When they circulated investment home, they made China a "world factory." Many Indian immigrants worked at Western multinational corporations (MNCs), connected their homeland with global funds and technology, and supported the global success of indigenous Indian firms. In short, diasporas are not miracle workers, but they are critical to economic miracles in the historic renaissances of the two Asian giants and ancient civilizations.

This book began as my dissertation project at Princeton University. Professors Lynn White, Atul Kohli, Kent Calder, and Thomas Christensen

MAP 1. Domestic Distribution of Foreign Direct Investment (FDI) Inflows in China (2011)
Note: China has twenty-seven provinces and four provincial-level municipalities. Foreign direct investment has concentrated in the coastal areas, marked in the dark shade, making this region the export hub of the nation. These are places that had substantial out-migration before reform and maintained strong ties to diaspora communities overseas, particularly in Hong Kong, Macao, Taiwan, and Southeast Asia.

have provided unending guidance, support, and encouragement at Princeton and beyond. Friends I made at Princeton continue to lift my spirits and offer companionship in the United States and in Asia. They are Ian Chong, Chunmei Du, Todd Hall, Scott Kastner, Ning Ma, Lanjun Xu, and Enhua Zhang. Most of the research and writing were done in Boston. Thanks to Boston University's leave policies, my colleagues, and the Princeton-Harvard China and the World Program fellowship, I was able to complete the research, write the book, and raise a new family. At Harvard's Fung Library, Nancy Hearst helped with collecting key archives and statistics used in the book.

Outside the United States, I drew on expertise and collections in China, India, Hong Kong, and Singapore while serving as a visiting scholar at the Chinese University of Hong Kong (CUHK), the Chinese Academy of Social Sciences, the Indian Council for Research on International Economic Relations (ICRIER), and the National University of Singapore. Ms. Jean Hung at CUHK availed me of the Universities Service Center's rich collection on China's economic reform. In India, I am indebted to two nameless women librarians at ICRIER and the Jawaharlal Nehru University library who compiled archives on Indian reform.

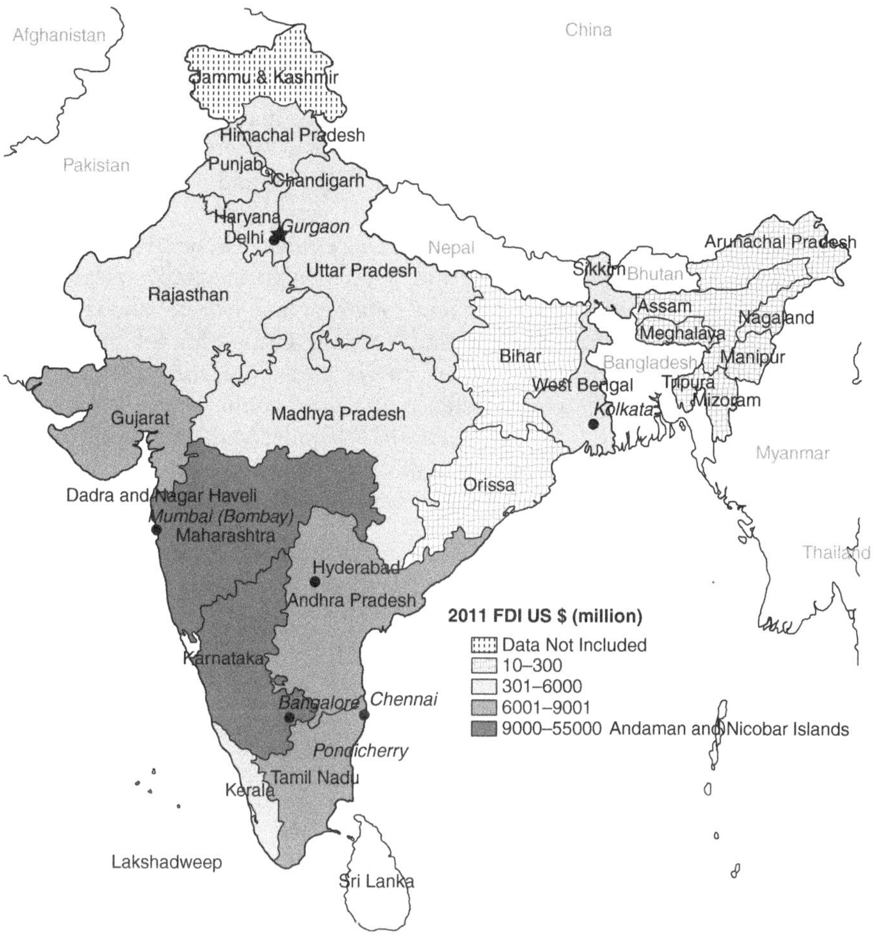

MAP 2. India and Regional Concentration of Foreign Direct Investment (FDI) Inflows (2011)

Note: India has twenty-eight states and seven union territories. Its private economy is most vibrant in South India. Since the 1990s, FDI inflows in India have concentrated in areas with strong indigenous capital such as Mumbai, Bangalore, New Delhi, Chennai, Hyderabad, and the state of Gujarat. Diaspora networks seem to facilitate FDI inflows in Gujarat, Andhra Pradesh, and Tamil Nadu, but not in West Bengal or Kerala.

Over the long years, the project has benefited from advice offered by Thomas Berger, Susan Eckstein, Joseph Fewsmith, Kevin Gallagher, and Williams Grimes at Boston University (BU); Iain Johnston, Tarun Khanna, William Kirby, and Liz Perry at Harvard; and Yongnian Zheng at the National University of Singapore and Devesh Kapur at the University of Pennsylvania.

At Cambridge University Press, I am thankful for senior editor Lew Bateman's interest in acquiring the manuscript and supervision of the review process. I also deeply appreciate Shaun Vigil for guidance throughout the production and the two anonymous reviewers of the manuscript for their comments to improve the book. My research assistants at BU, Sarah Chung, Joshua Lacey, and Damin Zhu, have helped with maps, figures, and statistics used in the book. Best wishes for their careers after BU.

A book project, in the midst of a ticking tenure clock, can be stressful, yet the births of my two daughters, Claire and Sophia (who inevitably delayed the project's completion), somehow made the long process a hopeful and enjoyable journey filled with laughter. My husband Yunrong Chai, a microbiologist, has played a central part in balancing my career and family life. An academic profession ultimately requires persistence and deep commitment, for which I am grateful to my parents who endured the havoc under Mao's rule, experienced dramatic change during reform, and still carry on with unyielding morality, discipline, gratitude, and a strong sense to serve their family and community. To them, I dedicate this book.

PART I

INTRODUCTION AND THEORY

1

Foreign Direct Investment in China and India

In late 1978, when Deng Xiaoping became the leader of the People's Republic of China (PRC), the country embarked on a persistent, and at times turbulent, course of capitalist economic reform. Foreign capital, once shunned in the country, was embraced. At about the same time in India (1980), Indira Gandhi launched a less noticed yet equally significant shift away from socialism toward capitalism. Foreign capital, however, was largely avoided in India until the 1990s. Even then, India's liberalization of foreign direct investment (FDI) was contested and remained constrained. The puzzle in comparing China's and India's economic reforms is not so much which one was doing better but why their paths of liberalization were so different, with one heavily reliant on external investment and the other largely promoting indigenous business.[1] To explain this critical divergence, domestic politics or globalization seems inadequate. Instead, actors transcending national boundaries – embedded in domestic politics yet blessed with global ties, the diasporas of these countries – have played important roles in forging pro-FDI reform in China and pro-domestic-business change in India.

China and India have both experienced substantial emigration for sustained periods throughout their respective histories. And, in both countries, immigrants have circulated back financial and human capital that has helped homeland economic reforms and late industrialization, albeit in different ways. The Chinese entrepreneurial diasporas contributed to their home country's initiation and consolidation of FDI liberalization. The Indian professional diasporas helped influence liberal policy making in their homeland and connected domestic business to global markets and resources. The Indian diasporas,

[1] Other comparative works include Friedman and Gilley (2005), Bardhan (2010), Khanna (2007), and Sharma (2009). There are also publications on China or India that make considerable reference to the other country. See Huang (2008) and Panagariya (2008).

however, have had less impact on FDI liberalization in India than the Chinese diasporas have had on FDI liberalization in China. Indian indigenous industries, although welcoming international funds, technology, and expansion into the world market, imposed more stringent terms on the entry and operation of FDI in the country.

DIASPORAS AND SOCIAL NETWORK THEORY

The study of diasporas' impacts on homeland reform is a lacuna in the literature in international and comparative political economy, and theoretical models that neatly capture and explain diasporas' homeland effects are lacking. To integrate diasporas into the politics of economic reform in China and India, I develop an interdisciplinary social network theory (SNT) that assesses policy makers' internal and external networks (diasporas being one such network) as two explanatory variables for FDI liberalization in developing countries undergoing economic reform. Internal networks in such countries are typically rooted in the previous economic structure, resist new liberal policies, and thus are called "domestic resistance." External networks, conversely, provide new ideas and resources necessary for FDI liberalization either directly or through domestic conduits to policy makers. Across countries, or across time and sectors within a country, these two variables' relative strength influences the prospects of FDI liberalization.

Meanwhile, the SNT posits FDI liberalization as a process of making and implementing new policies and incorporates a diffusion model that analyzes FDI liberalization in two stages: the initiation stage, in which external networks influence policy makers to initiate new FDI policies, and the consolidation stage, wherein policy makers expand FDI liberalization within the country. In the consolidation stage, the early success of the new policy is critical because this success helps policy makers broaden domestic support and overcome domestic opposition. Diaspora networks help in this stage of FDI liberalization by transferring knowledge and resources to those domestic actors who generate early success. By interacting with more domestic actors, diasporas facilitate the diffusion of FDI liberalization in their homeland. The SNT thus comprehensively captures the determinants and effects of FDI liberalization and social interactions among various actors: the state, domestic industries, and external networks (including diasporas).

China and India both have cultural and linguistic complexities that make understanding them and drawing common insights quite difficult. Yet such a comparison offers opportunities to revisit core theories in economic development studies, such as how FDI affects late development, how regime types shape economic reforms, and how states confront and leverage domestic and external networks in the process of globalization. And, as Tony Saich (2005, 227) remarks, "[L]essons about what has worked and what has failed may provide important learning experiences for other lesser-developed countries striving to get out of poverty through shifting to more sustainable economic growth."

Foreign direct investment in China and India speaks to a long-standing debate in the field. Some development scholars have argued against FDI because this form of capital opens a developing economy to powerful and profit-driven Western companies and is likely to increase the country's vulnerability to global market forces.[2] In Atul Kohli's words (2004, 382), foreign capital "can be a liability" because state autonomy weakens with increasing FDI. Some globalists, conversely, have celebrated China's FDI-reliant industrialization as a victory of globalization pursued by Western multinational corporations (MNCs) and international organizations (IOs).[3] More important, almost all debates and writings on FDI have treated such capital as coming from Western MNCs.

The SNT melds the views on economic development and globalization and examines both external and internal actors in shaping FDI liberalization, as well as the effects of FDI on economic development. It finds that external actors have indeed precipitated FDI policy changes in China and India and that the most influential external actors in these countries are their diasporas who have accomplished great success in advanced societies. The Chinese diasporas are primarily entrepreneurs in East Asia, and the Indian diasporas are primarily professionals working at Western MNCs and IOs. Furthermore, diasporas' policy influence was achieved through interactions with policy makers and domestic groups, transferring financial and human capital to produce early success and thereby broadening domestic support for FDI liberalization. Embedded in diaspora networks that possess ideas, technology, and capital, policy makers in China and India have pursued FDI liberalization with great success.

The diffusion analysis proffers that FDI liberalization begins with some domestic actors adopting new policies early on, creating early success that persuades more actors to emulate the policy. Diasporas that provide new ideas and resources help to initiate FDI liberalization, increase the chance of early success, and expedite the diffusion process. In the meantime, policy makers' internally oriented networks play important yet opposite roles. Under strong domestic resistance, FDI liberalization occurs either when external actors strengthen or when domestic resistance weakens or both. In such cases, FDI liberalization proceeds slowly, and crises are often needed to spur major policy change, with domestic networks continuing to contour postcrisis policy consolidation.

[2] The dependency literature in post–World War II decades and the developmental state literature from the 1980s to 1990s both argue against FDI. For more recent critiques of FDI, see Huang (2003) and Huang (2008).

[3] See Friedman (2005) and Gowan (1999). This stance is also expressed by IOs such as the IMF and World Bank, as well as in publications in the *Financial Times*, cited in Wade (2004).

The research finds that diaspora networks were the key drivers of FDI liberalization in China. The impact of the Chinese diasporas existed at both national and local levels: local officials in South China revived ties to diaspora entrepreneurs, with whose help they designed special economic zones (SEZs). Reformist leaders in Beijing also interacted with diaspora entrepreneurs and were positively inclined toward opening the country's economy. Despite strong conservative resistance in the national government, ideas and incentives provided by wealthy diaspora entrepreneurs supported local governments' pursuit of FDI and enabled SEZs to achieve early success, thereby strengthening the reformist coalition and sustaining FDI liberalization in the country. In the open coastal cities, high-tech development zones, and reform of state-owned enterprises, diaspora entrepreneurs were the external allies of the government at the local level, supplying capital, technology, and global commerce. The diffusion process also reveals the importance of the Chinese state that provided domestic opportunities to diasporas, encouraged diaspora networks to form, and relied on diaspora resources to generate industrial success. In short, the state's external embeddedness, fostered by the state itself, greatly enhanced its political strength in forging economic reform.

With regard to India, the relative strength of domestic resistance and external networks also explains the nonoccurrence and occurrence of FDI liberalization across time and sectors. The social network approach reveals that indigenous private producers influenced Mrs Gandhi's domestic deregulation in 1980. Yet indigenous producers also constituted the domestic resistance to FDI liberalization attempted by Rajiv Gandhi in the mid-1980s. In the 1990s, Indian policy makers were armed with liberal ideas and implemented FDI liberalization in the aftermath of the 1991 debt crisis. Yet postcrisis policy consolidation was again constrained by domestic resistance. Indian diasporas were primarily professionals in the West. Although supplying liberal ideas and at times bridging Indian industry with global markets, their developmental strength was less than that of the Chinese entrepreneurial diasporas and their effect on India's FDI was more limited.[4] After 2000, Indian indigenous industry, facilitated by diasporas, was transformed and developed robust external ties to Western companies; FDI liberalization moved forward but with clear constraints.

Understanding diasporas' central position and unpacking diaspora investment from other FDI leads to a more nuanced assessment of FDI and development. Many have argued that China's dependence on FDI is a source of domestic instability and have predicted large-scale nationalist backlashes against globalization.[5] By contrast, India's lesser reliance on FDI is viewed as a strength.[6]

[4] One of the main diaspora groups is contractual laborers in the Gulf. They are quite important in helping grassroots welfare by sending remittances. Their impact on FDI is minimal, however.

[5] See, for example, Huang (2003) and Gallagher (2005).

[6] See Huang and Khanna (2003).

However, because of their shared linguistic and cultural heritage, Chinese diaspora investors tend to work with domestic political and economic actors. Their operations in China have not roused domestic backlash and likely remain a stabilizing force in "Greater China."[7] In India, nonethnic investors dominate FDI. Although amounting to only a fraction of that in the PRC, FDI in India has been more contested. If nationalism does engender domestic backlash against FDI, it is more likely to occur in India than in China.[8]

FDI AND FDI POLICIES IN CHINA AND INDIA

China and India have comparable pre-reform economic-political conditions that make their divergence in FDI liberalization puzzling. First, both had large populations and territories, granting them similar factors of endowment (cheap land and low labor costs). Second, India and China both had poor infrastructure and dreadful living conditions, which discouraged Westerners from coming to these countries.[9] Third, both countries pursued socialism after independence, although China's Maoism was more extreme than Jawaharlal Nehru's system in India. Their prior institutional barriers to FDI were thus comparable. Fourth, the two countries have venerable traditions and have suffered from Western aggression in the modern era, making their elites intensely nationalistic. Ideological opposition to FDI and fear of foreign imposition were highly analogous. Despite all these similarities, FDI liberalization during their economic transitions has been decidedly different, and FDI has played a much stronger role in China than in India.

Contrasting FDI Liberalization in China and India

A narrow definition limits FDI liberalization to the passing of formal laws and regulations on the entry and operation of foreign companies. In this book, FDI liberalization is broader and refers to an economy's increasing openness to FDI and thus includes not only formal rules and laws but also policy implementation and other important provisions that matter to foreign investors. This broadening is necessary in transition economies where formal policies are often conflicting and have yet to establish credibility with investors. Informal institutions, perceptions, and attitudes are important supplements to and sometimes sufficient substitutes

[7] "Greater China" refers to areas surrounding southern China, including Hong Kong, Macao, Taiwan, and Southeast Asia (Naughton 1997).

[8] Exception should be made for Japanese investment in China, which is plagued by Chinese anti-Japan nationalism. Yet China's anti-FDI backlashes are few and not caused by diaspora investment in general.

[9] See, for example, Joydee Mukherji, "The Causes of Differential Development," and Subramanian Swamy, "Chasing China," in Friedman and Gilley (2005).

for official decrees. Dani Rodrik and Arvind Subramanian once explained, "[India's] government's attitudinal change toward business," prior to concrete policy measures, was a sufficient driver that "unleashed the animal spirits of [the] Indian private sector" (Rodrik and Subramanian 2004, 2).

Such a broad definition of FDI liberalization is consistent with the United Nations Conference on Trade and Development (UNCTAD), which surveys investors on factors determining their foreign investment decisions. The UNCTAD surveys find that formal regulations are but one of the five conditions to be considered: investors additionally examine whether the country offers preferential incentives, workable infrastructure, appropriate labor, and clear governing bodies that they can relate to. A pro-FDI regime thus strives to provide all these conditions to foreign investors. Conversely, a country that passes a bill allowing FDI and yet continues restrictions and fails to offer favorable conditions is hardly an FDI-welcoming site. The enduring divergence between China and India includes all the five factors and is summarized in Table 2.1 in Chapter 2.

Because of the intricate nature of formal policies and other conditions entailed in FDI liberalization, UNCTAD ranks nations by FDI performance and FDI potential and uses these indicators to measure the effect of policy liberalization and to categorize countries as front runners, above potential, below potential, and underperformers. The 2006 *World Investment Report* provides the specific ranking positions for China's and India's FDI liberalization in 1990 and 2004. Demonstrated in Table 1.1, China was persistently a front runner, and its ranking improved from 1990 to 2004. India was an underperformer in both years, and its ranking fell in the same period. In recent years, UNCTAD stopped providing countries' specific rankings but continued to categorize countries' attraction and performance regarding FDI.

The assessments of China and India in Table 1.1 still hold for the more recent categorizations by UNCTAD. According to the agency's 2012 *World Investment Report*, using FDI attraction (in place of the FDI performance score)

TABLE 1.1. *Ranking China and India's Foreign Direct Investment (FDI) Liberalization (of 141 countries)*

	FDI Performance		FDI Potential	
	1990	2004	1990	2004
China *Frontrunner*	52	45	41	33
India *Underperformer*	101	112	76	82

Note: Both developed and developing countries are included in the rankings. China, although ranked only forty-fifth in FDI performance and thirty-third in FDI potential in 2004, is one of the few frontrunners in the developing world. Most other developing countries categorized as frontrunners have economies solely based on resource production or tourism.

and potential indexes, India remains in the "way below expectation" category after controlling for its economic size, labor, infrastructure, geography, and so forth. The *Report* suggests that India "may wish to explore policy options and innovations in comparable economies" (UNCTAD 2012, 65). The same report finds that China not only remains "above expectation" in attracting FDI but also has higher per unit FDI contributions to employment, exports, revenue, research and development (R&D), wages, value, and capital formation than the normal rate in the world.

Statistical indicators suggest that China's FDI liberalization was clearly ahead of India's from 1980 to 2010. In terms of global shares of FDI inflows, China's starting rate in 1980 was below India's. With FDI liberalization, China increased its advantage over India rapidly. In 1994, the gap between FDI in China and India was 13 percent in China's favor. In that year, Chinese diaspora investment comprised 76 percent of FDI in the PRC. Since 2005, China has become an important source of FDI, and its global share of FDI inflows has gradually evened out. The gap between the two countries remains: In 2011, the PRC's global share was 8.1 percent and India's was 2 percent. Diaspora investment in China declined but remains substantial at 66 percent of total FDI.

Compared to other developing countries, FDI liberalization sets China and India as two outliers on the spectrum of FDI inflows. Figure 1.1 shows the trends in China, India, and three Latin American (LA) countries before and after 1990, respectively, because the FDI volumes of the two periods were significantly different. The first chart shows that, in the 1970s, both India and China had less FDI than the LA countries (Argentina, Brazil, and Mexico) but also that India had sizably more FDI than China. The 1980s, however, witnessed China surpassing the other countries by growing margins, whereas India's FDI remained significantly lower than all three LA countries.

In the second chart in Figure 1.1, showing the trends in the 1990s, the five countries have unanimously attracted more FDI; yet the Chinese FDI growth rate was remarkably higher than that of the LA nations, and India's growth rate was clearly lower, despite India's policy reform. Only after 2005 did India attract more FDI than Argentina and Mexico, as these two LA countries stumbled in their openness to foreign investment. Since 2008, India's FDI inflows have declined, whereas China's have increased further, widening the gap between the two countries.

These statistics, as well as those to follow, demonstrate the empirical contrast between China's and India's FDI liberalization. There are two possible concerns with these statistics: round-tripping and overreporting in China. Round-tripping refers to Chinese domestic capital flown out of China and then returning disguised as FDI. Yasheng Huang (1998) studied such round-tripping FDI and estimated it at roughly 25 percent of FDI in China in 1992–1994, a period when round-tripping was thought high. Round-tripping FDI, however, does not challenge the argument here but rather serves as evidence that policies toward FDI

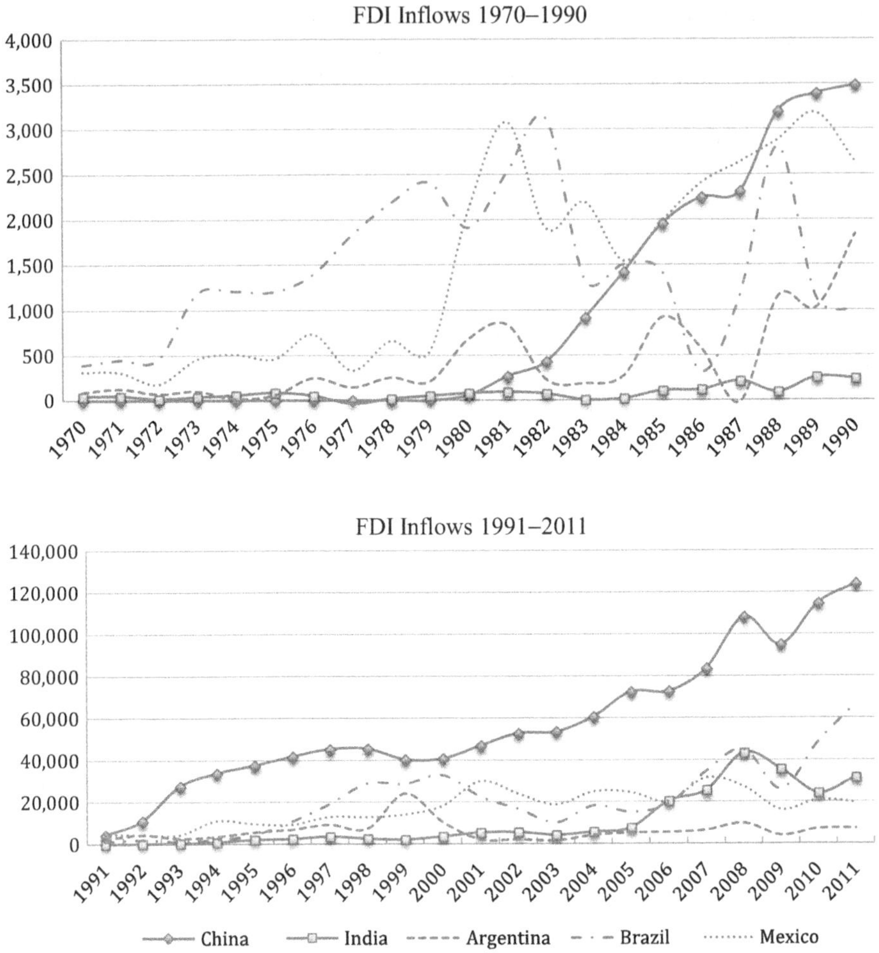

FIGURE 1.1. Foreign Direct Investment Inflows in Comparative Perspective ($Mi)
Source: Original data are from UNCTADstat.

were highly beneficial and that FDI liberalization was profound in China.[10] It also demonstrates that domestic investors could strategically exploit diaspora linkages to overcome institutional constraints and influence the home state in rather creative ways.

[10] Huang (1998) arrived at the figures by comparing the increase in FDI from Hong Kong with those from Southeast Asia and Japan and categorized the "extra" rate in Hong Kong FDI as caused by round-tripping. However, as this study hypothesizes and establishes, due to Hong Kong's geographic, ethnic, and political ties to the mainland, investors from Hong Kong were more forthcoming in China than were investors of other origins.

Several studies have noted China's overreporting of FDI. Guy Pfeffermann (2002, 2003) argues that actual inflows into China were only half the size that official statistics suggest. S. Srivastava (2003) and R. Nagaraj (2003) cited and circulated the Pfeffermann finding in India. A close examination of the International Finance Corporation (IFC) report, on which Pfeffermann's assessment was based, reveals that this halving of China's figure was done mainly by excluding FDI coming from Hong Kong and Macao.[11] Given that Hong Kong and Macao were the largest "foreign" investors in China, the drastic reduction of FDI was not surprising. Along the same line, an argument was made for reassessing India's reporting of FDI because India used accounting standards that were more restrictive than the International Monetary Fund (IMF) standards. India's underreporting has not been an issue since 2001, when India revised and updated its FDI statistics to be on par with global standards. Like round-tripping, overreporting FDI was not extraneous to FDI liberalization. Precisely because China had preferential policies toward FDI and government officials were desirous of FDI, overreporting occurred more frequently.

FDI Has Had Divergent Impacts on China and India

Foreign direct investment has played different roles in China's and India's national economies and their integration into the world. Prior to 1980, India had more FDI, and exports accounted for a larger share of its gross domestic product (GDP), than China. In 2000, when both countries were admitted into the World Trade Organization (WTO), India was significantly behind China in FDI inflows and openness. The WTO acceptance marked the general completion of their economic transitions from socialism to capitalism. The UNCTAD thus compiled detailed statistics on the roles of FDI in both countries, by assessing FDI inflows, stocks, and foreign affiliates in the countries, as well as FDI's contribution to imports and exports, and concluded that FDI had far greater effects on China than on India.

Table 1.2 updates the UNCTAD study with data from the 2013 UNCTAD database and comprehensively compares the roles of FDI in China and India. Such a comparison takes many data points, and the most current year for all data points was 2004. Since then, India has had more FDI, and China has also gained strongly from surging FDI in the country. The gaps between the two countries' FDI volume and performance persisted, as shown in Figure 1.1. The 2012 *World Investment Report* evaluated China as being "above expectation" and India as being "way below expectation" in FDI liberalization, as mentioned earlier.

In Table 1.2, China attracted more than ten times as much FDI inflow as India, and China's FDI stock was about seven times India's. As a share of GDP, FDI stock was about 13 percent in China and a little more than 5 percent in India. In regard to the number of foreign affiliates, China had more than 40,000

[11] See World Bank (2002). *Global Development Finance Report*. Washington, DC: World Bank

TABLE 1.2. *Comparing Foreign Direct Investment (FDI) in China and India*

FDI Statistics	*FDI inflows ($bi)*	*FDI stock ($bi)*	*FDI stock/ GDP (%)*	*FDI flows per capita ($)*
China	60.6	245.5	12.7	46.8
India	5.8	38	5.3	5.1
Foreign-invested firms (FIFs)	*Number*	*Assets ($bi)*	*Sales ($bi)*	*Profits ($bi)*
China	42,753	579	698.7	41.7
India	518	22	34	3.95
FDI-led Exports	*FDI-Exports ($bi)*	*FDI-Imports ($bi)*	*Share of national exports (%)*	
China	338.6	324.6	57.1	
India	3.8	5.7	5	

Source: Original statistics are from WDI database, UNCTAD, FDI/TNC database, 2013.

foreign-invested firms (FIFs) and India only around 500. The total assets, sales, and profits of these FIFs as a whole were much higher in China than in India. Table 1.2 also indicates that FDI has contributed to China's and India's external sectors rather differently. China's exports and imports by FIFs were both more than $300 billion.[12] The comparative numbers in India were barely $4 billion (exports) and $6 billion (imports). China's FDI-led exports accounted for 57 percent of its total exports. India's FDI-led exports accounted for only 5 percent. The gap between the two countries' exports persisted. In 2006, China overtook the United States to become the second largest exporter in the world, whereas India ranked twenty-ninth. In 2011, India became the world's nineteenth largest exporter. China has been the world's top exporter since 2009.

POLITICAL THEORIES OF FDI LIBERALIZATION

This book draws on insights from multiple disciplines: immigration, sociology, business, and public policy. The SNT, however, is posited as a political framework to analyze state–society interactions during economic reform. Its chief competing arguments are the political theories of economic liberalization available in international and comparative political economy. International political economy (IPE) publications emphasize global forces as driving liberalization in developing countries, and students of comparative political economy (CPE) stress domestic polity. They each present specific arguments that the following pages review. A number of works covering either China's or India's liberalization are further examined in the country-specific chapters.

[12] Unless specified otherwise, all currency ($) in the text refers to U.S. dollars.

First, IPE works strive to determine the global agents of liberalization in developing countries; focus on hegemonic powers, IOs, and MNCs; and generally neglect immigrants of developing nations. Immanuel Wallerstein (1979), for example, argues that advancement of nations from the periphery to the semiperiphery is difficult and happens through "accepting invitation from core nations." Robert Keohane (1980), Robert Gilpin (1987), Stephen Krasner (2000), and David Lake (2000) affirm America's role in spreading economic liberalism worldwide. John Williamson (2002) and Ngaire Woods (2006) point to the importance of international organizations. Robert Wade (1998–1999) suggests that America's MNCs heavily influenced the agenda of IOs and pressured for global financial liberalization. Beth Simmons and her coauthors (Simons and Elkins 2004 Elkins, Guzman, and Simmons 2006; Simmons et al. 2009) recently reported that U.S.-based financial regulators led the diffusion of financial liberalization in the world. Simmons and her coauthors concur that policy makers of developing countries are pressured to reform because they compete among themselves for financial resources available in advanced nations.

Second, students of IPE have noted the importance of crises, which often originate externally and reduce domestic resistance to liberalization. The mixture of precrisis social groups and postcrisis policy implementation are often not analyzed, however. Stephan Haggard (1990) sees crisis as the key condition of policy innovation and compares different responses to crises in East Asia. Because political leaders are crucial to rallying coalitional support for liberalization (Haggard and Webb 1993), crises enhance leadership and help them pursue difficult reforms (Haggard and Maxfield 1996). Peter Gourevitch (1986) centers on politics after crises: how crises cause policy change and how crises interact with underlying political factors – mechanisms of representation, the organization of the state, ideology, and coalition politics. Helen Milner (1988a; 1988b) examines domestic industries' responses to crises and argues that the more internationalized the industry, the more likely it advocates liberalization.

Third, IPE studies have also examined the relationship between political regimes and FDI flows. Different from comparative politics and SNT, these studies are interested in finding global patterns of relationship, and their arguments are quite divided. Arguing for democracy, Mancer Olson (1993) maintains that democracy enhances property rights for investors and therefore facilitates FDI inflows. Nathan Jensen (2004; 2008) also finds that executive constraints help democracies attract more FDI, using a large cross-time dataset. Sonal Pandya (2007) establishes that democratic politicians, in order to cultivate votes with consumers, are less likely to restrict FDI than are autocrats because FDI benefits consumers. Edward Mansfield, Helen Milner, and Peter Rosendorff (2000) and Milner and Keiko Kubota (2005) find that democratization is robustly associated with open trade policies. Arguing for autocracy, IPE publications cite Guillermo O'Donnell (1978; 1988) and Peter Evans (1979) in reporting that more FDI goes to autocracies because of collusion between foreign investors and autocrats in developing countries. John Oneal (1994) disproves democracy's positive impact, and Adam Resnick (2001) suggests that democratic transition even reduces FDI inflows. Li and Resnick (2003) find that only property-rights-related institutions in democracies are associated with more FDI inflows and that other democratic institutions have negative impacts.

The controversy on political regimes remains lively in IPE, and several recent publications question the arguments for autocracy. Using large-*n* statistics, John Ahlquist (2006) proves that stable democracy attracts FDI. Shannon and Robert Blantons (2007) find human rights, better in democracies than in autocracies, have a positive effect on FDI inflows. Choi (2009), especially, argues that the positive association between autocracy and FDI found in the earlier literature was due to China's outlier position.[13] A recent work even finds that common law systems attract more FDI than other legal systems.[14] Against such findings on a global scale, China and India are stark outliers. India is a democracy and arguably has better human rights and a more advanced judicial system than China, yet its FDI is only a fraction of China's.

IPE scholars investigate cross-national policy liberalization toward FDI and generally do not consider domestic diffusion of FDI liberalization. By contrast, the comparative literature takes domestic politics of liberalization seriously and offers mechanisms for how and why democracy slows policy change. The arguments fall into two forms. On the one hand, scholars emphasize the importance of leaders, their policy preferences and political strength. On the other, interest group political models stress the constraining effect of social forces. The intellectual base of both arguments is the same: state capacity and political regimes influence state capacity.

On leadership, Atul Kohli (1989) and Susan Shirk (1994) studied economic reforms in India and China, respectively, and arrived at analogous conclusions. Both argued that leaders' political intentions explained the initiation of economic reforms and the concrete policies that they adopted. Specifically, Indira Gandhi's intention to win business voters led to deregulation, and Deng Xiaoping's wish to weaken his more conservative political rivals led to liberalization that benefited local officials and diaspora investors. On the 1990s reform, Rob Jenkins (1999) and James Manor (2005) argue that Narasimha Rao's reign in India from 1991 to 1996 was the key factor in India's FDI liberalization. In China, Victor Shih (2008) examines elite politics as an explanation for China's financial liberalization or the lack thereof. Hongbin Cai and Daniel Treisman (2005; 2006) collaboratively argue for the centrality of Chinese leaders in spurring the country's economic miracle.

[13] Li (2009) later offered a rebuttal to Choi's criticism.

[14] See Staats and Biglaiser (2011).

The flip side of leadership capacity is "constraining social forces," again derived from political regimes. Comparative literature has blamed interest groups for blocking the adoption of liberal policies that political leaders try to promote. Adam Przeworski (1991), Pranab Bardhan (1993), and Kohli (2004) all point out that democracies are more susceptible to interest group pressure. For development to succeed, Bardhan argues that policy makers "need strong insulation against the ravages of short-run pork-barrel politics and the inevitable lobbies of group predation." He also observes that "this is unthinkable in India" (Bardhan 1993, 46). Similarly, Kohli (1987, 33) notes that "the democratic element of the regime tends to tie the state to organized social interests" and that over time, "the autonomy of the state typically declines." Philip Keefer and Stuti Khemani (2009) shed light on democratic capture by electoral dynamics and reveal that legislators provide more "pork" to their party weakholds to cultivate votes. Democracy, in their views, makes it harder to build durable policy consensus and sustain economic reform in India (with FDI liberalization being one part).[15]

The comparative literature seems to imply that in state–society interactions, states (or leaders) want reform but societal groups resist change. The literature also implies that democracies are less adept at economic reform and that autocracies, which are capable of forcing societal resistance into compliance, are better equipped to conduct policy innovations. The praise for authoritarianism and criticism of democratic weakness has a long origin among political scientists (e.g., Barrington Moore 1969; Samuel Huntington 1968). The implied conclusions based on regimes, however, fail to accommodate more nuanced similarities (and differences) between China and India. "After all," says Edward Friedman, "it matters that India is a democracy and China is not. But precisely how it matters or how much it matters is not obvious" (Friedman and Gilley 2005, 7).

Another drawback of the comparative literature is its failure to incorporate changes in the globalized world and how external linkages influence domestic politics of economic reform. Indeed, in both China and India, liberalization has varied considerably over time and across sectors. And with globalization, the incentives of domestic groups have shifted and their ability to influence the state has greatly varied from the past. With external linkages on their own, domestic actors can push back institutional constraints and profoundly transform existing institutions without fighting a head-on battle with the state. External actors, particularly diasporas, can thus play decisive roles in shaping domestic development by providing new ideas and incentives to indigenous players.

[15] Aseema Sinha's work on political decentralization in India offers a rebuttal to such arguments. Sinha (2005a) explains how subnational politicians formed "winners coalitions" with national leaders and helped to promote and sustain reform in India.

Political regimes are important, and authoritarian leaders may have more power than democratically elected officials, although they rarely use that power to pursue new economic policies due to economic uncertainties and the political risks of new policies. Joel Migdal (2001) theorizes that the state consists of different political coalitions, just as society is "a web of mélange" composed of diverse interest groups. A new policy inevitably has pros and cons and benefits some and harms others. If it challenges the core social groups, authoritarian leaders are just as likely, if not more likely, than democratic politicians to withhold its adoption. Policy makers' decisions on new policies draw on information and resources that are offered by some actors to neutralize the others, and that is where external networks can play crucial parts in economic transformation in both autocracies and democracies. By supplying new ideas and incentives, they influence the policy positions of key interest groups within the country.

Diasporas, due to co-ethnicity that may dictate similarity in language, culture, and ancestral localities, have an easier time forming ties to state and societal actors in homelands than do nonethnic foreigners. Operating between homelands and global markets, diaspora entrepreneurs are uniquely positioned to propel FDI liberalization in developing nations. Diaspora professionals, recipients of liberal ideas and knowledge from abroad, become agents in bringing such ideas back home. Charles Tilly thus views diaspora–homeland relations as likely "trust networks" and maintains that "by sniffing out the operation of trust networks," students of development "can have a splendid opportunity to illuminate fundamental social processes that go on throughout the world" (Tilly 2007, 16). Rubin Patterson (2006, 1894) concurs: "Strategic collaboration and brain circulation between diaspora and homeland" underlie successful late industrialization in the world. Anthropological and business studies have also supported that diaspora connections transform domestic views of globalization and affect firms' investment flows and strategies.[16] John Kao, policy advisor to Senator Hilary Clinton, has described cross-border diaspora investment as creating the "Chinese commonwealth" (Kao 1993, 32).

The globalization and political economy literature is yet to fully engage the policy role of diaspora networks.[17] The SNT of FDI liberalization analyzes the important yet somewhat different activity of diaspora networks during China

[16] An important message in Xiang (2006) is that India's information technology (IT) body shopping not so much transferred technology or resources to homeland but produced "the desire to go abroad" and the embrace of diasporas in India. For investment literature on diaspora networks, see Yeung (1997), Chen and Chen (1998), and Hsing (1996, 1998). Chen and Chen (1998), particularly, trace the locational choices and coping strategies of Taiwan-based investors on the Mainland. From an international finance perspective, David Leblang (2010) confirms that diaspora networks enhanced both FDI and portfolio investment from host to homeland.

[17] Kapur (2010) provides the long-awaited exception, profiling diaspora connections between India and the United States.

and India's reforms. By incorporating diaspora impact into state–society interactions in the two opposite political systems, it shows that political institutions and social networks are not mutually exclusive. Conceptually and empirically, they are interactive, and when their effects work in one direction we observe the most profound policy change and development results. Social network theory is thus an addition to political forces operating in China and India. By explicating the diffusion process, the theory also sheds light on decentralization and experimentalism as contributing factors to institutional innovation in the two countries.[18]

FDI liberalization embodies long-term policy change, and some variables in previous works may have influenced specific episodes. For example, leadership expedited China's FDI liberalization in 1984, and India's 1991 debt crisis (along with international pressure) clearly helped its liberalization. Furthermore, diasporas do not act alone but serve as channels for ideas and resources that help policy making and implementation. Although stressing diaspora networks, the empirical analysis extensively engages individual leaders, local governments, domestic industries, and Western MNCs. However, in explaining the persistently divergent pathways of FDI liberalization in China and India (one started early and advanced profoundly, and the other began slowly and proceeded haltingly), the two countries' capitalist social networks – diasporas and indigenous industry – need to be underscored. The interactive effect of diaspora and domestic industry further supports the policy impact of diaspora networks, which not only provide ideas to help policy makers initiate change but also help overcome domestic opposition by providing material incentives.

China and India are the two largest countries in the world, and each has unique historical circumstances and institutional legacies that shape its economic reforms.[19] How representative are their experiences against other developing nations in the world, and how generalizable are findings in this book? In the conclusion, I deal with these questions directly and explain the historical and institutional contexts of the two countries. Nevertheless, the key findings of SNT should apply to other countries' adoption of new liberal policies; namely, the importance of external ideas and resources, the early success and diffusion stages, and the critical roles of diaspora networks. In both China and India, one policy lesson is clear: Diasporas can be developmental. To international organizations and wealthy nations interested in helping late development: Allow immigrants from poor nations, and give them upward opportunities. And to developing countries keen on growth: Promote outmigration and embrace their return.[20] Chinese leader Deng Xiaoping was indeed a development expert:

[18] As provided in Weingast (1995), Sinha (2005a), and Heilmann (2008).

[19] See Roderick MacFarquhar, "Introduction," in Friedman and Gilley (2005).

[20] A similar thought was expressed strongly by Indian diaspora development scholar/policy adviser, Jagdish Bhagwati (2002, 315–373).

earnestly engaging the return of entrepreneurial émigrés while radically freeing outmigration to Western societies.[21]

CHAPTER OUTLINES

Chapter 2 explains SNT and specifies external networks and domestic resistance as two causal variables of FDI liberalization. Parts II and III offer the national comparison between China and India. Part II has two chapters – Chapters 3 and 4 – and explains the divergence in China and India's liberalization in the 1980s: One went for FDI, whereas the other pursued domestic deregulation. Part III also has two chapters – Chapters 5 and 6 – and compares the two countries' FDI liberalization since the 1990s. The two China chapters (3 and 5) demonstrate an ever-deepening diffusion of FDI liberalization since 1980, and the two India chapters (4 and 6) reveal a faltering process in comparison. These chapters suggest that policies adopted in different stages of liberalization are interconnected and that what happens in the more recent period has its origins in the early reforms.

Chapter 3 in Part II addresses how diaspora entrepreneurs contributed to the early initiation and rapid consolidation of FDI liberalization in China. Chapter 4 traces the growing private business networks since the 1970s and explains how these networks shaped Indira and Rajiv Gandhi's reforms in the 1980s. In Part III, Chapter 5 explains how Chinese entrepreneurial diasporas led to "zone fever" after 1992 and influenced the national government's effort to reform state-owned enterprises. Chapter 6 discusses India's 1991 debt crisis and the FDI liberalization that came in its aftermath. This chapter focuses on the impact of indigenous business on liberalization after the 1991 episode and demonstrates how these networks resulted in partial opening to FDI. The chapter then offers a discussion of the changed social basis of India's economic reform: inflows of Western MNCs, internationalized business elites, active local governments, and immigrant ties between India and the United States.

After these accounts at the national level, Part IV consists of two chapters that present paired comparisons of the electronics and automobiles sectors in China and India. By holding national polity constant, Chapter 7 focuses on how diaspora entrepreneurs shaped FDI liberalization in electronics and how the lack of diaspora networks and strong domestic resistance affected liberalization in the automotive sector. State preferences and initial policies were comparable in those sectors. Chapter 8 finds that FDI liberalization in India's informatics industry has been rapid thanks to strong diaspora networks and relatively weak domestic resistance. The automotive sector more closely follows India's overall

[21] Deng's personal request to President Carter upon the 1979 Sino–U.S. normalization was to open the door to Chinese immigrants as soon as possible.

difficulty in embracing FDI, in which domestic resistance supersedes diaspora networks. Subsector dynamics, especially between hardware and software in informatics, and other sectors are also included to add validity to social network analysis.

The last chapter concludes with empirical and theoretical findings and addresses policy implications. It once again situates this project in the reform literature in international and comparative political economy. Moreover, the last chapter synthesizes findings on diaspora and development and posits the significance of newly emerging transnational diasporas to development studies and how comparative diasporas may offer a new focus for future research.

2

Social Network Theory

Diasporas, Domestic Industry, and the Diffusion of FDI Liberalization

Sociologists have stressed diaspora networks and hypothesized their effects on homeland development. Charles Tilly (2007, 5) comments, "Migration flows are serious business, not only for the individuals and families involved, but also for whole national economies." Sidney Tarrow (2009, xiii) maintains, "The most effective transnational activists are people who grow up in and remain closely linked to domestic networks and opportunities even after moving away from their home country," those whom he calls "rooted cosmopolitans." Alejandro Portes, an immigration expert at Princeton University, synthesizes that different types of migrants (entrepreneurial vs. labor) and circularity (to what extent diasporas return to their homeland) have resulted in varied developmental effects in their homelands (Portes, 2013).

Specific cases of diaspora networks are abundant. Robert Smith (2000) shows that a hometown association connecting New York City with Ticuani in Mexico regularly intervenes in Ticuani affairs to the extent of financing water supplies and backing candidates for public office. Sarah Mahler (2001) finds that immigrants traveling between Salvador and New York City play crucial parts in moving goods, money, and information to homelands. Inbom Choi (2003) substantiates diasporas' role in facilitating foreign direct investment (FDI) into South Korea. Kirsten Schuttler (2007) and Bettina Schulte (2008) likewise support a facilitative role regarding Moroccan diasporas and Turkish migrants living in Germany. Even in Cuba, immigrant ties have shifted the economic practices of local actors without transforming the state (Eckstein 2004; 2013). Several studies relating to Asian capitalism have noted diaspora investment in South China and how the social capital of overseas Chinese became drivers of commercial activities across borders (Vogel 1989; Hamilton 1991; Weidenbaum and Hughes 1995; Hsing 1998; Wang Hongying 2001).[1]

[1] On the importance of informal institutions, see also Kellee Tsai (2004; 2007) on informal coping strategies of private business, and Lily Tsai (2007) on solidary groups as a remedy for local accountability in social provision.

Vanita Shastri (1997) and Devesh Kapur (2010) document the importance of diaspora–domestic elites' connections to India's economic policy and development.

The political literature on economic reform, as reviewed in Chapter 1, has not adequately accounted for such diaspora phenomena for a number of reasons.[2] One, the types of diasporas emphasized in this book (those who succeeded in amassing financial and human capital in developed economies and then circulating it back to homelands when opportunity rose) are more recent developments, driven by technological breakthroughs in global transportation and communication.[3] Two, the continuing divide between international political economy (IPE) and comparative politics (CP) creates hurdles because IPE focuses on global forces and CP stresses domestic actors and institutions, whereas diasporas are in-between. And finally, policy studies normally focus on policy makers' interest calculations and political capacity and have not taken relational factors seriously.[4] It is thus difficult to operationalize the influence of diasporas that are external but possess considerable ties with domestic actors and, although material incentives play a part, are "dedicated" to homeland development.

Compared to nonethnic external actors, diasporas are potentially stronger policy networks in the homeland. First, diasporas are likely to engage their homelands earlier and with more dedication than are nonethnic investors (Patterson 2006) because coethnic ties typically produce "a sense of sympathy and solidarity" (Safran 1991). Second, interactions between diaspora and domestic actors are likely to be more trusted and lasting, constituting what Charles Tilly (2007) calls "trust networks." Good relations facilitate the transfer of ideas and resources from outside to domestic actors. Third, as economics and business scholars find, diaspora networks help to overcome institutional and infrastructural barriers and reduce transaction costs in investing in underdeveloped homeland markets (Chen and Chen 1998). Last, there is a coalitional effect of diaspora networks. By sharing linguistic convenience and local norms (Hsing 1998), diasporas are more likely to involve local officials and smaller economic actors, whereas, conversely, Westerners prefer dealing with national bureaucracies and leading corporations. And multilevel domestic support enhances economic liberalization.

Diasporas may not possess these prescribed characteristics and may fail to play the development roles hypothesized here. To start, diasporas may not have the new ideas and resources that are instrumental to policy making. Numerous labor immigrants who struggle at the bottom strata of Western societies are unlikely to facilitate policy innovations in their homelands. Only diasporas who make head way in such societies have access to more advanced ideas and more

2 New studies have begun to rectify this gap. See McClurg and Young (2011), Kahler (2009), and Mercer (2010).

3 The previous migration scholars were critical of out-migration, and only in the new millennium have scholars and policy makers noted its potential positive roles. See Cohen (2008); Eckstein (2013).

4 Mark Blyth (2002) offers a systematic criticism of these assumptions. Kapur (2010) also criticizes the missing leg in globalization literature – immigration across borders.

abundant resources. Second, diasporas may not want to return, let alone form "trust networks." The Cubans living in the United States harbor animosity toward their homeland government and are unlikely to circulate ideas and resources that may help the regime to grow. Third, homeland institutions and opportunities directly shape the ties that diasporas build with domestic elites and can amplify or lessen diaspora impacts. The state and domestic interest groups emphasized in previous political studies are the integral and interactive conditions of diaspora networks and constitute the other explanatory variable of social network theory (SNT).

SNT AS A NEW POLICY FRAMEWORK

Social network theory is proposed as an interdisciplinary policy framework that expands conventional state–society models with two perspectives from sociology: one, the importance of social relations to decision making, and two, the diffusion process of adopting new technology and institutions. Like earlier state–society models, policy makers remain the central actors in social network analysis. Building on that, the new approach investigates how the circulation of diasporas critically shapes state–society interactions surrounding policy making during China's and India's reforms.

On the importance of social relations to decision-making, Mark Granovetter (1985) has strongly established that embedded social networks shape individual behaviors. The stronger interpersonal ties triumph.[5] Brian Uzzi (1996) studies corporate decisions in New York City and confirms that companies frequently resort to "special" and "close" relations with other firms in conducting economic transactions. John Padgett and Christopher Ansell (1993) qualify the conventional account of the Renaissance state in Florence that attributed state building to the grand design of Cosimo de' Medici, and instead they emphasize the ratchet mechanism of elite network transformation that underlay Medici's actions.

In SNT, social relations play important roles in new policy making. Internal and external networks provide ideas, information, and resources that directly help policy makers to rank and formulate specific policies. Furthermore, during the interactions between state and societal actors, power and interest alone do not decide who has more influence on the resultant policies. The quality of ties between state and societal actors often has a decisive impact. SNT thus incorporates the quality of social relations between policy makers and specific social groups (external as well as internal) as an important variable to assess policy options and results. In FDI liberalization, because FDI and liberal ideas are new to the country and because domestic networks often offer opposing ideas and influence, the quality of external ties is even more important to policy makers' reception of new policies.

[5] Granovetter (1983) also explains the strength of weakness when information flows via strong ties are routinized and weak ties are more likely to channel new ideas and resources.

The second conceptual origin of SNT is in diffusion studies that stress stages of innovative adoption (Carrington, Scott, and Wasserman 2005). Everett Rogers (1995) offers three conclusions of innovative diffusion across many issue areas, including machinery, laws, and public health. First, individuals' decisions to adopt new ideas and practices are "socially driven." A change agent for a new technology, practice, or policy has greater success in convincing the target if he or she uses social relations rather than "rational reasoning." Second, different relations with external agents determine the rate at which members of a group adopt new ideas or practices. Thus, innovative adoption by a group does not happen at once but rather involves diffusion from early adopters to "laggards." Three, in adopting an innovation, individuals face a counterforce rooted in the old practice. The stronger the counterforce, the slower innovative diffusion takes place. Good social relations with change agents help overcome the counterforce against innovative adoption.

Foreign direct investment liberalization involves policy makers – political leaders and bureaucrats whose motivations and calculations are more complex than those of individuals or companies, but nevertheless shares considerable traits with other innovative diffusions. To start, the adopters (policy makers) need the input of new ideas to initiate liberalization: what ideas are provided and who provides them matter. Interpersonal ties and trustworthiness influence policy makers' reception of new ideas. Thus, although policy makers are provided with the common econometrics of FDI, their assessments of liberalization likely differ depending on their relations with external and internal actors who provide competing views. Second, adopting a new policy has different stages: initiation, challenge, and consolidation. The diffusion perspective in SNT stresses the interconnectedness of major policy change, particularly the importance of early success and the expansion of pro-change coalitions. Third, the counterforce of policy diffusion is composed of domestic groups that oppose change. If such domestic resistance is strong, diffusion relies on their transformation, and the process is likely lengthy.

SOCIAL NETWORKS AND DIFFUSION OF FDI LIBERALIZATION

The SNT incorporates insights from sociology and makes three additions to the politics of economic reform. First, state–society interactions include external actors in the age of globalization. For countries undergoing economic reform, new ideas and resources typically come from external actors who change domestic political dynamics. Second, conventional interest group models view society as opposing change, yet as cross-border mobility of people, technology, and goods intensifies, domestic interests are subject to change and, in many cases, they become drivers of policy innovations. Last, the study of politics and policy making needs to integrate relational factors because ties between policy makers and social groups vary and shape the policy options and results. Particularly in policy innovation, the quality of ties with external actors determines domestic reception of new policy ideas.

There are two broad explanatory variables in SNT: policy makers' external and internal social networks. These two sets of social networks provide competing ideas and resources to influence policy makers in deliberating on and implementing new FDI policies. The relative strength of these two networks determines the speed and outcome of FDI liberalization. External networks originate from the outside and pass ideas and resources directly or indirectly to policy makers. They tend to facilitate the adoption of new, liberal economic policies. Internal networks consist of preexisting interests and ideas before reform and likely oppose pro-FDI policy change and are thus called "domestic resistance." In a country undergoing reforms, both external networks and domestic resistance exist in varying degrees. Due to homeland ties, diasporas, if present, are often the early external networks in the country.

Neither external networks nor domestic resistance can be considered monolithic or static. Members of external networks may seek protectionist goals, especially after they gain preferential treatment through ties to policy makers. Conversely, some members of domestic resistance may actually support FDI liberalization, given their own interests in and ideas of foreign commerce. With liberalization, domestic actors' ideas and stances on FDI are likely to change. This description of external networks and domestic resistance is the starting point of the SNT. The diffusion model, as indicated in Figure 2.2, has a built-in, interactive mechanism between the two types of networks, and a reinforcing loop between liberalization and external networks.

The SNT is expressed in the two graphs below. Figure 2.1 diagrams the occurrence and nonoccurrence of FDI liberalization, with the relative strength of external networks and domestic resistance. It illustrates two pathways of FDI liberalization, with strong external networks and domestic resistance respectively. Figure 2.2 portrays the diffusion process, with its stages and steps. In this process, Figure 2.2 offers three mechanisms for external networks to influence FDI liberalization: demonstration, persuasion, and co-option, and explains how

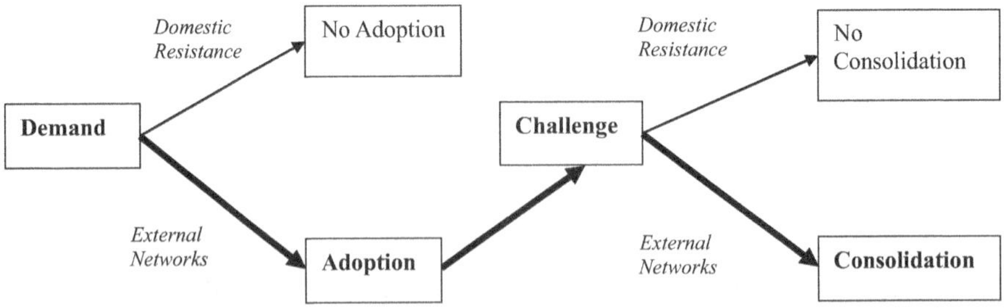

FIGURE 2.1. Occurrence and Nonoccurrence of Foreign Direct Investment Liberalization

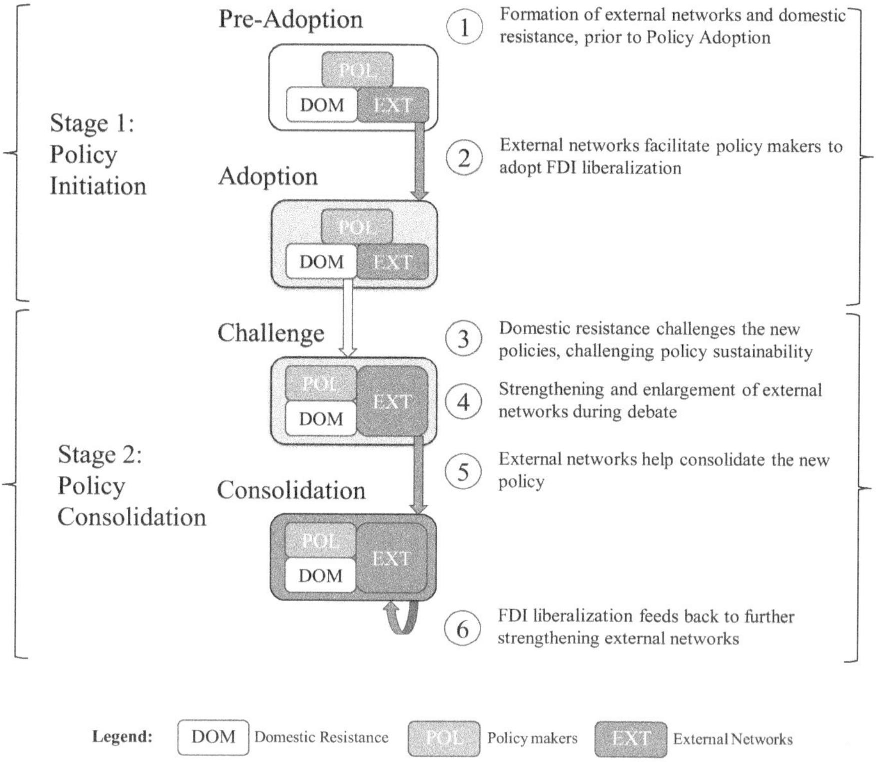

FIGURE 2.2. The Diffusion Model of Foreign Direct Investment Liberalization: Stages and Steps

external networks interact with policy makers, domestic support groups, and opposition during different stages of FDI liberalization.

FDI Liberalization: Uncertain Pathways

Foreign direct investment policy making consists of four phases: demand, adoption, challenge, and consolidation, as demonstrated in Figure 2.1. Demand has two components: one, a country's actual need for external technology and capital in order to achieve economic development; and two, the policy makers' recognition of that need. Although almost all developing countries can benefit from having access to foreign technology and capital, their policy makers may not pursue external inputs but attempt to develop those needed via measures such as domestic accumulation and indigenous innovation. After independence, many developing countries, including China and India, pursued import-substituting industrialization that sought to reduce foreign inputs. Thus, one crucial precondition of FDI liberalization is a change in top leadership that creates, at a policy level, a demand for foreign technology and capital.

Demand does not necessarily lead to policy change, however, as many developing countries linger in this stage for years. It is also possible that late developers transfer foreign technology and capital separately, without adopting FDI liberalization, as the developmental states in East Asia have successfully done in the decades since World War II. Thus, the particular external networks that help to initiate liberal policies toward FDI are important for the first transition from demand to adoption. Policy makers' internal networks harbor old ideas and protectionist interests when transition starts, although some members may form external networks and support the initiation of liberalization. During this transition, ideational transfers are critical: external actors interact with domestic supporters of FDI liberalization and transfer information and knowledge of FDI. Whether ideational transfers are effective and durable, however, is conditioned on external actors' relations with policy makers and material resources. More trusting interpersonal relations make persuasion easier, and material interest alignment enhances the formation of networks.

After the new policy is adopted, domestic resistance challenges the consolidation of FDI liberalization. If domestic resistance – the potential and actual losers of FDI liberalization and nonbelievers in FDI – is strong, the challenge to FDI gains momentum. If the new policy does not deliver early success, domestic resistance grows, and consolidation is left uncertain. Moving from challenge to consolidation requires additional input from external networks. During this transition, external networks help to consolidate the new policy by providing resources (finance, technology, expertise, etc.) to facilitate early success. Without resource input, social relations alone cannot create early success. Without early success, ideational appeal of the new policy diminishes and domestic resistance gains strength. Thus, the transition from challenge to consolidation is uncertain and more difficult when external networks fail to provide resources. The diffusion model (Figure 2.2) explicates how external networks help a developing country undertake FDI liberalization. The next section explains that such external networks are likely to form with former immigrants of the country.

The Diffusion Model: Stages and Steps

As a new policy paradigm, three developments typically happen upon the initiation of FDI liberalization in a country. First, policy makers' economic beliefs are influenced to favor liberalization. Second, implementers of liberalization (economic bureaucrats and local officials) acquire certain knowledge about the new policies. And third, resources or the prospect of resource transfers are useful in generating incentives. Because FDI liberalization is new to both policy makers and domestic actors, these developments are usually enabled by external networks that bring in new ideas, knowledge, and resources. External networks can demonstrate the value of liberal policies in promoting economic growth, persuade policy makers (or other domestic groups) to initiate FDI liberalization, and co-opt domestic resisters by providing material incentives. External networks' ability to play these roles depends on their ideational superiority, material resources, and access to policy makers (and other elites) – a measurement of network strength to be explained shortly.

Figure 2.2 expands on the liberalization pathway presented in Figure 2.1 and details the mechanisms through which external networks help the diffusion of FDI liberalization. Policy change proceeds in two stages. In the first, external networks facilitate the initial adoption of the new policy. In the second, they sustain the new policy against opposition and push for its consolidation. In the first microprocess, from demand for foreign capital to adoption of FDI liberalization, information flows and ideational influence dominate interactions between external actors and policy makers. In the second microprocess, from challenge to consolidation of liberal FDI policies, material transfer is essential because it offers incentives to reduce domestic opposition and also helps to generate the early success critical to broadening domestic support. Material incentives and ideational persuasion are not separate and exist in both stages. In the initiation stage, material consideration serves as a powerful motive to connect external and domestic actors, and incentive alignment makes ideational persuasion more effective. And, in the consolidation stage, apart from direct material contributions, external actors help FDI liberalization by continuing to transfer ideas and knowledge to more domestic actors. External networks help to consolidate FDI liberalization if they have broad ties to domestic actors.

The two-staged diffusion of FDI liberalization breaks into six steps, marked by interactions among policy makers, domestic resistance, and external networks. It begins with external actors providing information/ideas to policy makers and/or domestic support groups. This step describes the formation of external networks that channel favorable information about FDI (indicated in Step 1). Here, we begin to see bifurcation in internal networks: some domestic actors (although a small number) become part of external networks and support liberalization. In the meantime, however, opposing networks also exist between domestic resisters and policy makers.

In Step 2, external networks influence policy makers who adopt the new liberal policy. Again, those domestic actors incorporated into external networks in Step 1 are salient in pushing/lobbying policy makers to implement or sanction legislation to implement the new policy. Given the newness of the liberal policy and domestic resistance to FDI, early FDI liberalization is typically narrow in scope. Yet limited liberalization still encounters opposition from domestic resistance, resulting in an uncertain period that challenges the consolidation of the new policy, as indicated in Step 3.

Whether FDI liberalization overcomes domestic resistance depends on the interactions of external networks and domestic resistance and whether members of domestic resistance change their position and join the expanding pro-FDI coalition. Strong external networks facilitate the diffusion process by providing information and resources that spur early success and thereby co-opt members of domestic resistance to support the new policy and as a whole strengthen external networks at the expense of domestic resistance, as indicated in Step 4. Early success is critical to incorporating more domestic actors, shaping the outcome of policy contestation, and resulting in the final consolidation and diffusion of FDI liberalization in the country (Step 5). This outcome reinforces the pro-liberalization coalition within the country, as well as its external networks, in a feedback loop marked in Step 6.

Again, external actors (such as diasporas) do not act unilaterally. In the two critical steps (Steps 1 and 4), external actors' influence is in persuading policy makers, often via domestic advocates, as well as in co-opting domestic resistance. Thus, in examining the interplay occurring during that particular stage, domestic actors appear as the chief players, with external actors in supporting roles. Yet, by contributing ideas and resources and forming ever-increasing social networks with domestic actors, external actors shape the deliberation prior to policy initiation, the outcome of policy contestation, and ultimately the emergence of a new policy paradigm. The "supporting actors" are indeed one key factor to explain the cross-national divergence between China and India, their different domestic institutions and interests notwithstanding.

EXTERNAL NETWORKS AND DOMESTIC RESISTANCE

In SNT, the relative strength of external networks and domestic resistance determines the diffusion of FDI liberalization. Strong external networks help to initiate and consolidate the new policy, whereas strong domestic resistance prohibits or slows liberalization. The strength of external and internal networks is measured by ideas, resources, and access combined. External networks and domestic resistance do not operate in separate spaces but instead interact among themselves while competing to influence policy makers. When applied to diaspora networks, these three components – ideas, resources, and access – sufficiently capture different characteristics of diasporas and their relationships with homelands and empirically reveal the varied effects of diaspora groups on homeland liberalization.

Diasporas Likely Form Earlier External Networks

An external network consists of an external actor, an internal actor, and a tie connecting them. External actors can be individuals, agents of international organizations, members of multinational corporations, or politicians and bureaucrats of foreign countries. Internal actors include policy makers, bureaucrats, local officials, managers of domestic companies, and other individuals. If the external actor of the network is coethnic, the network is here called a *diaspora network*. Diaspora networks in China include ties between Deng Xiaoping and Hong Kong billionaire Y. K. Pao and Nobel Laureate physicist

Chen–Ning Yang, as well as those ties between Hong Kong businessmen and local officials in Guangdong. In India, examples of diaspora networks include connections between Rajiv Gandhi and Shankar Acharya who worked for the World Bank, as well as those between Silicon Valley Indian entrepreneurs and Wipro in India. Thus, diaspora networks are a subgroup of external networks but are likely to form sooner than nonethnic external ties in nascent transition economies.

Conventional migration literature makes distinctions among groups of diasporas, such as immigrants, settlers, and sojourners, as well as their offspring of different generations. The term "diaspora" is used to cover immigrants who stay outside of their homelands. The transnational migration literature, as cited shortly, emphasizes transnational diasporas, who, with improvements in transportation and communication technologies and legal status, have the ease and willingness to go back and forth between host societies and homelands. The conventional concepts cannot really capture the relationships such transnational actors build with home and host societies.

This book does not make intragrouping among immigrant bodies, despite the different characteristics and homeland connections that will be examined in later empirical chapters. There are three reasons: first, the explanatory model hypothesizes on the *aggregate* strength of external networks compared to domestic resistance, not diasporas per se. Second, SNT measures network strength by ideas, resources, and access combined, already capturing the differences among diaspora networks. And last, but not the least, avoiding inner distinctions mollifies subgroup identities that likely create unnecessary barriers to diasporas' interactions with the home state and society. Political leaders in China and India have not, quite prudently, stressed inner groupings in the countries' diaspora policies.

The reason for émigrés being earlier entrants than nonethnic foreigners is that the latter tend to be quite reluctant to get involved in underdeveloped countries, despite globalization of capital and improvements in technology. In the late 1980s, almost a decade into China's reform, Hsing (1998, 63) finds that Western managers hesitated to "go along the bumpy roads in rural China, nor to stand the dull evenings in the midst of rice fields." Similar hesitation existed among foreign investors in India, and much reluctance still remains. Agents of international organizations (IOs) may form aid-based contractual ties with developing nations, but such ties are likely short term. Once a mission concludes, the tie breaks down (Tilly 2007). After the countries make sustained progress, nonethnic external networks become more available – Shanghai and Mumbai today attract many Western visitors.

Even today, "brain circulation" involving diaspora professionals greatly exceeds that of nonethnic others. For example, China has made efforts to attract "global talent" since 2008 with aggressive compensation that is typically more generous to "non-Chinese" talents; however, only four of the 126 "foreign talents" who responded within a year were nonethnic Chinese (Zhao 2009). In embryonic reforms where policy makers deliberate whether or not to embrace FDI, diaspora networks (as a subgroup of external networks) are probably the only external networks building ties to policy makers and domestic actors and willing to contribute to their homelands.

The definition of diasporas here follows migration scholar William Safran (1991): "immigrants and descendants of immigrants, who are dispersed from their original homeland yet possessing a collective memory and myth about and sentiment and/or material links to that homeland." In the People's Republic of China (PRC), diasporas include Chinese living in Hong Kong, Macao, Taiwan, Southeast Asia, North America, Europe, and other parts of the world. The total number is staggering, and internal variation is clear. The Chinese government has not distinguished subgroups of diaspora networks and has offered uniform incentives for their return. Those who circulated back ideas and early investment were mostly émigrés in the Mainland's vicinity, who were born in China and became successful entrepreneurs before the PRC's opening and who, using the measurement of network strength, constituted strong diaspora networks with superior economic ideas, substantial resources, and extensive ties to domestic actors in the homeland.

Indian diasporas are composed mostly of early immigrants to the United Kingdom, Indians with education and work experiences in the United States, and indentured labor in the Gulf (some who rose to become entrepreneurs). Ideas, resources, and access embodied in network strength also account for the different policy effects of diaspora subgroups in India. For example, diasporas of different professions (entrepreneurs, professionals, and labor) or at different distances from homeland result in a varied mix of ideas, resources, and homeland connections. On FDI liberalization, entrepreneurs are likely to have more impact than professionals and laborers. In other policy innovations, professionals with specific skill sets may have stronger effects. As to grassroots well-being, remittances from overseas laborers may be more immediate than the other two types of diasporas. In SNT, the main concern is diaspora networks' aggregate strength compared to domestic resistance, which together shapes FDI liberalization; subgroup variations reveal themselves in empirical discussions.

Diasporas Constitute Stronger External Networks than Nonethnic Foreigners

SNT combines relational and material factors and measures the strength of external networks with three indicators: ideas, resources, and access. Ideas are measured by the extent that external actors' ideas are perceived as superior, or "the relative advantage" of an innovation (Rogers 1995). Apparent ideational superiority inspires domestic actors to follow and emulate. Ideational appeal is enhanced by three conditions: one, the material possession of external actors, which serves as evidence to domestic actors that their practice/ideas may be superior; two, economic crises or problems calling existing institutions into question; and three, early success in the initial implementation of the new policy. Holding all these constant, coethnicity enhances ideational superiority: if fellow Chinese or fellow Indians excel in business, they have a stronger appeal to individuals in their homelands because diasporas' success is considered more relevant for learning and emulation.

Early success is crucial to sustaining and enhancing ideational appeal, which in turn expedites innovative policy adoption. Peter Hall has established the importance of early success to economic paradigm shifts. On studying how Keynesian ideas emerged as a new economic paradigm in advanced countries, Hall (1989) finds that the Great Depression discredited old ideas, leading governments to implement moderate Keynesian experiments. The impressive early success in a limited policy experiment led President Roosevelt to pursue much bolder Keynesian economics. In addition, Hall (1993) highlights "learning" in policy paradigm shifts, as policy makers learn from the early experiences of their own and others. Domestic actors also observe, learn, and continuously debate competing ideas in the country. Economist Jagdish Bhagwati put it succinctly: "[N]othing succeeds like success. If reforms could produce quick and substantial results, that would certainly help" (Bhagwati 1993, 94).

The importance of early success to lasting reform highlights the second component of network strength: the material resources transferred from external networks. Resources include personal wealth, advanced technology, and/or market access. These resources are fungible, and external networks need not provide all types of resources to be influential. Resources strengthen the other components of a network: ideas and access. More resources on the part of external networks enable them to offer incentives to domestic support groups, who can lobby on their behalf and thereby enhance their influence on policy makers. Resources also enhance ideational appeal: on the one hand, resources are evidence of idea superiority, and, on the other, input of resources makes early success more likely and helps to sustain ideational superiority.

Diasporas, compared to other foreigners, may not necessarily have more ideas or material resources in total terms, but they are more willing to supply ideas and resources to the homeland than are nonethnic foreigners. Prosperous Western societies offer potential for latecomers to draw on, but the "foreign" actors who actually come to underdeveloped nations are likely these countries' immigrants making inroads in such societies. Business scholars find that FDI in "primitive markets" is difficult because Western companies are unfamiliar with these markets and encumbered by poor institutions and infrastructure (Chen and Chen 1998). Edward Steinfeld (2010) was puzzled as to why FDI was so substantial in China given the enormous difficulty in setting up subsidiaries in developing countries. International finance studies confirmed that firms' investment decisions have a "home bias" (Leblang 2010). Indeed, the majority of FDI in the world takes place within developed economies. Inferring from these works, diasporas form stronger external networks in their homelands than do Westerners partly because resources from/via them are more forthcoming.

The third source of diasporas' strength is the access to domestic ruling elites, which serve as channels for external ideas and resources. The quality and density of ties determines the effectiveness of ideas and resource transfers via such channels. If the ties are more trusted, then the ideas and resource flows will be smoother. If there are more ties between external and internal actors, the influence can be multiplied. Even when ideas flowing through these ties are the same, the presence of more domestic supporters enhances the appeal of the new policy in the eyes of policy makers. *Homophily*, a social term to describe similarities between individuals within networks, considerably strengthens the quality and density of transnational relations (Rogers 1995, 17). Co-ethnicity is a powerful homophily, as it implies similar language, culture, norms, and physiological attributes. Homophily is particularly important to forming subnational external networks.

Diasporas with ideas and resources can potentially form three levels of domestic access. At the top level, accomplished diasporas with policy ideas establish interpersonal ties to political leaders and senior bureaucrats. Such ideational transfers are likely to have a direct impact on the initiation of new policies. Below the national level, diasporas can form ties to the substate apparatus. Networks at this level are important because provincial heads are key constituencies of national leaders and often implementers of national policies in the provinces. Policy ideas appealing to top politicians but not convincing to provincial chiefs have a hard time materializing or persisting. Below the provincial level are societal levels, including low-level officials and indigenous business. At this level, establishing nonethnic external networks is difficult because language, norms, and infrastructure prevent foreigners from establishing interpersonal ties. Diasporas, conversely, can build ties to these local actors. At times, diaspora networks at this level are more pronounced due to the émigré's deeper dedication to his or her hometown than to the home country. And although ties to higher governments are critical to the initiation of a new policy, societal connections, or ties to grassroots governments, deepen the diffusion of FDI liberalization.

In China, as the policies of special economic zones (SEZs), open coastal cities (OCCs), "zone fever," and state-owned enterprise (SOE) reforms demonstrate, entrepreneurial diasporas have strong ties at all three levels: top leaders, provincial governments, and societal actors (local officials and entrepreneurs). In the early period, the interactions between diasporas and national and provincial leaders were critical to the initiation of FDI liberalization. Yet the rapidly growing interactions between diaspora entrepreneurs and local actors became vital to the early success of FDI and to the profound diffusion and consolidation of FDI liberalization in the country. In India, although the top-level diaspora networks seemed quite robust, diasporas at the state-level were limited to only a few states, and diaspora networks at the grassroots level were severely undersupplied.

The emphasis on diaspora networks in SNT does not mean that all diasporas play policy roles in their homelands. Some may not have homeland ties – when refugees uproot, for example, there is nothing that they can return to. Some may not have the skills or resources to help their homeland, as is the case of labor migrants from the poorest to poorer places without upward mobility. Some immigrants have negative impacts: when mothers in the Philippines go abroad as domestic help, family structures in the homeland are destroyed and children suffer. When Salvadorian men leave, they circulate HIV and other diseases back to their homeland. Or, when illegal Mexican youngsters in Los Angeles are deported back to their hometowns, they bring gangs and street violence home with them.[6] And, as long suggested, Cuban immigrants in America have worsened their home country's isolation by lobbying *against* the United States lifting economic sanctions against Cuba.[7]

The social network framework is conscious of these complexities and measures network strength by the combination of ideas, resources, and access. Diasporas highlighted in SNT encompass those from poor to prosperous societies, acquiring skills, expertise, and financial resources, as well as legal standing and social connections to go back and forth between host and homelands. They are diasporas, but also transnational actors that serve as conduits of ideas, expertise, and resources from developed host regions to underdeveloped homelands.

Furthermore, the importance of diasporas to FDI liberalization does not negate the importance of states or political institutions. Politicians' and elites' views of diasporas determine the scope of immigrants' contribution to their homelands. If the state sees diasporas as beneficial to its development goals and embraces their return, diaspora networks at national and local levels are more likely to flourish. Conversely, if the state views diasporas as unwelcome or unwanted, diasporas find it difficult to form policy networks that facilitate liberalization – although covert grassroots diaspora linkages still operate. Devesh Kapur (2010) thus concludes that the conditions shaping Indian diasporas' homeland effects were internal to the home state. Alejandro Portes (2013, 53) maintains that homeland governments "must be proactive in creating suitable conditions" for the circulation of émigrés, and "a *laissez faire* approach that merely waits for the market to work out its 'magic' through spontaneous remittances and knowledge transfers will not work. Governments must meet their half of the bargain since, in the absence of suitable conditions that only they can create, the best-intentioned transnational projects cannot succeed."

Countries with abundant diasporas but no reforms are not uncommon. Cuba, North Korea, and Pakistan are among these, to name a few, because leaders of these countries are yet to make the historic shift from political survival to development. The pro-growth government in China, which implemented proactive policies to engage entrepreneurial immigrants, was thus the key to the emergence of diaspora networks and their contribution to China's late development. India, learning from the Chinese experience, is implementing

[6] For a cross-national study on immigrants' impacts on homeland, see Eckstein (2013).

[7] Eckstein (2013) has noted key differences between the new and old generations of Cuban immigrants in America. The more recent immigrants maintained strong homeland ties and are shaping Cuban economic institutions under Castro.

favorable policies toward its professional immigrants. If sustained, such efforts will pay off. Yet India still has a lot to learn from China to spur entrepreneurial diaspora involvement in the country. And, for a large number of developing countries where late industrialization appears elusive, entrepreneurial and professional diasporas can play crucial roles, helping to initiate a new policy, generate some success, and consolidate a shift in economic orientation. After all, more than half of all immigrants from less-developed countries today go to developed nations, and transnationalism created by such South to North human mobility perhaps bodes critical potential for world development.[8]

Domestic Resistance and Its Strength

Domestic resistance refers to policy makers' internal social networks that oppose policy liberalization. If these internal networks are strong, they constrain FDI liberalization; hence, in countries with strong domestic resistance, the pace and pattern of liberalization differ from countries with weak domestic resistance, other things being equal. It should be said, however, that not all domestic actors are against liberalization. Some domestic actors are advocacy groups for liberalization. Such actors usually have external ties. Further, internal networks' ideas and influence change – voluntarily due to external interactions or involuntarily due to crisis and leadership change that disrupts their preexisting ties to policy makers.

Previous interest-group political models have highlighted domestic opposition, but included opposition mainly based on material interests: owners of scarce capital and technology, immobile sectors, and bureaucracies and labor in charge of these sectors (Stolper and Samuelson 1941; Rogowski 1990; Frieden 1991). In SNT, there are two kinds of domestic resistance: one is driven by material interests, and the other is driven by ideology. Material-based opposition can be reduced with economic incentives, but ideology-laden opposition, which is influential in transition economies, requires a different means to effect change. To bring ideology-based resisters into pro-FDI courses, material incentives may not be effective or sufficient. Relational-based interactions and persuasion have a long way to go.

Furthermore, policy implications of interest groups are not static and may change as a result of external networks channeling new ideas and resources. Take capital and technology owners as examples. Before a country's opening, they oppose FDI and foreign goods that present competition to their domestic interests. Yet, in the age of globalization and in interaction with external networks, they may recognize the need for new capital, technology, and the possibility of new markets. Their positions on liberalization are not predetermined. Furthermore, capital owners are no longer a coherent group. Some may be early adopters of innovation and achieve success, and others have to follow or otherwise lose out. As a class, their opposition to FDI liberalization likely weakens.

[8] In Latin America and the Caribbean, East Asia, and Middle East, the ratio is more than 80 percent. See Ratha and Shaw (2007).

External networks and domestic resistance interactively shape FDI liberalization. The same indicators – ideas, resources, and ties – also measure the strength of domestic resistance. In the case of economic failure, ideas held by domestic resistance are undermined, and new views come to take hold. If the number of domestic resisters is small and their resources constrained, the aggregate strength of domestic resistance is limited, and the opposition can be co-opted relatively easily by liberalizing forces. Moreover, if domestic resisters have limited access to policy makers, during leadership or regime changes for example, their preference for protectionism cannot win. Thus, crises and leadership change may predate some liberalization episodes, but the interactions and relative influence of external and internal social relations shape long-term policy transformation. In the context of strong external networks, diffusion of FDI liberalization likely ensues, and, conversely, with powerful domestic resistance, it will be a protracted process if it happens at all.

COMPARATIVE CASES AND HYPOTHESIZED EXPLANATIONS

This book is foremost a comparative research of China's and India's reforms. It develops the SNT to examine the causes and processes of FDI liberalization in the two Asian giants. It involves three types of investigation: first, a *structural* analysis of diaspora networks and domestic resistance assesses the relative strength of these networks. Second, a *process* analysis of the interactions between policy makers and external and domestic actors tracks the origin and scope of policy change. And third, a *diffusion* analysis of liberalization episodes illustrates how earlier policy liberalization influences later policy change and how social structure varies during liberalization. The empirical testing is conducted across three dimensions: national, across time, and across sectors.

The first and general comparison in the book is divergent FDI liberalization in China and India. Table 2.1 offers a comparison of five aspects of FDI liberalization. Before reform, the two countries were highly comparable in infrastructure,

TABLE 2.1. *Foreign Direct Investment (FDI) Liberalization in China and India (1980–2010)*

Aspects of FDI Liberalization	China	India
Incentives for FDI	Yes	No
Infrastructure	Yes	No
Skills training	Yes	No
Governing agency	No (until the 1990s)	No (until the 1990s)
Regulations	Yes	No (until the 1990s)
Hypothesized causality	Diaspora networks	Indigenous industry
Alternative arguments	Political regimes: Leadership and Interest group politics	

labor, and policies. The table also lists the hypothesized social network explanation, focusing on diasporas and indigenous industry, respectively, and alternative political explanations for China and India's divergence – derived from political regimes are differences in leadership and interest group politics. Social network theory, to be sure, also explores leadership and interest group politics, but by integrating diasporas into the state–society analysis, it demonstrates divergent policy choices and consequences in the two Asian giants.

The aspects of FDI liberalization are summarized by the United Nations Conference on Trade and Development (UNCTAD 2006), which finds that foreign investors consider five elements in the recipient nation: incentives, infrastructure, labor skills, governing agencies, and transparent regulations. Clearly, investment decisions go beyond formal rules and laws, and a country's FDI liberalization entails other provisions than making formal FDI policies. Starting from a comparable status in 1980, China strived to supply all these conditions to attract foreign investors, absent an overarching governing agency.[9]

Interregional variations were present in 1980s China. Some areas passed remarkably favorable policies toward FDI (or interpreted national policies flexibly) and improved infrastructure and labor supplies, whereas other regions did not do so. In the 1990s, China's FDI regulations were more consolidated and transparent than before, and infrastructure and labor policies were greatly improved. India supplied none of these conditions until the 1990s. Even then, India was slower in improving infrastructure and labor supplies.

On infrastructure and labor, India's democracy was often criticized as the culprit because democracy prevents the state from forceful land seizure or involuntary layoffs, which had occurred rather extensively in China since the late 1990s. Yasheng Huang (2008), however, has established that China's recent decade was the least developmental period since 1979. Economists find that per unit return on infrastructure investment in China is very low and much lower than in India. A bigger cost, to be sure, is political, and bubbling social instability is engendered by land seizure and dislocation (Fewsmith 2013). In India, Columbia University anthropologist Partha Chatterjee (2011) observes that the lack of funding and jobs for the dislocated peasants were the root problems, and democracy was the key social insurance against such displacement – thus making the reform process more sustainable in that country.

Beyond these countering views, attributing China's infrastructure and labor supply entirely to autocracy is not accurate for most the reform period. Youtien Hsing (1998) has documented that diaspora-invested companies drove the aggressive recruitment (and training) of migrant workers from afar, hiring former military personnel with networks in inland regions. Mary Gallagher

[9] A web of intervening agencies handled FDI disputes. The underdeveloped national FDI institutions in China in the 1980s led Western observers to conclude that China's FDI liberalization was not substantial, a pattern at odds with local practice and geographically concentrated drastic openness often tailored to diaspora investors.

TABLE 2.2. *Cross-Time Analysis of China and India's Foreign Direct Investment (FDI) Liberalization*

Time Periods	China	India
The early 1980s	Special Economic Zones (SEZs)	Domestic Deregulation
Mid- and late 1980s	Open Coastal Cities (OCCs)	Failed (and limited) FDI liberalization
Early 1990s	Deng Xiaoping's Southern Tour*	New Industrial Policy: major opening
1993–1996	"FDI fever": High-tech development zones	FDI resisted: Bombay Club
1996–1998	National policy transformed: State-owned enterprise reform	National policy compromised: "Calibrated globalism"
2000s	FDI-led export success	The globalization of domestic industry
Hypothesized causality	Diaspora capital	Domestic business
Alternative arguments	Leadership choices Geostrategic environment	Interest group politics Crises; external pressure

Note: * It initiated new FDI policies and thus was seen as a major policy liberalization episode.

(2005) establishes that, thanks to FDI, voluntary transfers of socialist labor to capitalist sectors took place before state-forced layoffs in the late 1990s. Chapters 3 and 5 here confirm that diaspora funding was directly responsible for rapid infrastructure improvement in China until the late 1990s, when the state took over property development. When this happened, one could argue that abuses occurred to the detriment of national development.

Table 2.2 summarizes major reform episodes in China and India and elaborates on their key differences. In China, they include the SEZs (1980), OCCs (1984), Deng Xiaoping's Southern Tour (1992), the high-tech development and economic zones (1993–), and SOE Reform (1996–1998). In India, the focus is on Indira Gandhi's 1980 liberalization, Rajiv Gandhi's 1985–6 budget, the 1991 balance of payments (BOP) crisis and subsequent reforms, the antiliberalization Bombay Club (1993–96), and the "Calibrated Globalism" at the end of the 1990s. The comparison continues into the recent decade: FDI helped China's export success, and Indian domestic business went through globalization. The relative centrality of diaspora and domestic capital remains in China and India; FDI liberalization continues to diverge.

Table 2.2 additionally lists the hypothesized causality according to SNT, which argues that diaspora networks shaped China's FDI liberalization and indigenous companies influenced India's. The prevailing alternative explanations include leadership choices and geostrategic context in China and interest group politics and external pressure in India. These alternative variables are relevant to specific episodes, and, more importantly, they work interactively with social network variables. The analysis suggests that dominant social networks – diasporas in China and indigenous industry in India – sometimes directly influenced FDI liberalization, whereas, at other times, their impact was strengthened or overcome by other conditions. Social network theory investigates the interactions of external and internal actors and the process of diffusion and aims to account for the long-term divergence in China's and India's FDI liberalization. Such persistent pathways are more than the aggregate of individual episodes and are rooted in changes in these countries' social structures: the large-scale circulation of diaspora entrepreneurs in China and globalization of indigenous companies drawing on diaspora professionals in India.

Finally, I add to the discussion of policy diffusion at the national level a set of cross-sector comparisons. Sectors with strong diaspora networks are compared with those with weaker external networks to see whether these sectors have been liberalized more fully. Sectors with powerful domestic opposition are contrasted with those with weaker opposition. I use paired comparisons and focus on the electronics and auto sectors in China and India. In Figure 2.3, Chinese hardware manufacturing has strong diaspora networks but weak domestic resistance, whereas India's software services had a similar social structure. Both industries, although of different national polities and periods, experienced successful and rapid FDI liberalization. India's hardware manufacturers, on the other hand, had difficulty opening up. China's automobile industry was dominated by SOEs, and India's automakers were mainly private. Yet because external players were predominantly Western multinational corporations (MNCs), cooperation with Western automakers was difficult to persevere in both countries.

The sectoral analysis goes into liberalization from 1980 to 2010, and much change has occurred in the external and internal linkages of dominant players in

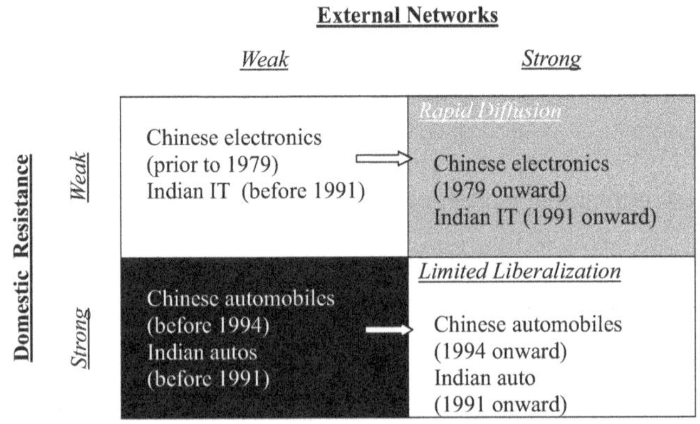

FIGURE 2.3. Industries and Foreign Direct Investment Liberalization

these industries. External linkages seem to have resulted in liberalization also in the auto industry since the 1990s, yet the salience of diaspora networks and domestic producers with MNC partnership in electronics and automobiles, respectively, has continuously influenced the dynamics of sectoral liberalization. Anti-FDI nationalism is strong in China's automobile industry but nonexistent in electronics, and similar resistance is present in many industries in India, although not in software services. Divergence between India's software and hardware industries additionally supports the importance of diaspora connections.

EMPIRICAL MATERIALS

The China and India comparison is most challenging in collecting empirical materials: in China, information on policy making was rarely recorded in the early period and was kept secret for the more recent periods. In India, first-hand information is more available but remains scarce and scattered. The comparative research is also most rewarding in gaining knowledge of policies, state–society interactions, and the empirical results of their reforms. The materials in the empirical chapters are based on research in China, India, Hong Kong, Singapore, and the United States over several years. The archives and collections at the Chinese University of Hong Kong and Harvard University are most useful for the Chinese case and those at Jawaharlal Nehru University and ICRIER in New Delhi for India's. The materials are both archival and statistical and supplemented with interviews with officials, scholars, and corporate representatives based in China and India. Together, these materials break down into five categories to explain how diaspora and indigenous industry interactively influenced FDI liberalization.

The first consists of reform policies in China and India from 1980 to 2010. I focus on the FDI policies of the two countries but also include policies on trade, domestic companies, labor laws, tax codes, and investment regulations when necessary. These policies are often interconnected and together give distinct reform pictures in China and India. Using this information, I show how priorities over reforms, the pace of liberalization, and the scope of policy change differed across the two countries and how they changed during different periods.

The second category of materials concerns policy making of key reforms. I researched official documents, primary archives, newspapers, and journals in China and India and used interviews to shed light on policy-making processes and determinants. The resultant information summarizes policy debates and options available to policy makers and includes the names of the proponents of various policy options, when possible. After each reform was inaugurated, I also studied the debates and controversies on the new policy in order to gauge the relative strength of support for and opposition to the policy, as well as the arguments presented by each group.

The third dataset comprises economic statistics from China and India. The FDI data are systematically differentiated by sources in both China and India. By unpacking FDI, I show that Chinese FDI was for the most part diaspora investment, whereas Western MNCs made up the lion's share of flows into India. Macroeconomic statistics such as exports, imports, account balances, and growth are extensively used to assess the development effects of FDI and provide macroeconomic conditions for policy making.

The fourth category of materials consists of subnational information about FDI liberalization. Making up the first part of the set are FDI policies, information about external networks, FDI inflows, and macroeconomic statistics for two sectors – electronics and automobiles – in both China and India. To create the second part of the set, I compiled data to analyze selected localities in China and India.

The final part of the empirical materials offers case studies of corporations in China and India. Companies constitute key domestic groups in the two countries, and an investigation of their history, growth, and globalization illustrates the dynamic of state–business interaction in the countries and their evolving exchange with global forces at the corporate level, which will likely have significant policy implications in the future. In China, diaspora investors worked closely with Chinese indigenous companies and helped them to become national and global players. In India, private Indian companies, including traditional business families and new entrants in the 1980s and the 1990s, had more complex relationships with foreign investors. Before 2000, these companies viewed FDI primarily as a threat to the domestic market. They have since successfully used partnerships with Western MNCs to acquire technology and financing and to expand internationally. Domestic companies, however, maintain substantial control over India's domestic and export markets, with foreign investors entering on the terms agreed by them.

CONCLUSION

Works in sociology, anthropology, and even international business have noted diasporas' roles in homeland development. Yet the political studies of China and India and FDI in general have not incorporated diasporas' impacts. Social network theory expands the political models by drawing on insights from the other fields. It makes two propositions: one, policy makers' internal and external social relations influence their policy choices regarding economic liberalization. And, two, innovative policy liberalization follows a diffusion model in which early success helps to broaden domestic support for the new policy.

Due to shared ethnicity, diaspora networks are uniquely important among external linkages as liberalizing agents in their home countries. Although external networks help liberalization, domestic resistance – policy makers' internal networks that oppose FDI – prevents or delays FDI liberalization. Domestic resistance, however, is subject to influence by external networks. Diaspora networks are more likely to form ties to domestic opposition than are nonethnic foreigners. Other things being equal, diaspora networks are stronger than nonethnic external networks because they are more willing and more likely to transfer ideas and resources and build broader ties to domestic actors. Openness to FDI is thus different in cases with strong diaspora networks and those with strong domestic resistance. The comparison of China and India in the following chapters exemplifies two pathways of FDI liberalization and validates the critical role of diaspora networks and domestic industry in homeland reform.

PART II

REFORM STAGE I

Diffusion of FDI Liberalization in China
Domestic Deregulation in India

3

Diaspora Entrepreneurs and Diffusion of FDI Liberalization in China

> I was born in China, and my roots are in China. I will do whatever I can to help motherland to develop.
>
> – Y. K. Pao, 1978

China began to prioritize economic growth in 1979 when it initiated new trends that moved away from socialism and isolationism. Not long after, in 1980, the national government approved the special economic zone (SEZ) bill and authorized the construction of four SEZs in South China. At the time, SEZs did not cause much reaction from Western observers, and within China they were seen as an experiment in narrowly bounded areas far from political-economic centers in the nation. The diffusion of foreign direct investment (FDI) liberalization, as initiated in four SEZs, was remarkably rapid: in 1984, fourteen open coastal cities (OCCs) were announced; in 1988, a coastal development strategy was promoted; in 1992, almost all of China was opened to FDI; and in 1993, China emerged as the largest recipient of FDI among the developing countries.

What accounted for the rapid diffusion of FDI liberalization? Why was the People's Republic of China (PRC) able to pull off a shift of this magnitude, from economic isolation to deep integration via FDI? Students of Chinese political economy have offered explanations focusing on either authoritarian leaders (Shirk 1994; Cai and Treisman 2006; Shih 2008), or communist institutions (Shirk 1994; Huang 2003; 2008), or local governments (Weingast 1995; Segal 2003; Thun 2006). David Zweig (2002) explores the combined effects of central government and local officials, and Mary Gallagher (2005) offers the process of capitalist "contagion" of labor practices through the strategic use of FDI.[1] Yet, in none of these works were diaspora networks present.[2]

[1] A similar idea was expressed by Barry Naughton, who popularized the phrase of "growing out of the plan" (Naughton 1996). Other works that are not directly about FDI liberalization but on reform in general include Michel Oksenberg and Kenneth Lieberthal's notion of "bureaucratic authoritarianism" (Lieberthal and Oksenberg 1988); Harry Harding's (1987) and Joseph Fewsmith's (1994) research on elite politics, Dali Yang's work on competitive lobbyism (Yang 1997), Yongnian Zheng's argument about globalism as new ideology (Zheng 2004), Lynn White's work on non-state power (White 1998), as well as Audrey Donnithorne's work on the "cellular society" (Donnithorne 1972) and Sebastian Heilmann (2008) on experimentalism as a policy process that facilitates institutional innovation.

[2] Huang (2003) treats the dominance of diaspora investment as a result of China's communist economic pecking order and does not discuss the policy influence of diasporas in China.

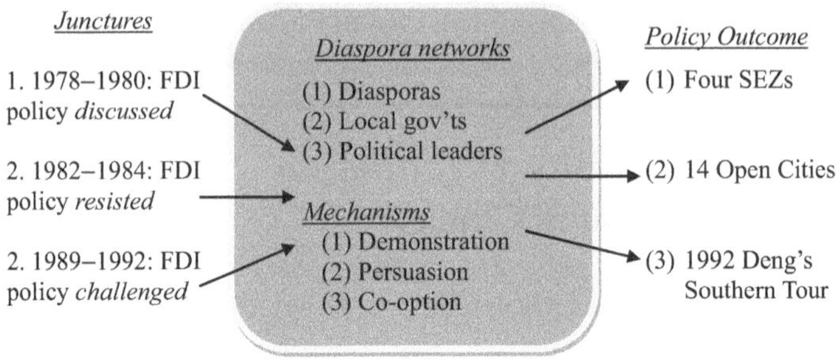

FIGURE 3.1. China's Diaspora Networks and Foreign Direct Investment Liberalization, 1978–1992

This chapter applies the social network theory (SNT) to China's FDI liberalization in the period from 1978 to 1992. It has two goals: first, systematically differentiating diasporas from other investors and demonstrating the significance of entrepreneurial diasporas to the PRC; and second, process-tracing the diffusion model and revealing diasporas' influence on China's pro-FDI policy shift – the initiation, contestation, and consolidation of FDI liberalization.

Figure 3.1 follows the diffusion model spelled out in Chapter 2 and presents three key episodes in China's FDI liberalization: (1) 1978–1980, the deliberation of various policy options and the initiation of FDI liberalization; (2) 1982–1984, challenges to FDI and the affirmation of liberalization; and (3) 1989–1992, a political crisis that emboldened opposition and the ultimate broadening of FDI liberalization in China. Each of these episodes began with a critical juncture (opened by leadership change, policy debates, and political crisis, respectively) and ended with more profound openness to FDI. Connecting these junctures to pro-FDI policy outcomes were interactions among diasporas, local governments, and policy makers.

Diaspora networks influenced policy outcomes through mechanisms of demonstration, persuasion, and co-option. And in each reform episode, diasporas interacted with policy makers and local governments. More importantly, the three reform episodes should not be read as separate events, since the outcomes of the latter two junctures were critically decided by the experience of the first. Diffusion analysis stresses the interconnectedness of sequential policies. Compelling early success changed leaders' views of FDI and brought more local governments on board with liberalization. Diaspora entrepreneurs who enabled such success should thus be viewed as doubly important to China's FDI liberalization in this period.

The contribution of diasporas is evident by their dominant shares in FDI in China, greatly surpassing those of Japan and the United States, the two largest international investors in the world.[3] As Table 3.1 demonstrates, between 1978

[3] Keep in mind, Sino-Japanese relations were exceptionally strong throughout the fifteen years, and Sino-U.S. ties were also strong in the 1980s, described by some as de facto alliance (Mann 1998).

TABLE 3.1. *Sources of Foreign Direct Investment (FDI) in the People's Republic of China (PRC), 1978–1993 Combined*

	No. of FIFs*	%	Registered capital ($billion)	%
Hong Kong**	106,914	63.8	103.9	72.7
Taiwan	20,612	12.3	13.2	9.3
Macao	4,116	2.5	4.1	2.9
Singapore	3,037	1.8	3.3	2.3
Thailand	1,361	0.8	1.6	1.1
U.S. United States	1,1554	6.9	8.2	5.7
Japan	7,096	4.2	5.2	3.6
Total Diaspora (%)		81.2		88.3

* FIFs refer to foreign-invested firms.
** Hong Kong's shares do not include investments made by Hong Kong subsidiaries of other nations. Investments made by Japanese companies via Hong Kong, for example, were counted as FDI from Japan. Due to political difficulties between Taiwan and the Mainland, Taiwanese investments via Hong Kong in the 1980s were included in the Hong Kong FDI.
Source: Jingji yanjiu cankao [Report on Economic Research], Beijing, China, October 12, 1994.

and 1993, investment from Hong Kong accounted for almost three-quarters of total FDI in China. Taiwan provided almost 10 percent.[4] Macao, with a population of less than 500,000, provided 3 percent of FDI in China. Japan and the United States combined account for the same share as Taiwan (9.3 percent). Table 3.1 adds up the diaspora investment and arrives at two staggering ratios. In terms of the number of firms, diasporas accounted for 81.2 percent of FDI, and by capital, diasporas' share was 88.3 percent.

The following five sections expand on the ideas presented here. The first sets up the political context of China's FDI liberalization; namely, the post-Mao government and the policy options under Deng's leadership. The next section traces the formation of diaspora networks at the national and local levels. The third section examines how diaspora entrepreneurs influenced the initiation of SEZ policy. The last two sections examine challenges to FDI liberalization and how diasporas helped the pro-FDI coalition to overcome them. The first significant challenge occurred in 1982–84 and ended with the construction of OCCs; the second was brought on by the 1989 Tiananmen crisis and concluded with the reassertion of FDI liberalization in 1992. In policy analyses, this chapter examines interactions among diasporas, policy makers, local governments, and domestic resistance, and emphasizes the sequential interconnectedness in the diffusion model.

[4] The actual contribution of Taiwanese was larger because some Taiwan-based FDI came through Hong Kong.

THE NEW GOVERNMENT AND POLICY OPTIONS

Most discussions of China's reform invariably start with Deng Xiaoping, who had a long and illustrious political career prior to reform – including twice being demoted by Mao due to his economic pragmatism.[5] China's open-door policy, however, involved more than just one man. According to Ezra Vogel (1989), pre-Deng bureaucrats were already pursuing openness to world capitalism, and the local government in Guangdong was "one step ahead" of the nation in inviting FDI. The new archives made available in 2005, one year after Deng's 100th birthday, support that when Deng assumed the leadership in late 1978, the preferred policy within the national government was not FDI liberalization but "socialist industrial policy," which was implemented in the following years and dismantled only after a nonsocialist economy took root.[6]

Mao died in September 1976, and a power struggle ensued between the "Gang of Four" and Hua Guofeng. Hua was more pragmatic and inclined to promote economic development, and thus he gained support from moderate forces in the Party, with whose assistance Hua ousted the radical faction. Deng was still in exile. Hua reoriented the country toward growth and industrialization, and his government was eager to learn from abroad. In late 1977, Hua sent four high-ranking delegations overseas to study other countries' development experiences. These delegations returned to China with two key conclusions: one, China was vastly behind others in development; and two, the capitalist countries were willing to help (Deng et al. 1979).

Meanwhile, Deng managed to end his exile in 1977. Under Hua, he focused on education and technology. Deng was proactive in meeting with foreign visitors to discuss ideas for industrialization and made particular efforts to befriend representatives of overseas Chinese. He interacted with diaspora tycoons Y. K. Pao, Henry Fok, Stanley Ho, Ma Wangqi, An Zhijie, Tang Xiangqian, and Lee Kashing, among others. From March 1978 to June 1983, Deng was the chairman of the Chinese People's Political Consultative Conference (CPPCC), a political organ at the level of the National People's Congress. The aforementioned diasporas were members of CPPCC. In late 1978, Deng visited Japan and Singapore and was impressed with growth there. Yet FDI liberalization was not a chosen industrial strategy.

The CCP Central Committee Work Meeting [*zhonggong zhongyang weiyuan gongzuo huiyi*] was held from November 11 to December 15, 1978. Deng's supporters staged a political coup to elevate Deng as the new leader of China. Participants at the meeting then discussed development policy options and particularly deliberated the four reports produced by the four delegations sent

[5] In his political career, Deng experienced three downs and three ups [*sanqi sanluo*]. The first down occurred in the 1930s due to his support for Mao. The latter two occurred because of Mao's purge.

[6] See also Heilmann (2008). For the most comprehensive account of Deng Xiaoping, see Vogel (2011).

TABLE 3.2. *China's Developmental Policy Options in 1979*

Time	Leader	Destination	Policy Suggestions
Early 1978	Deng Yingchao	Yugoslavia Romania	(1) adjust state-owned companies (2) transfer advanced technology (3) stress domestic saving and production
March – April 1978	Lin Hujia	Japan	(1) transfer technology (2) use foreign capital (3) use foreign loans
April 1978	Gu Mu; Duan Yun (Vice Chairman, SPC)	Hong Kong, Macao	(1) use foreign capital (2) exploit cheap labor (3) develop special economic areas in Shenzhen (4) decentralize trade, currency regulation, personnel, tax, etc
May 1978	Gu Mu	Western Europe	(1) develop technology (2) exploit the desire on the European side to trade with China (3) use promised loans from Germany and France, in the form of compensatory trade

Sources: Compiled from issues of *Jingji yanjiu cankao* [*Report on Economic Research*], 1979–1980. Specific titles are as follows: Deng Liqun, "Jiangjiang wode xuexi tihui" [On My Thoughts], no.1, January 1, 1979; "Zhongguo caizheng jingji kaochatuan fangwen baogao: Nansilafu he Luomaniya" [Report from Visits to Yugoslavia and Romania], no.8, January 12, 1979; "Dongou geguo gongye guanli qingkuang" [Industrial Management in East Europe], no.22, February 5, 1979; "Riben jingji zhuanjia zuotan yijian" [Japanese Economists' Workshop Report], no.30, February 17, 1979; Ma Hong, "Zenyang liyong xianggang wei woguo sige xiandaihua fuwu" [How to Take Advantage of the Hong Kong Economy to Serve our Four Modernization Development], no.39, March 8, 1979.

overseas.[7] Table 3.2 summarizes the four delegations and their findings. The first delegation went to Yugoslavia, led by Deng Yingchao, wife of China's first Premier Zhou Enlai and herself a well-respected, revolutionary elder. Deng

[7] The Work Meeting had more discussion of economic policies than the Third Plenum of the Eleventh Party Congress, which was credited as the beginning of economic reform. See, "1978 Zhongguo dazhuanzhe xiezhen" [The True Reflection of China's Turning Point in 1978]," *Yanhuang Chunqiu*, No. 10, 1998.

Yingchao was to become the Chairwoman of CPPCC, succeeding Deng Xiaoping in 1983. The second delegation, which went to Japan, was led by Shanghai Party boss Lin Hujia. Vice Premier Gu Mu led the third and fourth delegations touring Hong Kong and Macao, and Western Europe, respectively.

The four reports, as discussed at the November 1978 CCP Work Meeting, covered development experiences in Yugoslavia, Japan, Hong Kong and Macao, and Western Europe and synthesized three policy options – Japan, France, and Germany were viewed as similar. The first option was to uphold the socialist economic structure while rationalizing central planning, following the model of Yugoslavia. This report argued that mobilizing domestic resources to reduce economic distortions caused by the Cultural Revolution, combined with aggressive adoption of more advanced technology, would be sufficient to improve China's economy.[8] The new rulers also liked the second option, based on the developmental experiences of Japan, West Germany, and France. Using Japanese-style industrial policy, the PRC could strengthen state intervention in industry, proactively join the global economy, and strategically utilize foreign capital and technology.[9] Propaganda Minister Deng Liqun paid an eye-opening visit to Japan in late 1978, further enhancing the appeal of Japanese industrial planning. The new leaders at the Work Meeting discussed but largely dismissed the third option – FDI liberalization, drawn from the experiences of Hong Kong, Taiwan, and Singapore.[10] Such preferences are clear from the length and wording of these reports.

The report on socialist adjustment – option 1 – was the longest, and in its conclusion it used the strongest Chinese word for learning [*xuexi*]. The Japanese model – option 2 – was appealing, and the lessons could be "partly borrowed" [*jiejian*]. FDI-led development was said to be "worthwhile to study" [*yanjiu*], a phrase with an unimpressed and dismissive connotation. The preference for socialist adjustment resulted in the "socialist industrial policy," combining Yugoslavia's socialist rationalization and the "strategic decoupling" employed by Japan. Under this policy, Chinese state-owned enterprises (SOEs) would borrow funds and transfer technology from abroad separately and strategically (Luo 1980). The merits of this policy were obvious: China could contain and minimize foreign influence while benefiting bureaucrats and SOEs with international exchange (Gu 1998). Within a year, the country had signed dozens of contracts with foreign countries to transfer advanced technology and equipment for the use of SOEs.[11]

[8] Reports produced were "Why Did Romania and Yugoslavia Grow Rapidly?" and "How the Soviets Utilized Foreign Capital and Technology for Domestic Growth," see Huang (2005).

[9] Report, "How Did Japan, West Germany and France Develop Rapidly after WWII?,"Ibid.

[10] Report, "How did Hong Kong, Singapore, South Korea, and Taiwan Grow Rapidly?,"Ibid.

[11] "Zhongguo jishu yinjin de jinzhan he zhanwang" [Progress and Prospects of Technology Transfer in China], *Jingji ribao [Economic Daily]*, No. 1630, August 1, 1979.

The socialist industrial policy continued well into the 1980s, but from its start it incurred a number of difficulties, and economic performance under this strategy was sliding.[12] The SOEs, as the main users of foreign technology and loans, could not increase exports fast enough to reimburse the costs of the technology and to repay the loans.[13] China's international debt increased rapidly. Furthermore, technological and financial collaborations between Chinese and foreign companies were difficult and complicated by mistrust on the part of China. Finally, increasing debt and negative reporting of foreign projects enhanced domestic resistance to liberalization. Chen Yun, the conservative leader, challenged the openness strategy (Chen 1986); in response, Deng unilaterally cancelled or downsized some foreign collaborative projects (Chen Jinhua 2005).

The socialist industrial policy was not abandoned, however. The national government continued to transfer foreign technology and loans to strengthen the SOEs; SOE reforms only began in the mid-1990s (see reform stage II, Chapter 5). A separate development path focusing on FDI was rising to prominence with the help of diaspora entrepreneurs. The leading members of diasporas provided important new ideas to national leaders; at the local level, South China revived immigrant ties and experimented with SEZ policy. Diffusion continued the momentum from there. The SEZs were so successful that national leaders were convinced of their superiority, domestic support for FDI was broadened, the reformist faction was strengthened, and over time this growth model won over the alternatives. The contribution of diaspora entrepreneurs was the basis of such rapid diffusion.

THE RISE OF DIASPORA NETWORKS IN POST-MAO CHINA

How did overseas Chinese return and contribute so strongly to the PRC, given that Maoist China shunned them and discriminated against the relatives they left behind? The change in leadership was critical to the rise of diaspora networks. The end of Mao's rule and the emergence of Deng's era marked a turning point; with Deng came four pivotal changes in domestic politics and foreign policy that ultimately served as felicitous conditions of FDI liberalization. First, Deng Xiaoping and his associates were eager (and desperate) for economic growth, after the lengthy havoc under Mao. Second, Deng's leadership was concurrent with the overhaul of personnel filling positions in the national and local governments, more or less sharing economic priorities. Third, Deng normalized relationship with the United States, improved ties to Japan, patched diplomacy with the Southeast Asian nations (with the exception of Vietnam), and as a whole

[12] On formal documents in this period and the problems in socialist industrial strategy, see Reardon (2002).

[13] The planners had hoped to use oil exports to reimburse expensive machinery imports (Lardy 2002). Their plans became futile as their oil exploration in the Bohai Gulf failed to yield positive results.

stabilized China's geostrategic environment. This, on the one hand, relieved the country from military buildup and, on the other, strengthened foreign investors' confidence in China's economy. The last, but most important condition for the rise of diaspora networks was that the PRC embraced diasporas and corrected the harm done by Mao. As shown in his frequent interactions with accomplished diasporas, Deng took personal pride in diasporas' success and asked for their contribution in any possible way to China's development.

As in India and many other developing countries in the postcolonial period, entrepreneurs (and assets) fled when the communist regime was founded in 1949, and many achieved business success in their new environment. Overseas Chinese in particular benefited from high growth in East Asia and amassed formidable capital, technology, and access to global markets.[14] In 1979, overseas Chinese were immensely richer than Mainlanders. Based on gross domestic product (GDP) per capita, Hong Kong and Singapore were 100 times wealthier than China, and Taiwan and Malaysia were 50 times wealthier.[15] As China was turning toward economic growth, diaspora business was interested in investing: in late 1978, for example, Hong Kong-based Henry Fok and Macao-based Stanley Ho founded an investment company targeting China and invited other leading diaspora businesses to join.[16]

The sharp contrast between wealthy immigrants and impoverished Mainlanders helped to change the PRC's diaspora policy from Maoist discrimination to admiration. Overseas Chinese affairs were back on the country's key foreign policy agenda.[17] At the national and local levels, Offices of Overseas Chinese were founded, revived, and given new mandates. Chinese newspapers began to publish editorials praising the achievements of overseas Chinese (Chang 1980). The national and local governments were eager to receive diasporas, calling on their empathy and offering incentives. When possible, they recovered their properties previously confiscated by Mao and gave their domestic relatives some privileges. These efforts paid off. Overseas Chinese returned, first tentatively and then in increasingly large numbers. Such a revival of immigrant ties was particularly vibrant in areas in South China, where most Chinese immigrants claimed their ancestral home.

Struck by the huge gap in development and living standards between their new lives and their homeland, diasporas made large donations and built ties to government officials in Beijing and their hometown localities. Via those ties, they passed ideas and resources and encouraged Chinese officials at both levels to open to foreign investment. Hong Kong had direct ties to Beijing even before

[14] See works on overseas Chinese capitalism, Hamilton (1991), Kao (1993), and Weidenbaum and Hughes (1995).
[15] See statistics in *Penn World Table*.
[16] According to *Shijie huaren nianjian [Yearbook on Overseas Chinese in the World]*, 1995.
[17] Guowuyuan qiaowu bangongshi (2001).

1979 because many national ministries and SOEs had outposts there.[18] With the government keen on growth, these former ties were strengthened. Hong Kong became the epicenter of diaspora networks shaping China's FDI liberalization.

Deng Xiaoping was remarkably open to diaspora contacts (Vogel 2011). In the early days of reform, he interacted with Y. K. Pao, Lee Kashing, Gordon Wu, Henry Fok, Stanley Ho, and many others. While building interpersonal ties with top leaders, these diasporas also made strong connections to the localities in South China where they claimed ancestral linkages. The interactions between Deng and the diasporas described herein epitomize a much larger diaspora network phenomenon at the local level, where diaspora entrepreneurs flocked.

Deng Xiaoping's relationship with Y. K. Pao was among the best recorded. Pao, born in Ningbo, Zhejiang Province, was a successful financier in Shanghai before 1949 and fled to Hong Kong after the Communist Revolution. While in Hong Kong, he built a shipping empire in East Asia and delved into real estate and infrastructure development in the 1970s. His initial motivation to return to the PRC was sentimental, but as the founder of a major business empire, he quickly spotted investment opportunities in the opening of China.

In 1978, Pao visited Beijing for the first time after the revolution and made a large donation to build the first modern hotel in Beijing. Pao arranged to meet with Deng Xiaoping, the Chinese signatory of his donation, and forged what would become a long-term relationship with the Chinese leader (Yu 2000). The hotel construction, however, was severely delayed by the lack of expertise and bureaucratic inefficiency in China. Y. K. Pao revisited China, was welcomed as a national guest, and had individual meetings with Deng. He even dined at Deng's own residence (Yu 2000). When Deng asked Pao's opinions on developing China's shipping industry, Pao responded, "I was born in China. My roots are in China. I will do what I can to help the motherland to develop." Pao collaborated with the Ministry of Machine Building [*Jixie zhizao bu*] and Ministry of Ship Building [*Chuanbo jianshe bu*] to help them gain funds and access to global markets.[19]

Y. K. Pao's involvement in his birthplace was deep. He donated funds to build a university named after his hometown Ningbo. By the mid-1980s, Y. K. Pao had invested extensively in shipping, real estate, hotels, roads, education, and other social programs. Pao's investments, especially the earliest ones, revealed "empathy and dedication" only available among immigrants (Patterson 2006), which buttressed his continual engagement after his hotel project went sour for

[18] Stanley Ho, the Casino King in Macao, resumed his business in the Mainland in 1970 and began to advise the PRC's political leaders on policies regarding Hong Kong and Macao well before the PRC opened its doors (Huang and Lawrence 1995).

[19] Chinese industries were under a huge credit crunch and backward technology constraints. See commentaries in *Renmin Ribao [People's Daily]*, May 23, 1978, 2; *Renmin Ribao [People's Daily]*, June 4, 1978, 2; *Renmin Ribao [People's Daily]*, July 3, 1978, 1, 3. The impact of diaspora networks was shown in the shifted views on FDI liberalization in state industry. See, *Renmin Ribao [People's Daily]*, November 17, 1984, 2.

years.[20] As a "primitive market," 1980s China was full of daunting problems that discouraged foreign investors: although SEZs did not set up hurdles against nonethnic investment, the majority of FDI came from diaspora entrepreneurs.

Another important contributor was Gordon Wu, whose father migrated from Guangdong to Hong Kong. Wu built his business in infrastructure and property development during Hong Kong's high-growth era. When China began its reform, Wu helped the development of infrastructure in Guangdong and served as policy advisor to the national government. In 1979, he contracted with the Guangdong government to build a large electrical power plant, which came to supply 35 percent of Guangdong's electricity, fueling industrial takeoff in the province. In the 1980s, Wu's company built the China Hotel in Guangzhou, the Customs and Immigration building between Hong Kong and Shenzhen, and the massive superhighway from Hong Kong through Guangzhou to Macao. In Beijing, Wu was a permanent policy advisor to the State Council and a member of CPPCC. As an influential reform advisory body chaired by Deng Xiaoping from 1978 to 1983 and Deng Yingchao from 1983 to 1988, the CPPCC produced regular policy proposals on economic reform.[21]

Lee Kashing, a Guangdong-born immigrant who left China as a destitute teenager, was the richest overseas Chinese. On October 1, 1978, he visited Beijing at the invitation of the State Council to celebrate the national holiday. Lee assessed Beijing's political atmosphere and also visited his home province. In September of the following year, Lee made a large donation to set up a university in the province. In Hong Kong, Lee maintained close ties to China's SOEs operating there, such as China Venturetech, Citic Pacific, and Shougang. He was involved in these companies' growth during the reform era (Lever-Tracy 1996). He formed long-term, personal relationships with business-minded family members of top political leaders in addition to regular contacts with national officials.[22] The political elites with whom Lee networked were key advocates for deepening FDI liberalization in the early 1990s, after it was halted in the wake of the 1989 Tiananmen Crisis. Lee's company also profited from his political connections and was involved in many high-profile infrastructure projects in

[20] In 1978, when Pao made a substantial donation to the PRC, there was no proper protocol in place to receive such donations. Only with Deng Xiaoping's intervention was Pao given a ceremony for that significant contribution. Shortly thereafter, Pao donated funds to build a modern hotel in Beijing, in honor of Pao's father who stayed in China after 1949. Yet bureaucratic delays rendered the hotel incomplete for years. When it was finished, Pao's father had passed away. Despite frustration, Pao continued to invest in China and advise policy makers on economic policies. See Li (2008).

[21] See member lists and proposals at CPPCC, compiled by Qu Yuan, a research analyst at CPPCC.

[22] According to Lee, he was deeply committed to China's economic success, and he committed over a third of his investable capital in the Mainland by the early 1990s (Huang and Lawrence 1995). Through his business and personal networks, Lee was especially close to Deng Xiaoping's son, Deng Zhifang, Deng Xiaoping's son-in-law, Wu Jianchang, and Chinese Vice President Yang Shangkun's son, Larry Yang.

Shanghai, ports along the Yangtze River, and property development in Beijing, as well as in SOE reforms in the 1990s.

The contrast between diaspora investment and non-ethnic FDI was clear. Japan's Nippon Steel and American Occidental Petroleum are examples. Both had the endorsement of Deng Xiaoping, home governments (Japan and America respectively), and top CEOs with strategic visions. Yet both failed to persevere.[23] Nippon Steel and Oxy incurred substantial losses, and the Chinese weren't happy either. In the auto industry (see Chapter 7), the three early entrants – French Peugeot, American Motor Company, and Japanese Isuzu – failed and withdrew. Furthermore, the early, nondiaspora investment projects had negative demonstration effects and discouraged Western investors' entry into the Chinese market (Lardy 2002).

Lee Kashing, Gordon Wu, Y. K. Pao, and the diaspora members of the CPPCC were not the only overseas Chinese interacting with mainland actors during the 1980s. Many more diaspora businesses operated between world markets and homeland, bringing new ideas and resources to China. Diaspora entrepreneurs in the vicinity of the homeland were engaged in manufacturing for Western markets. Thus, when they invested in China, they also brought global commerce to China-based industries – in some cases, global commerce was the underlying force for their massive relocation, as in the case of the toy industry in Hong Kong and the footwear industry in Taiwan. Diasporas' influence, exemplified by these individuals but also by thousands on smaller scales, was extremely important in regions with strong immigrant ties. Diasporas' policy impact was more direct at the local level. The central government suffered from faction politics and broader political concerns, whereas local governments were pragmatic and less encumbered by ideology-based opposition (White 1998).

SPECIAL ECONOMIC ZONES AND THE INITIATION OF FDI LIBERALIZATION

In the early years of the post-Mao era, both Hua Guofeng and Deng Xiaoping opened China to capitalist countries under the "socialist industrial policy," which allowed China to receive foreign technology and loans, as well as limited joint ventures, as early as 1977. FDI liberalization, which conceded considerable autonomy to foreign investors, began with SEZs. The SEZs provided open and concessionary conditions to foreign companies, directly contradicting communist ideology and existing institutions. It was on this policy that diaspora networks had a central influence.

The national government reluctantly passed the SEZ bill in 1980. The actual constructions of Shenzhen and Xiamen SEZs, as well as investment

[23] For the Occidental case, see Lardy (2002, 1–2).

contracts with overseas Chinese, had begun earlier, however, with the other SEZs being completed later. In the process leading to the SEZ bill (1978–1980), overseas Chinese supplied ideas and information that helped to draft the bill and provided technology and capital indispensable to jump-starting the operation of the SEZs. The national government, meanwhile, continued to pursue the "socialist industrial policies" that transferred foreign loans and technology for the use of SOEs.[24]

The idea for SEZs first appeared in correspondence between Hong Kong and local officials in Guangdong. Reliant on information flows from Hong Kong and anticipating significant diaspora investment, Guangdong officials lobbied national leaders for liberal policies. In October 1977, at the Military Commission Meeting [*Junshi weiyuan huiyi*] held in Guangzhou (capital city of Guangdong), local officials suggested the openness strategy to Deng to attract diaspora entrepreneurs, even before Deng's leadership was established. Their hope was clear: to build Bao'an (today's Shenzhen) and Zhuhai as export zones to Hong Kong and Macao. In April 1978, after vice Premier Gu Mu and his delegation returned from Hong Kong and Macao, Guangdong local officials held another advising session with these national policy makers, making a strong case for FDI liberalization.[25]

In June 1979, the national government passed the joint venture law (JVL), which conformed to the "socialist industrial policy." The JVL signaled China's willingness to invite foreigners, but set out stringent (and ambivalent) terms for foreign companies' entry and operation in the PRC. The JVL was improved in 1986.[26] Nevertheless, even before the 1979 JVL, Hong Kong investors had already contracted hundreds of merchandise assembly orders with the Guangdong government for investment exceeding $30 million – this in addition to the famous Zhongshan Hotel contracted with Henry Fok. In November 1979, Guangdong party boss Xi Zhongxun asked Beijing to authorize the proposed SEZ. This move was followed by a group of Hong Kong businessmen sending a joint letter to Deng Xiaoping asking for authorization to set up factories in Guangdong and pledging to bring concrete benefits to the local economy (Xiao 2005).

Before the approval from the central government, local officials proceeded in constructing the SEZs with the help of diaspora networks. The first, Shekou, was

[24] Chinese high politics was complex in the 1980s. Although Deng Xiaoping had top political authority, his rival Chen Yun, who had long-term work experience in economic planning, weakened his control over economic policy, and Chen's followers occupied key positions in economic bureaucracies. For a glimpse into this polity, see Zhao (2009).

[25] See "Gu Mu yu Yuan Geng," *Yanhuang Chunqiu*, No. 8, 1998. The Guangdong Party boss Xi Zhongxun was originally from Shanxi, but on his arrival in Guangdong, local officials persuaded him of the importance of diaspora networks and how diaspora investment might improve Guangdong's development.

[26] Complex reform politics influenced ambivalent and contradictory liberalization policies and, in Westerners' eyes, resulted in too much uncertainty for them to commit; see Pearson (1992).

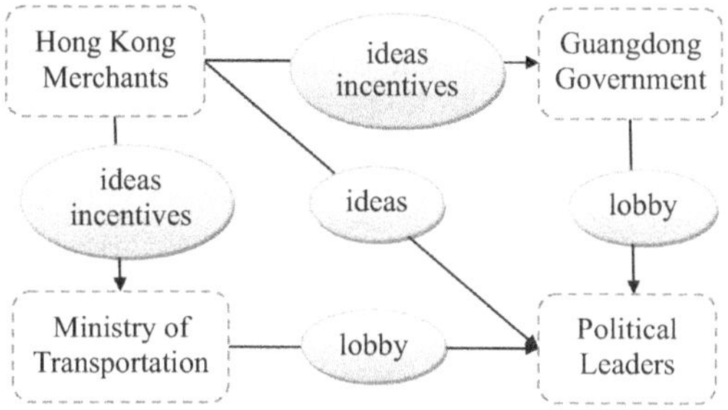

FIGURE 3.2. Shekou Industrial Export Zone, Guangdong, January 1979

in operation a year ahead of the 1980 SEZ Bill. Figure 3.2 shows how Yuan Geng, head of Hong Kong Merchants' Group, initiated the Shekou export zone. Yuan was born in Guangdong and developed deep roots in Hong Kong's business communities, as well as with political elites on the Mainland.[27] Yuan proposed the establishment of an export-processing zone in Shekou (part of Shenzhen) to Zeng Sheng, the chairman of Guangdong Revolutionary Commission [*gewuihei*], and then to Fujian native Ye Fei, the Minister of Communications [*Jiaotong bu*] the establishment of an export-processing zone in Shekou (a part of Shenzhen). The three collectively asked national leaders for approval of the Shekou project.[28] Driven by this three-way policy advocacy, the Shekou zone received approval from Beijing, although Vice President Li Xiannian warned that no central funding be spent on the project (Li 2008, 73).

In early 1979, Hong Kong businessmen suggested that the Shekou zone be expanded to encompass property development and tourism, suggesting the name "Special Economic Zone" to reflect this broader scope (Ho and Huenemann 1984, 49). Deng Xiaoping finalized the name in April 1979 in a meeting with Guangdong party boss Xi Zhongxun. In the proposed SEZ, a 15 percent corporate tax rate was applied to match the tax rate in Hong Kong (Sung 1991, 13). Officials in charge of developing the SEZ were armed with new ideas such as efficiency, taxation, contracts, and the like and promises of capital and technology inflows from Hong Kong. Several national leaders, including head of state and Guangdong native Ye Jianying and Guangdong vice governor and military chief Yang Shangkun played a positive role. Both Ye and Yang were allies of Deng and connected diasporas, local governments in South China, and Deng's coalition more closely.

In August 1980, under Ye Jianying's pressure, the National People's Congress approved the Guangdong government's SEZ proposal, which included extensive

[27] Hong Kong's Merchants Group was a company established by the Qing Dynasty in the 1800s. The PRC took ownership in 1949, yet left the company to operate in Hong Kong. Similar China-owned companies included China Resources. These companies were deeply embedded in the Hong Kong business world and played important roles in connecting Hong Kong with the Mainland after 1976.

[28] *Renmin Ribao [People's Daily]*, July 21, 1989, p. 4.

and detailed incentives for diaspora investors (Lu 2005). The draft incorporated substantial input from diasporas in the business world. The 15 percent corporate tax, for example, was insisted upon by Hong Kong business representatives, who succeeded in convincing the Mainland drafters to give up on the original rate of 33 percent (a common rate in the PRC) (Li 2008). At the time of the SEZ bill, Deng Xiaoping and other national leaders perceived SEZs as "experiments," bounded in small, remote, and politically inconsequential areas in the southern tip of the nation. Official documents underscored the "experimental" nature of SEZs.[29]

Like Guangdong, Fujian province also benefited from strong diaspora networks. It had an emigrant population of 30 million in Hong Kong, Macao, Taiwan, and Southeast Asia. Between 1952 and 1967, these emigrants invested RMB 70 million (equivalent to $54 million in 1981) in sixty-two firms in twenty-seven cities across Fujian and made generous contributions to education, road building, and social welfare (Ren 1999). Such diaspora links ceased during the Cultural Revolution (1966–1976). The end of Mao's rule revived these pre-reform ties, and Fujian local officials were in close consultation with their successful emigrants (Wang 2005). They quickly created plans to develop export and light industries reliant on overseas Chinese and began to send development reports to Beijing in late 1978. Before the central government's approval, the local government had approved joint ventures with foreign firms. Diaspora investors played the role of go-between in these ventures, in addition to being major investors themselves.

Diaspora connections facilitated the reemergence of private enterprises in China, contributing to pro-FDI practices at the societal level. In 1980, with the influence of diaspora networks, the State Council passed a document encouraging joint ventures between overseas Chinese and their relatives and friends on the mainland. It stipulated that overseas Chinese could transfer equipment valued under RMB 100,000 (equivalent to $59,000 in 1981) to their relatives or personal associates on the Mainland free from customs duties. Both Fujian and Guangdong experienced a revival of private enterprises. Early private factories were established by relatives and friends of overseas Chinese, who provided technology, capital, and even market access (Zheng 2006). Li Ping, a diaspora entrepreneur from Indonesia, for example, brought two machines to Fujian in 1980, and within one year, his company grew from thirty workers to more than 200 workers. He also helped local entrepreneurs set up seven factories and provided them with equipment and knowledge, even sharing his international orders with them.[30] The township and village enterprises (TVEs) in South

[29] These documents were the July 15, 1979 "Approval by the Central Committee of the Chinese Communist Party and the State Council Concerning the Adoption of Special Policies and Flexible Measures in External Economic Activities" and the May 16, 1980 "Written Instructions of the Central Committee of the Chinese Communist Party Provincial Authorities," See, "Implement the Policy of Readjustment, Ensure Stability and Unity," December, 25, 1980. (http://english.peopledaily.com.cn/dengxp/vol2/text/b1480.html)

[30] *World Chinese: Business Legend*. 1995, II, p. 150.

China in the 1980s had connections to diaspora entrepreneurs – that is, if they were not diaspora-invested firms to begin with.

In South China beyond the designated zones, private entrepreneurship burgeoned thanks to hometown networks with diaspora entrepreneurs. Small towns like Dongguan, Guangdong, were not designated SEZs but had substantial numbers of emigrants to Hong Kong and Taiwan. Local cadres attracted considerable diaspora investment, growing rapidly from 1978 to 1983.[31] The ties between local officials and diaspora investors, who spoke the same dialect, were incredibly personal, and local officials interpreted policies flexibly to suit the needs of diaspora investors (Hsing 1998). The lure of Guangdong and Fujian had two important effects: first, labor and talents in other regions were eager to join diaspora-invested companies in SEZs; and second, local officials elsewhere were eager to emulate pro-FDI policies within their jurisdictions. From 1979 to 1981, local officials outside Guangdong set up fifty nationally licensed trading companies in Hong Kong and another 300 without authorization from the national government.[32]

Diaspora entrepreneurs were important players in SEZs. They were early entrants and provided the majority of investment. An August 1981 report disclosed that in the Shenzhen SEZ, 90 percent of FDI was from Hong Kong, 6 percent was from other overseas Chinese, and only 4 percent was from non-Chinese foreigners. Hong Kong investment built the three largest projects in Shenzhen. In Zhuhai SEZ, a 1984 statistic suggests that 92.2 percent of FDI was from Hong Kong. In Xiamen SEZ, over three-quarters of foreign visitors were overseas Chinese. And in Shantou SEZ, a Thai-Chinese established the first of the so-called foreign companies (Chen 1984).

Ezra Vogel (1989) has suggested that, although originally envisioning SEZs as small experiments, the national leaders were convinced of their great success by the end of the decade. They cost the government practically nothing and were able to generate remarkable growth. In Shenzhen, more than 85 percent of investment in infrastructure from 1979 to 1984 came from FDI, whereas domestic funds, including national and local government allocations and bank loans, amounted to less than 15 percent. And in the SEZs' first three years (1979–1982), almost all investment in infrastructure came from diaspora funds.[33] Table 3.3 shows that diaspora investors contributed the majority of FDI to the earliest zones.

Between 1979 and 1983, more than 90 percent of FDI in Shenzhen was from Hong Kong. Singapore was the second largest investor in Shenzhen. The United States and Japan followed as a distant third and fourth, respectively. In Shekou, the earliest export zone located in Shenzhen, diaspora investment also accounted for the majority of FDI. Using the 1984 statistics, Hong Kong, Singapore, and Thailand together accounted for almost 70 percent of FDI. The United States

[31] *Renmin Ribao [People's Daily]*, March 20, 1983, p. 2.

[32] *Hong Kong jingji shibao* [*Hong Kong Economic Times*], October 4, 1988.

[33] *The Yearbook of China's Special Economic Zones, 1984*, Hong Kong: China SEZ Yearbook Publisher, 1985, p. 198.

TABLE 3.3. *Foreign Direct Investment (FDI) in the Shenzhen and Shekou Zones in the Early Period (%)*

	Hong Kong	Singapore	Thailand	United States	Japan	Europe
Shenzhen SEZ	>90	3.2	~	1.8	0.7	1.2
Shekou	45.5	4	17.7	21.5	5.9	5.4

Data for Shenzhen are for the period 1979–1983; those for Shekou are for 1984 only.
Source: The Yearbook of China's Special Economic Zones, 1984, Hong Kong, China SEZ Yearbook Publisher. 1985, pp. 231, 202.

was a major contributor of funds, at 21.5 percent, and Japan brought up the rear with 5.9 percent. Other than supplying funds, overseas Chinese investors also brought sales channels and helped to make these SEZs a manufacturing basis for exports. Having close ties to local governments and entrepreneurs, diasporas bolstered developmental proclivity in South China, and other localities soon began to emulate this region's development.

OPEN COASTAL CITIES OVERCAME CHALLENGE TO FDI LIBERALIZATION

Recall the pathways of FDI liberalization described in Chapter 2 (Figure 2.1): once a new policy is initiated, challenges to it ensue, and the policy's consolidation is uncertain. In China, there were several roadblocks to FDI liberalization. From 1982 to 1984, opposition to FDI was strong because the conservative forces in the national government were concerned with losing control. Diasporas helped to overcome domestic resistance in two ways. First, diasporas made more contacts at the national and local levels. Many served as policy advisors of the State Council and members of the National People's Congress and CPPCC. Second, their investment was forthcoming and helped to establish SEZs as a symbol of economic success, which laid the basis for the pro-FDI coalition. The passage of OCC laws signaled the victory of such coalition.

Studies of elite politics have established the existence of conservative and reformist factions in China and how their rivalry shaped economic policies (Shih 2008; Vogel 2011). Shortly after the passing of the SEZ bill, conservative resistance to SEZs and FDI mounted. Chen Yun, the head of the Central Advisory Commission (which consisted of revolutionary elders) led domestic campaigns against SEZs and FDI (Schran 1984). Chen instructed the national government to implement a rectification campaign [*zhengdun*] in response to a growing sense of "ideological dissolution" in the country (Dittmer 1982, 39). Rising debt incurred under the socialist industrial policy enhanced conservative resistance to opening, including resistance to SEZs. Corruption and smuggling emerged in South China, leading many in Beijing to resent liberal FDI policies, subscribing that SEZs were havens of economic crimes. Deng Xiaoping worried and concurred that "the steps taken and methods used should be subordinated to the current readjustment, and the pace should be slowed somewhat."[34] Deng's remarks further strengthened opposition to pro-FDI groups.

In 1982, the CCP Propaganda Department [*Xuanchuan bu*], under the influence of the conservative faction, launched the "anti-spiritual-pollution campaign" targeting SEZ policy. Deng Xiaoping shifted further toward the opposition group (Dittmer 1982, 43). Overall, Beijing pursued a more restrictive economic policy and focused on the dangers of "bourgeois liberalization" (Lieberthal 1983). Although a general focus on economic development remained, the national government as a whole emphasized recentralization. Financial control shifted back to Beijing, heavy industries received a larger share of government investment than in the previous two years, and economic reform slowed down (Lieberthal 1983, 35). By 1983, ideological debates and political turmoil seemed to have obstructed China's FDI liberalization (Kallgren 1984).

Because of domestic uncertainties over the direction of economic reform, Western investors became more cautious, adopting a wait-and-see approach. The locally rooted diaspora networks, in contrast, remained robust. Through 1984, their investment continued to flow into China. Local governments, driven to develop their local economies and increase revenues, were eager to facilitate the entry of diaspora investors and used mainstream news outlets to demonstrate the advantage of the SEZs.[35] In Beijing, although conservatives were critical of FDI, others were praising the apparent economic gains in South China. Further, representatives of diaspora networks, such as Henry Fok, Stanley Ho, Ma Wangqi, An Zhijie, and many others, served in the CPPCC and regularly attended the annual meetings of the National People's Congress. Consulting diasporas on China's economic reform was normal and frequent in the mid-1980s.[36]

To personally assess the operation of SEZs, Deng Xiaoping conducted a Southern Tour. The tour lasted twenty-seven days and was publicized within China alongside the economic success visible in SEZs.[37] The daily accounts of Deng's tour suggest that he was uncertain of FDI's effect in the first days of the visit; in his own words, he was there "to watch with his own eyes" [*qinzi kankan*] whether or not SEZs worked.[38] His misgivings were quickly dispelled. When he was invited to the Presidential Suite on the top floor of Guangzhou's White Swan

[34] "Implement the Policy of Readjustment, Ensure Stability and Unity," December, 25, 1980. (http://english.peopledaily.com.cn/dengxp/vol2/text/b1480.html)

[35] See a series of publications in *Renmin Ribao [People's Daily]*, January 11, 1983, p. 4; January 15, 1983, p. 4; February 4, 1983, p. 4; March 15, 1983, p. 2; March 20, 1983, p. 2;

[36] China's negotiation with Great Britain over Hong Kong's reversion in 1984 and the agreement reached in that year served as an important, additional impetus to enhancing interactions between Mainland leaders and Hong Kong business representatives.

[37] Reporting of the tour also suggests the importance of Hong Kong media. In the first days of the Southern Tour, the Beijing-based reporter accompanying Deng's tour was not authorized to publish in the Mainland, whereas the Hong Kong media reported profusely.

[38] Zhonggong zhongyang wenxian yanjiushi (2004, 954–983).

Hotel, built by Henry Fok, Deng was clearly impressed. He held Fok's hands and said "thank you."[39] So convinced, Deng endorsed every SEZ with strong remarks in his own calligraphy. When he returned to Beijing, he summoned the Politburo members and instructed them that, "The open door policy should be expanded rather than contracted ... SEZs should be windows for technology, management, knowledge, and open policies."[40]

Other political leaders on the tour were equally impressed. Wang Zhen, an otherwise politically conservative elder, spoke enthusiastically in 1984 about the extraordinary achievement in Shenzhen. He explained that he had visited Shenzhen four times from 1979 to 1984, and each time he was struck by its improvements. "In 1979," Wang noted, "the Shekou industrial area was nothing but dark marshes, barren hills, and rugged roads. By 1984, it had risen as a modern city with highways, an airport, electricity, water, nice residential areas, properties, shopping malls, and diverse industries."[41]

Deng's 1984 Southern Tour and its publicity had two positive effects on FDI liberalization in China. On the one hand, it showed outside observers that Deng Xiaoping remained supportive of openness. Diaspora entrepreneurs responded to this message more quickly than other foreign investors. When FDI flows increased in 1984, most of these funds came from overseas Chinese. On the other hand, Deng's tour suggested to officials in other parts of China that FDI was an effective means to industrialization. Other localities became more motivated to implement openness policies and to attract foreign investors. Among them, local officials in Shanghai took note and began to construct infrastructure projects that would facilitate FDI while lobbying the national leaders for similarly liberal policies.

In April 1984, Beijing granted open policy to fourteen cities along the coast from north to south.[42] A high-level forum on OCCs was held in Beijing. The attendants at the Forum exchanged their views on the Shenzhen SEZ marvel. A Symposium on Investing in China's Open Cities was concurrently held in Hong Kong. Diaspora entrepreneurs, domestic companies, financial institutions, local governments, and ministerial officials attended and discussed collaborative business opportunities (Jin 1984). By the time the symposium concluded on November 15, 1984, the Chinese side had contracted $2.2 billion in diaspora investment for the OCCs.[43] Subsequently, the State Council solicited Y. K. Pao as its official advisor on coastal development (Li 2008).

[39] See *World's Chinese: Business Legend*, Xinua News Publisher, 1995.

[40] Ibid.

[41] "Wang Zhen Gives Impression on Tour of Special Economic Zones in the Company of Deng Xiaoping," *Liao Wang [Outlook]*, Staff Reporter, No. 16, 1984.

[42] Ministry of Foreign Economic Relations and Trade, *Guide to China's Foreign Economic Relations and Trade: Cities Newly Opened to Foreign Investors* (Beijing: Economic Information and Agency, 1984).

[43] *Renmin Ribao [People's Daily]*, November 17, 1984, p. 2.

Among the fourteen coastal cities, twelve were located in provinces that served as major sources of Chinese out-migration (Guangdong, Fujian, Zhejiang, Shanghai, Jiangsu, and Shandong). Even before 1984, many of them had been involved in covert economic activity with overseas Chinese through immigrant ties.[44] Tianjin, outside Beijing, and Dalian in northeastern China were the two exceptions. Yet, as two major port cities in northern China, they had attracted a significant number of visitors and tourists from Hong Kong since the early 1980s (Yeung and Hu 1992). Once they became OCCs, investment from diasporas in these cities skyrocketed. In 1985, for example, six hotel projects in Dalian worth a total of $100 million, including the Dalian International, Dalian Forama, Qing Gang hotel, and Dalian Dayang Mansion (itself a $10 million joint venture) were agreed upon by Hong Kong investors and the Dalian government (Yeung and Hu 1992, 34).

From 1982 to 1984, the PRC was involved in lengthy negotiations with Great Britain over Hong Kong's reversion. The countries signed a treaty in 1984, in which Britain agreed to return Hong Kong and the PRC promised to guarantee Hong Kong's socioeconomic systems for fifty years after reversion. This broad, strategic background played a facilitative role in Mainland–Hong Kong relations as China's top leaders intensified engagement with representatives of diasporas. The archival materials available today, however, demonstrate more clearly that the remarkable early success achieved in SEZs and intensified diaspora engagement in the homeland precipitated and deepened FDI liberalization in China.

As the FDI-led economy took off in SEZs, other localities in China established footholds there. By 1987, twenty-seven of China's twenty-nine provinces and many municipalities had established offices (as well as their own provincial guesthouses) in Shenzhen (Vogel 1989, 141). Some twenty-five different central ministries established over 2,000 "domestic link" ventures under their Shenzhen offices. These domestic linkages helped to expand pro-FDI coalitions within China. As many localities set up their own "open areas" with or without central endorsement, the reach of diaspora investors increased considerably. Overseas Chinese typically entered the new open areas sooner than other investors.[45] Infrastructure development offered business opportunities for diaspora entrepreneurs who built Hong Kong, Taiwan, and Singapore in the post–World War II decades. Because immigrant investors relied heavily on interpersonal relations, they helped to transform the ideologies and incentives of mainland actors at both national and local levels.

[44] "Shadow trade" with overseas connections contributed to the growth of early entrepreneurs in Wenzhou, Zhejiang, for example.

[45] In 1990, for example, although the overall environment for FDI deteriorated, overseas Chinese investment in the OCCs remained steady. In that year, more than one-third of foreign invested firms were from Taiwan. Keep in mind, Taiwanese investment was only allowed beginning in 1988. See *Renmin Ribao [People's Daily]*, October 31, 1990, p. 2.

In 1984, the success of OCCs did not end debates over FDI. Challenges continued to rise because FDI liberalization was inchoate, and external shocks and crises strengthened domestic resistance. In the mid-1980s, for example, resistance to SEZs resurfaced as a major smuggling ring in Hainan was disclosed. Deng Xiaoping, going against his strong support of SEZs in early 1984, recanted in June 1985, saying, "It still needs time to judge whether SEZs work for China ... It is OK if they fail, as they are just experiments."[46] Again, overseas Chinese and their networks at the national and local levels gave reformers an upper hand and helped to sustain FDI liberalization.

Success in SEZs sufficiently co-opted local officials in other parts of China. The importance of these local networks and dynamics was clear in the wake of 1989 Tiananmen Crisis, which additionally challenged the diffusion of FDI liberalization. The Tiananmen Crisis was acute, and the consolidation of FDI liberalization followed a similar dynamic as it did 1984: policy debates within the national government favored the conservative camp, whereas local governments continued to embrace openness. Diaspora entrepreneurs continued to invest in China and built more extensive ties to local governments, and Deng Xiaoping once again toured South China to mobilize pro-FDI coalitions. Openness to FDI continued and profoundly expanded in the early 1990s.

REASSERTING FDI LIBERALIZATION AFTER THE TIANANMEN CRISIS

In June 1989, a major student demonstration in Beijing led to nation-wide political protests. The government decided to call in the military and crushed the demonstration with force. Once political order was restored in the country, party leaders conducted a stringent rectification campaign, systematically undermining reformist officials in the government because the more powerful conservative faction viewed reform and openness as underlying causes of Tiananmen.[47] Zhao Ziyang, the General Secretary of the CCP and a main supporter of opening China to FDI, was stripped of his position and placed under house arrest. Countless bureaucrats and local officials with whom Zhao associated stepped down. Deng Xiaoping's authority was tarnished. In public discourse and official documents, critiques of liberal economic reform as inviting Western "peaceful evolution" were pervasive (Jiang 1991).[48] Overall, the Tiananmen Crisis strengthened the power of conservatives, and liberalization was put on back burner for eighteen months.

In early 1992, Deng Xiaoping orchestrated the second Southern Tour. Unlike his 1984 Tour, this time he needed no convincing that openness was critical to economic growth. Everywhere he visited, he said he wanted to "reignite fire for

46 Zhonggong zhongyang wenxian yanjiushi (2004, 1055).

47 For a detailed account of elite politics in the wake of the Tiananmen crisis, see Fewsmith (2001).

48 See also titles in *Renmin ribao [People's Daily]*, September to November 1989.

opening" [*dianhua*]. Although Deng's personal authority was instrumental, it was more important that he correctly assessed the expansive pro-FDI coalition in the nation, based on three developments during the 1980s. First, diasporas on a large scale provided favorable ideas and strong incentives. Second, rapid industrialization in South China made FDI liberalization the preferred economic model for other localities. Finally, growing industries cooperated and drew benefits from diaspora networks and external exchange. By mobilizing these incentives and interests, Deng reconsolidated FDI liberalization and his political power.

Prior to Deng's 1992 Southern Tour, three developments shaped the coalitional politics of FDI liberalization. First, diaspora investment and trade had become important to local development. From 1979 to 1988, China's foreign trade increased fivefold, going from \$20.6 billion to \$102.8 billion.[49] Even though there were absolutely none in 1978, foreign capital inflows in 1988 amounted to \$16 billion, with more than 6,000 foreign-invested firms operating in China.[50] Open areas expanded from four SEZs to fourteen open cities along the coast, plus Guangdong, Fujian, and Hainan provinces, three delta regions, and various border areas, covering a total area of 320,000 km^2 and boasting a population of 200 million.[51] The open areas experienced significant improvements in industrial output, infrastructure, and living standards. The local governments became richer and more influential in the country.

Foreign direct investment's direct contribution to local economy was remarkable for most coastal areas. In 1992, for example, in new technology and development zones, 59 percent of GDP and 34 percent of exports were produced by foreign-invested firms (FIFs). In OCCs and SEZs, 13 percent of GDP and 35 percent of exports were produced by FIFs. In Fujian, 33 percent of GDP and 45 percent of exports were produced by FIFs. In Guangdong, FIFs accounted for 19 percent of GDP and 29 percent of exports. In Shanghai and Zhejiang, relatively late in opening, FIFs' shares were also impressive: they accounted for 17 percent of GDP and 22 percent of exports for Shanghai, and 16 percent of GDP and 12 percent of exports for Zhejiang.[52]

Second, driven by earlier success in the open areas, local governments launched campaigns to support continued FDI liberalization. They used impressive statistics and graphs in official media to showcase the phenomenal economic achievements in their areas. Guangdong and Fujian led the pro-liberalization campaign. Guangdong showcased its "golden era" of economic development in *Renmin Ribao* [*People's Daily*] in September 1989: from 1978 to 1989, Guangdong's GDP increased by more than 300 percent, its industrial output by more than 400 percent, and its government revenue by 170 percent, whereas

49 *Renmin Ribao [People's Daily]*, September 18, 1989, p. 6.

50 *Zhongguo tongjinianjian, 1995 [China Statistical Yearbook, 1995]*.

51 *Renmin Ribao [People's Daily]*, September 18, 1989, p. 6.

52 *Zhongguo tongji nianjian, 1993 [China Statistical Yearbook*, 1993]; *Zhongguo duiwai maoyi nianjian [China's Statistics Yearbook of Foreign Trade]*, 1993 edition.

foreign investment and trade rose by almost 600 percent and more than 400 percent, respectively.[53] In Shenzhen, GDP grew to 42 times its 1979 level. Fujian used similar tactics. It contrasted its industrial backwardness in 1978 with new images of booming manufacturing sites in *Renmin Ribao* [*People's Daily*]. Statistics demonstrated that from 1978 to 1986 industrial output in Fujian increased sevenfold, GDP increased sixfold, and savings increased fourteen times, which correlated with rising trade and increased foreign investment.

Economic statistics were persuasive, but local governments also assured political leaders that FDI strengthened socialism and facilitated national "reunification" [*tongyi daye*]. Guangzhou advertised itself as the "smiling city" in service to the people [*fuwu renmin*]. According to these pro-FDI articles, Hong Kong compatriots not only set up factories, but also built universities, hospitals, kindergartens, and nursing homes, as well as roads, bridges, buildings, dams, and power plants. The slogan "socialism is progressing" [*shehui zhuyi shiye zai qianjin*] marked the core theme of these local governments' lobbying efforts.

Finally, the strength of diaspora networks was rapidly increasing. The Hong Kong business community maintained strong economic, social, and political ties to Beijing. Hong Kong representatives Henry Fok and Stanley Ho served as standing members of the National People's Congress in China and were directly involved in the legislation concerning Hong Kong's reversion and postreversion institutions. An Zhijie, Ma Wangqi, Tang Xiangqian, and others all served in CPPCC. Tang Xiangqian's father was the vice Chairman of Shanghai's CPPCC and played an influential role in Shanghai's FDI liberalization.

The economies of Hong Kong and the Mainland had become more interdependent by 1989. Hong Kong's imports from the Mainland more than tripled between 1984 and 1989, and exports quadrupled.[54] Diaspora visitors to the PRC increased rapidly. From 1980 to 1990, the number of diaspora visitors grew from 5.14 million to 25.6 million. Taiwanese visitors became an important group. After the ban on travel across the Taiwan Strait was lifted in late 1987, more than 55,000 Taiwanese visited Fujian in 1988. Furthermore, diasporas maintained strong investment in the period 1989–1992, whereas other investors halted or reduced investment.

Even before Deng's 1992 Tour, these forces had led local governments outside South China to embrace foreign investment, with the national authority engulfed in debate and uncertainty. Beijing municipality anxiously courted foreign investment. Inland cities, such as those in Shanxi province, were likewise eager to attract foreigners. Thus, actual and contracted FDI in China rose steadily from 1989 to 1991. Most of this increase came from diaspora investors, as Western capital sharply declined. In Guangdong, for example, American investment decreased from $307 million in 1989 to $64 million in 1991, whereas investment from Hong Kong increased from $1.8 billion to $4.2 billion in the

[53] *Renmin Ribao [People's Daily]*, September 11, 1989, p. 4.
[54] *Zhongguo tongji nianjian, 1995 [China Statistical Yearbook, 1995]*.

same two years. Taiwanese investment in the province also more than doubled, and Japanese investment likewise increased, although on a smaller scale than diaspora investment.[55]

Shanghai in particular raced ahead with FDI liberalization and vowed to promote foreign investment and exports. Developing Pudong had been Shanghai's priority since the mid-1980s and persisted through the Tiananmen crisis.[56] Shanghai began the construction of a bridge linking old Shanghai with Pudong in 1989, paving the way for rapid development to follow.[57] Shanghai had traditionally been the hub of global commerce and diaspora networks. Many entrepreneurs in Hong Kong and Taiwan were based in Shanghai before 1949. Residents of Taiwan, newly allowed to visit and invest in the Mainland, were drawn to Shanghai. Areas near Shanghai became the foci of FDI inflows and emerged as the new growth pole in China.

The emergence of Shanghai proper and China's deepening FDI liberalization in the 1990s are investigated in Chapter 5 of Part III. It's now time to examine the less noted but globally consequential transformation happening in Asia's other giant: India. There, democratic institutions did not prevent policy makers from implementing pro-growth policies, yet it was the rise of private business networks that shaped the government's reform plans. Diaspora professionals, although supplying ideas to policy makers, were not able to provide resources to either co-opt indigenous industry or produce compelling early success. Local governments were either nondevelopmental or closely embedded in indigenous business networks and thus opposed FDI. Reform in 1980s India took a different form than it did in China – domestic deregulation without FDI opening.

CONCLUSION

This chapter affirms the importance of individual leaders, local governments, and an improved geostrategic environment as described in earlier publications, but revisits such political arguments with network and process analyses and demonstrates the indispensable role of diaspora entrepreneurs. In China, diaspora networks had a strong impact on FDI policy making and made the largest contribution to FDI's early success, upon which pro-FDI ideas, incentives, and coalitions developed in the country. Between the national and local governments, the process analysis uncovers that local governments were more proactive than the national government. Diaspora networks initially and more strongly worked with provincial governments in South China, who lobbied for the initiation of FDI liberalization and then continued to embrace FDI against domestic resistance in the national government. The grassroots governments

[55] Ibid., pp. 401–407.

[56] Pudong is a district of Shanghai. Since the initial stages of its development in 1990, when plans were first announced, Pudong has emerged as China's financial and commercial hub.

[57] *Shanghai duiwai kaifang [Shanghai Opens Up]*. Shanghai, Shanghai People's Publisher. 2000.

within provinces were key economic actors in China, and they readily discarded socialist economic institutions and embraced partnerships with diaspora entrepreneurs, thus greatly expediting the diffusion of FDI liberalization.

This process supports the diffusion model of FDI liberalization. Ideas and incentives from diasporas helped China to initiate its open policy with SEZs. Stellar gains exemplified the effectiveness of FDI in introducing industrialization and expanded openness to OCCs in 1984 and more open areas in 1992. Foreign direct investment liberalization and diaspora networks were mutually reinforcing in China and demonstrated a virtuous cycle: more diaspora networks, speedier FDI liberalization, and greater economic success led to more diaspora networks and more profound FDI liberalization. The diffusion process clearly demonstrates that the fundamental transformation of large economies, like China's, can be introduced through incremental changes in policy enabled by resourceful and engaging diasporas with pragmatic and responsive governments.

The Chinese government's openness to diaspora influence was also due to weakness in domestic resistance. Despite socialist beliefs held by conservative factions in the national government, interest-driven local governments were largely pro-FDI, and SOEs were shielded from direct competition in the 1980s. Domestic industries were quite different in India, however. When they influenced deregulation in the early 1980s, they were not ready to share domestic markets with foreign investors and thus opposed external opening in the decade. The lack of entrepreneurial diasporas that could have offered incentives to change stances additionally hurt Rajiv Gandhi's external liberalization. India's returned diaspora were accomplished professionals in the West. They helped India's macroeconomic policy making but were unable to supply resources to jump-start FDI liberalization. Their ties did not go beyond the national government and limited their ideational influence on a broader scale.

4

Deregulation without Openness in India

India's reform experience provides an intriguing comparison and contrast with China's. Both countries started implementing reforms at almost the same time; yet they ultimately diverged in key contents of change. In 1980, Indira Gandhi returned to power and launched a pro-growth agenda. Deregulation was seriously pursued in India, just as the Chinese were constructing pro-foreign direct investment (FDI) special economic zones (SEZs). In 1984, Rajiv Gandhi succeeded his mother in premiership and announced liberalization with an external flare. His internal deregulation was implemented, but external opening was stalled; in the same year, the Chinese increased the number of open zones from four to fourteen. When Rajiv Gandhi stepped down in 1989, FDI liberalization hardly existed in India. This same year, the Tiananmen Crisis erupted in China and put FDI liberalization to a halt; yet the People's Republic of China (PRC) was already opened to FDI, which helped to revive liberalization in 1992. How did India's reform begin? Why did it not open to FDI?

Main political explanations are based on state capacity. One argument looks at individual leaders only (e.g., Harriss 1987; Manor 1987), and the others combine political institutions (Kohli 1990; 2004; 2006a) and interest group politics (Bardhan 1984). Specifically, these arguments suggest that Indira Gandhi implemented pro-business changes because she wanted to gain electoral leverage, and Rajiv attempted openness to FDI because of his personal penchant for technology (Kohli 1989). Extant works have explained that FDI liberalization was not implemented because democratic institutions limited these individual policy makers' ability to effect change or because interest groups could not unify their interests, and their internal strife derailed lasting reform (Bardhan 1984). These arguments also point to the role of bureaucracies and how senior economic bureaucrats devised policy liberalization toward private business as an act of state autonomy.

Like these extant works, the social network analysis examines actions and stances of key actors – policy makers, bureaucrats, and business groups – but stresses the importance of ties and interactions between policy makers and private businessmen. It also notes that economic bureaucrats were products of leadership preferences, as the prime ministers picked their cabinet members. The ties between policy makers and domestic business were formed and became salient in the 1970s and led to pro-business deregulation in the 1980s. Domestic interest groups stood against FDI in the latter half of the 1980s, but their victory was also partly due to weak external networks – the diaspora professionals transferred ideas but possessed few resources or ties outside policy makers.

In the chapter, macroeconomic statistics indicate that under Rajiv Gandhi's tentative opening, economic performance was not visibly improving. Instead, liberalization worsened national account deficits and engendered the specter of debt crisis a few years later. In China, by contrast, diaspora networks were willing and able to contribute technology, capital, and global commerce to make FDI liberalization successful from the bottom up. India's democratic institutions and social groups were important venues for arguments that deemed FDI liberalization largely unwelcome and unsuccessful. And the roots of opposition lay in the mixture of external and internal networks in 1980s India.

INDIA STARTED REFORM IN THE 1980S

India's liberalization in the 1980s was relatively narrow compared to its post-1991 reform, but it is significant when compared to the pre-1980 period, and it paved the way for more drastic liberalization in later years.[1] Within elite circles, concerns about economy overshadowed a commitment to socialism, and some form of external engagement was seen as necessary, in contrast to earlier ideas of economic isolationism. The government introduced a number of new cornerstone policies that continued into the post-1991 era. Ideas about reform, domestic industrial interests, and growth patterns were consistent from 1980 onward, and all represented obvious breaks from pre-1980 periods. Gross domestic product (GDP) growth, for example, averaged 5.8 percent per year in the 1980s, but only 2.9 percent in the 1965–1979 period. Annual growth between 1991 and 2004 averaged at 5.6 percent, similar to that of the 1980s.

Table 4.1 suggests a shift in the growth patterns of public and private companies starting in 1980. Before then, public sectors had a rising advantage over private sectors. In the 1960s, public companies increased paid-up capital by 14 percent annually, whereas private companies increased only 7 percent annually. In the 1970s, public companies' capital grew 19 percent annually, whereas the rate for private companies stayed more or less the same, and the gap between

[1] This view was commonly expressed by former officials that I interviewed and also confirmed with publications, Kohli (1989, 1990), Rodrik and Subramanian (2004), Panagariya (2008).

TABLE 4.1. *Annual Growth Rates of Public and Private Companies in India, 1961–1996 (%)*

	Public companies		Private companies	
Period	*Paid-up capital*	*Number*	*Paid-up capital*	*Number*
1961–1971	14	8	7	1
1971–1981	19	11	7	8
1981–1991	16	3	14	14
1991–1996	7	1	33	13

Source: Government of India, *Annual Report on the Working and Administration of the Companies Act*, New Delhi (various issues); CII, *Handbook of Statistics*, various issues.

the annual growth rates of each increased to more than 12 percent. Their rates per number of companies were also unbalanced and significantly favored the public sectors.

When reform started in the 1980s, public sectors stayed largely the same but private sectors gained enormously. In terms of paid-up capital, public companies' annual growth rate was 16 percent, whereas that of private companies increased rather significantly to 14 percent – significantly closing the gap between the two. In terms of the number of companies, the private sector made decisive gains over public companies in annual growth rates: 14 percent for private companies versus 3 percent for public ones. The same trend continued in the 1990s. The annual growth rate of the public sector halved in capital and stagnated in number. Private companies, by contrast, had rapid annual growth: 33 percent in capital and 13 percent in the number of companies.

Figure 4.1 graphs the changes in external sectors, where trends were far less clear. Imports as a share of GDP grew at first but then quickly evened out. Exports as a share of GDP fell consistently until 1990. The gap between imports and exports was substantial throughout the 1980s. FDI inflows did not gain much during the decade. In Figure 4.1, FDI's share of GDP was next to zero from 1980 to 1985, the same trend as in the mid-1970s; then in 1986, the share reached 0.1 percent, in 1987, 0.2 percent. It reverted back to 0.1 percent in 1988–89, until a sharp reduction in 1990, right before the financial crisis in the country.

Compared to Table 4.1, Figure 4.1 suggests two things: first, in contrast to the clearly pro-private trend in domestic sectors, changes in external sectors were more limited and less persistent; and second, when external sectors did open (for example in trade), results were not visibly positive, as seen in the persistently large trade imbalances and limited FDI inflows.

The sections to follow examine the reform episodes initiated by Indira and Rajiv Gandhi. In the first episode, I highlight the influence of domestic business groups on Mrs. Gandhi's decision to implement a particular type of economic liberalization – domestic deregulation. In the second, I stress the ideational

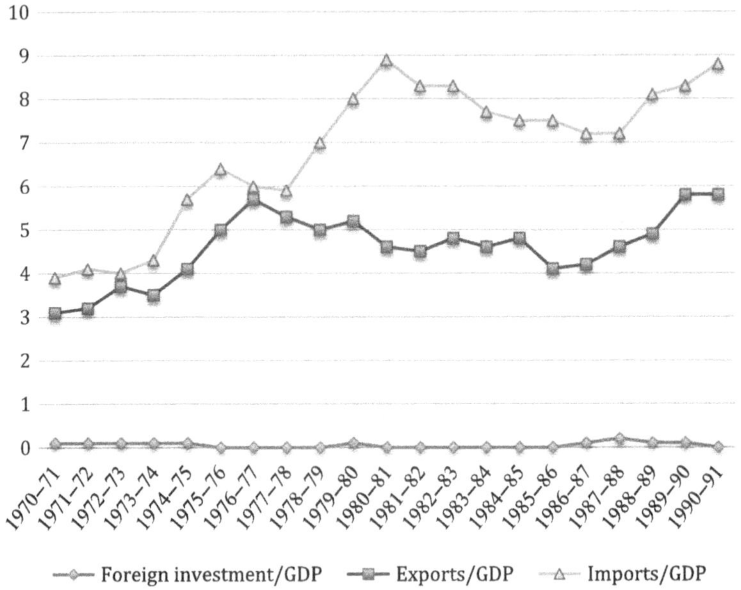

FIGURE 4.1. Volatile External Sectors (Share of GDP %)
Source: Raw data from Ministry of Commerce and Industry, Government of India, *Balance of Payment*, various years.

influence of diaspora professionals, which operated through Rajiv Gandhi's bureaucratic "change team," on his policy choices. The final section assesses the effect of 1980s reforms on the state and business in India and how these changes precipitated FDI liberalization in the subsequent era.

INDIRA GANDHI'S BUSINESS NETWORKS AND DEREGULATION

Indira Gandhi was in power from 1966 to 1977, during which time she pursued populism, promoted public sectors, and resisted external pressure for change. When she returned to power in 1980, however, she was "a changed Prime Minister" (Panagariya 2008, 79) who set out on a new economic direction for India (Gupta 1981). A 1981 *Times of India* editorial read, "A change of considerable significance is taking place in India ... the emphasis has shifted from distributive justice to growth."[2] According to her economic advisors, Mrs. Gandhi was "determined to get back to the firm foundation of economic reform" (Sengupta 2001, 55). Consistent with these policy priorities, Indira Gandhi promoted new political and economic advisors and bureaucrats, such

[2] *The Times of India*, February 22, 1981.

as L. K. Jha, P. C. Alexander, and Arjun Sengupta, who had considerable experience in business and extensive networks in private industry. The new administration then devised and announced new industrial policies that contained favorable changes toward private business in India.

What caused Indira Gandhi to change course? The seeds of her decision were planted in two developments in the 1970s that deepened Gandhi's relations with domestic private business. First, her second son Sanjay Gandhi emerged as a major player in business and fostered close ties with leading figures of Indian capitalists. And second, when Indira Gandhi was voted out of power between 1977 and 1980, private businessmen provided financial support for her livelihood and re-election, thus strengthening Indira's ties to business people.

Before the rise of private business networks under Indira Gandhi, private business communities largely stayed away from the government, and the main business sites were concentrated in South India. Government–business interactions were knit within the stricture of the *license-raj system*, with the state imposing extensive regulations on private business activities. Where policy makers sought to reduce protection, either by external pressure or persuasion, domestic industry acted against such efforts to change (Kochanek 1987). Indigenous industry's roles in post-1980 India have been different. Although resisting rapid FDI liberalization, they were nevertheless agents of economic change due to their globalization of talents, funds, and markets.

India's License-Raj and State–Business Relations before Reform

Postindependence India pursued socialism and set in place extensive control over private business, including the Industries Development and Regulation Act, the Monopolies and Restrictive Trade Practices Act (MRA), import and price controls, and various financial institutions (Eliot 1971). This system was generally called *license-raj*. The license-raj system hurt entrepreneurship and distorted interactions between state and business. The two operated in separate worlds, with business hiding assets from the state as much as possible. Ingenious and wealthy business families, however, were able to exploit the license raj to their own advantage and grew steadily.

Business houses, such as Tata and Birla, controlled Indian private business through holding directorships in a wide range of companies and associations. In the early 1950s, for example, ten Indian families, including the Birlas and the Tatas, held a total of 619 directorships (Chaudhuri 1975, 26), and in the mid-1960s, seventy-five leading business groups controlled 47 percent of the total assets and 44 percent of the paid-up capital of all nongovernmental and non-banking companies (Chaudhuri 1975, 18). They not only received the majority of licenses issued by the government, but also revoked or modified those licenses to suit their operational needs (Ghose 1974). Eager to expand, business houses invested capital in any field in which they could establish a business, regardless of its relation to their primary business, as long as there was potential for profit, creating what Asim Chaudhuri called "tycoon capitalism" (Chaudhuri 1980).

Furthermore, many of the assets held by these houses were acquired with money borrowed from public banks and financial institutions (Chaudhuri 1980, 39). For large houses like the Tatas, Birlas, and Mafatlals, there was no real barrier to their securing licenses except for opposition from the other houses (Kochanek 1987). To be sure, politicians' perennial need to raise funds enhanced the influence that Indian business elites exercised over policy making (Arora 1981; Kohli 1987). In many cases, politicians used licensing to extort funds from business, whereas businessmen used licensing to pressure bureaucrats, causing Dennis Encarnation (1979) to lament, "Indian bureaucracy: responsive to whom?"

Despite mutual capture in the license-raj system, private industrialists maintained an arms' length relationship with the government before the 1970s. In terms of power relations, they appeared subordinate to political elites (Arora 1981). As Dhirubhai Ambani, founder of Reliance, notes, "The government of India is the most important external environment [of my company]. I am willing to salaam anyone [in the government]."[3] Private business, concentrated in South India, also maintained its distance from politicians in New Delhi. Although competing with one another, private business families were in a cozy structure of jointly monopolizing domestic markets. In the auto sector, for example, the Tatas and the Birlas held unequivocal control over passenger vehicle manufacturing and sales, whereas Bajaj Autos monopolized the production of two- and three-wheelers. All the major auto-making companies and industrial associations were located near either Mumbai or Chennai, far from policy making in New Delhi. This would change in the 1970s, when Sanjay Gandhi became involved in business.

Indigenous Business and Sanjay: The Emergence of New Policy Networks

Sanjay Gandhi was Indira Gandhi's second son and reportedly her favorite. Despite his political pedigree, he was more interested in business than politics. In 1971, he founded the state automaker, Maruti Udyog, and used his political connections to acquire virtually unlimited government resources, including land, capital, and technology, for Maruti. Yet the company could not produce any vehicles and ran at a loss throughout the 1970s. Sanjay's business endeavors, however, helped forge close relationships with business people in India. K. K. Birla, for example, had advised Sanjay on his Maruti project since the beginning. Via Sanjay, Birla gained more access to Indira (Abbas 1985; Birla 1987). With Birla's advice, Sanjay divided Maruti Udyog into Maruti Technical Services and Maruti Heavy Vehicles and delved into a wide range of sectors

[3] Cited in Rosen (1992, 12).

including banking, import licensing, marketing, bus body production, chemical sales, and business consultancy.

Sanjay maintained a firm grip on Maruti and developed extraordinary business connections that incorporated both South India and New Delhi. Maruti became a powerful lobbying organization for various domestic companies and foreign multinationals such as International Harvester and Piper Aircraft (Frank 2001, 393). Local governments near New Delhi were brought into the new business networks. Bansil Lal, Chief Minister of Haryana, for example, developed strong personal ties to Sanjay Gandhi and provided Sanjay's business ventures with enormous amounts of land in that state, just a few minutes' drive from Delhi.

The formation of business networks and interactions with private businessmen changed Sanjay's views on socialism and capitalism. Sanjay developed a strong dislike for bureaucracy, the public sector, and government control and regulation of the economy, and he acquired a reputation as the "voice of big business" (Abbas 1985, 11–15; Hardgrave and Kochanek 1993). On August 6, 1975, when Sanjay was interviewed by Uma Vasudev of *Surge*, he denounced India's socialist economic policies, praised big business and multinational corporations, and declared that he favored removing all economic controls. He went so far as to pronounce that the public sector should be allowed to die "a natural death." The interview was quickly covered by ninety American newspapers and the British press, in addition to making headlines in all the major Indian newspapers.[4]

Maruti's corporate history and Sanjay's business activities demonstrate that there was a concealed and yet important shift in government–business interactions in the 1970s. Before that time, private business communities were concentrated in Mumbai, Chennai, and Calcutta, all in South India, and they kept their distance from policy making in New Delhi, where public sectors and socialist ideology had dominated economic policies since India's independence. Via the rise of Sanjay and operation of Maruti, private businessmen now acquired better access to government and developed stronger ties to policy makers. Influential business networks began to emerge around New Delhi (Hardgrave and Kochanek 1993). Even during the 1975–77 Emergency, business's influence began to show in economic policies toward private capital and foreign markets.

Strengthening Business Networks during Indira's Political Fall

Nobody knows precisely why Indira Gandhi called a national election in 1977, but she lost it and rendered herself powerless for three years while the Janata government sought revenge against the former PM. The Left and socialists

[4] In the interview, Sanjay levied attacks against the Communist Party and conservative members of Indira Gandhi's cabinet. Later, pressured by the Communist Party and the cabinet, Sanjay published a clarification of his statements.

deserted Indira and complied with the government's wishes. With the help of several businessmen, Indira's financial state was maintained, and with Sanjay and his business associates, Indira staged a successful comeback. The experience was important; Indira seemed to gain new business friends and a new appreciation for private capitalism – not to mention that it intensified the power of Sanjay and his pro-business orientation. These shifts were reflected in Indira Gandhi's parliament and cabinet choices and were responsible for significant deregulation measures in 1980.

Indira Gandhi was a private person and did not write about her experiences during her fall from political power. She did relate this to her friends, however, and according to them, Indira was "deeply disappointed" at the communists who did not stand by her when she was persecuted by the Janata government (Parthasaradhi and Prasad 1985). Her usual sycophants before 1977 were no longer frequent guests at Indira's new residence; many joined the repressive hands of the government. Sanjay's business friends, on the other hand, lent her sympathy and financial support. Many even suffered with Indira as targets of the government (Birla 1987). A businessman and family friend offered the Gandhis a place to live. Several others, including a young man who owned a soft drink company in Delhi and was a personal friend of Sanjay, sustained Indira's family with generous financial backing (Frank 2001, 417). Indira's business sympathizers, such as R. P. Goenka, M. V. Arunachalam (president of FICCI), Joet Pal of Apeejay & Co, and K. K. Birla, were arrested or harassed by the Janata government – yet they stayed loyal to the former PM. Such experiences strengthened the ties between Indira and private business communities (Pande 1989).

The ruling Janata Party's persecution of the Gandhi family backfired and generated sympathy for Indira in India and abroad. Although the government restricted Gandhi from traveling abroad, the British government successfully pressured it to issue her a diplomatic passport valid only for Britain. Her visit to the United Kingdom was a great success; she surrounded herself with nonresident Indians (NRIs) in London and reconnected with wealthy Indian industrialists. Swraj Paul, an Indian immigrant in the United Kingdom, arranged her stay at the Claridge's Hotel in the same suite she had occupied when she was prime minister and paid all the expenses associated with her elaborate "come-back tour" in London. Paul proved himself an invaluable fundraiser in England and orchestrated Indira's political rehabilitation there. During Indira's visit, Paul organized numerous support rallies for her and attracted large numbers of NRIs to attend. The London tour generated positive feedback in India.

As Indira's ties to the business world strengthened, her dependence on Sanjay also deepened. Sanjay built a formidable political machine to organize Indira Gandhi's campaign for her return to power. Contrary to his earlier image as a somewhat corrupt, abusive figure, Sanjay became "to some a fearsome, and to others an inspiring, character."[5] Many observers viewed the stunning Congress

[5] "Sanjay Gandhi: Fearsome and Inspiring," *The New York Times*, June 26, 1980.

Party victory in state elections in May, 1980, as belonging solely to Sanjay Gandhi, who approved the nominations and sent personal lieutenants to drum up support in "trouble spots." Sanjay also seemed to expand his formerly narrow constituency into a vast nationwide network, with a new generation of young politicians looking to him for guidance.[6] A large number of Sanjay's associates ran for office in 1980 and won.[7] Of the 351 members of parliament with the Congress Party, 234 were new to Parliament, and at least 150 were ardent Sanjay followers (Malhotra 1989, 215).

There was a clear change in the new Parliament in 1980 reflecting the growing power of private business networks. Socialism was declining, and new politicians with strong business ties were rising. Among Sanjay's associates, Bansil Lal became Defense Minister; Om Mehta took charge of Home Affairs; K. Brahman and A. Reddy served in the Information Ministry; Vidya Charan Shukla was charged with directing the media; and Mohammed Yunus, Yashpal Kapoor, and R. K. Dhawan all became ministerial-level bureaucrats influencing economic policy making (Jha 1985; Kidwai 1996). Indira Gandhi also appointed individuals with strong business and international connections to key positions in her cabinet, including P. C. Alexander, Pranab Mukherjee, P. V. Narasimha Rao, and R. Venkataraman.[8] Ms. Gandhi announced that her government did not believe in doctrinaire (socialist) theories and would instead prioritize productivity and efficiency (Andersen 1982).

To leading business figures, Indira Gandhi showed appreciation upon her return to power. In 1980, she invited K. K. Birla and J. R. D. Tata to the National Integration Council, a prestigious government body chaired by prime ministers. This was the first time that any business people had ever served as Council members. K. K. Birla's nephew Aditya Vikram was made the Board Director of the Reserve Bank of India (Birla 1987, 146). The appointment of P. C. Alexander, a specialist in development and international trade expert, as the Commerce Minister particularly demonstrated new thinking on Indira's part. Alexander was not part of Indira's inner circle before 1980. He worked at the United Nations (UN) for three terms and also held jobs at the International Monetary Fund (IMF) and the World Bank. According to Alexander's recollection (1991), his experience with international organizations was the chief reason that Gandhi offered him the job. Being an outsider with enormous external and corporate ties, Gandhi hired Alexander to make economic changes in her new government.

6 Ibid.

7 During Indira's campaign in 1980, Sanjay's Youth Congress provided her organizational support, and his business networks lent financial backing. These associates later became active in Indira's premiership.

8 Before 1980, Mukherjee was in charge of industrial development; Rao was famous for his reforms and positions on foreign affairs; and R. Venkataraman had ample experience at the IMF and Asian Development Bank.

This narrative demonstrates the strengthening of policy makers' business networks in the late 1970s and how these networks influenced government personnel and policy orientation when Indira returned to power in 1980. This account qualifies the two main explanations in the literature: one, Indira implemented economic deregulation to win business votes, and two, senior Cabinet members were mainly responsible for Indira Gandhi's economic reform. It clarifies that Indira's business connections formed prior to her electoral victory and drove both reform policy and bureaucratic appointments. With new interests and ideas prevailing in New Delhi in 1980, pro-business economic reform was a natural course of action in Indira Gandhi's new government.

Indira Gandhi's Economic Deregulation

In 1980, Indira set up a massive Prime Minister Secretariat with 200 members to monitor government performance, coordinate macroeconomic policies, and generate ideas to stimulate the economy. Presiding over the Secretariat was P. C. Alexander. Along with Alexander, other economists with exposure to outside ideas took on increasing significance in the government. The PM declared 1982 "the year of productivity" and inaugurated a new industrial policy to stimulate this idea. The new policy, announced in April 1982, was welcomed by industry as "economic pragmatism" and a "dilution of dogma."[9]

Gandhi then launched three powerful committees to study how economic transition could be better performed: the L. K. Jha Committee to study the overhaul of economic administration, the Abid Hussain Committee to review trade, and the M. Narasimha Committee to oversee financial reforms. The three senior bureaucrats who led the committees and for whom they were named were well regarded by the Indian business community (Kohli 2006, 1256). The specific policy measures adopted suggest that considerable attention was paid to the interests of Indian big business (see Table 4.2). These policies included relaxed control over private business and increased support for industry.

The measures infer two points: first, the policy changes undertaken during Indira Gandhi's 1980–1984 administration demonstrate a clear shift toward private business interests. Second, these proposed changes had a limited impact on India's overall economic structure. The private sector was a priority, but the public sector did not experience a significant decline. The government, for example, reduced tax burdens and loosened credit controls over private business, but did not reduce financial obligations to public sectors. Absent substantial input of external funds, the country was unlikely to sustain these policies. Furthermore, despite the new favorable policies, the private sector did not improve performance noticeably because it took time for efficiency to grow. External sectors remained uncompetitive, and exports were sliding. The government's enlarged financial commitment to the private sector, on top of continual

[9] *Hindustan Times* (New Delhi), August 19, 1982.

TABLE 4.2. *Indira's Pro-Business Deregulation*

Summary Policy Changes	
I. Deregulating private business	(a) control over steel and cement prices was loosened (b) manufactured imports were liberalized (c) controls on both entry and expansion by national firms were relaxed (d) twenty selected industries were placed under automatic licensing (e) the antimonopoly act was diluted, allowing private expansion in chemicals, drugs, ceramics, cement, and power generation
II. Supporting private industries	(f) financial support and incentives were provided: credit for big borrowers was liberalized, and big business was offered tax reliefs
III. Suppressing labor	(g) labor activism was discouraged by official statements and legislation
IV. Limiting the public sector	(h) limited new investments into public sector enterprises and cut subsidies to the public distribution system.

Source: Drawn from Frankel (2005) and supplemented with the author's own archival materials.

investment in the public sector, created the specter of debt crises in the subsequent years. In the interlude, the Indian government ran a dangerously large and growing deficit.

RAJIV GANDHI'S DIASPORA NETWORKS AND THEIR ROLE IN LIBERALIZATION

Policy makers make policies, but their social networks provide information and incentives to rank different policy measures. Rajiv Gandhi had external networks that channeled liberal ideas to support economic change in India. He married an Italian wife and worked as a professional pilot for British Airways. He was thrust into the limelight of politics after his brother Sanjay died in a plane crash in 1980. Sanjay was the General Secretary of the All-India Congress Committee – a position Rajiv took over after Sanjay's death. Although new to politics, Rajiv demonstrated an uncanny knack for political maneuvering. He masterfully replaced most of Sanjay's cronies with people who shared his own beliefs in developing a modern economy in India.[10] Compared to his mother, Rajiv had a strong propensity for Western technology and was eager to develop India's technological edge. His association with private business families was thus completed with ties to diaspora professionals who had extensive education and work experiences abroad.

[10] See also, "Silent Hand of Son Helps Mrs. Gandhi," *The Globe and Mail* (Canada), April 17, 1981.

Upon assuming premiership at the age of forty, Rajiv surrounded himself with advisors with foreign educations and work experience, appointing them to key positions in his Cabinet. In 1985, he initiated a new industrial policy, centered on ambitious plans to permit more foreign products and foreign companies to compete in the Indian market while continuing measures that would help domestic companies to grow. Support for domestic companies was warmly received, but openness to foreign investment and goods was resisted. Macroeconomic statistics also suggest that external openness failed to generate early success, which strengthened domestic resistance to such opening. By the mid-term elections in 1987, Rajiv had significantly toned down his plans for external liberalization.

Rajiv Gandhi's Change Team

As the son of Indira and grandson of Nehru, Rajiv grew up with scions of prominent business families in India.[11] He additionally became a part of diaspora networks that shaped his policy ideas when he became prime minister in 1984. Table 4.3 lists Rajiv Gandhi's main advisors, including returned diasporas

TABLE 4.3. *Rajiv Gandhi's Economic Team and Diaspora Networks*

Name	External experiences	Positions in the government
Arun Nehru	MNC in Calcutta	Minister of Energy
Arun Singh	MNC in Calcutta	Union Minister of State
Montek Singh Ahluwalia	UK education, World Bank	Special secretary
Manmohan Singh	UK education	Planning Commission chairman
Bimal Jalan	UK education, IMF and World Bank	Banking secretary
Jayanta Roy	U.S. education, World Bank	Economic advisor, Ministry of Commerce
Rakesh Mohan	U.S. education, World Bank	Planning Commission Advisor, Ministry of Industry
Shankar Acharya	U.S. education, World Bank	Chief Economic Advisor, PMO
Vijay Kelkar	U.S. education	Planning Commission Advisor
Jairam Ramesh	U.S. education, World Bank	Planning Commission Advisor, PMO
Nitin Desai	U.S. education, World Bank	Planning Commission Advisor, PMO
Madhur Srinivas	World Bank	Planning Commission

Source: Drawn from Shastri (1997) and supplemented with the author's own archival materials. MNC, multinational corporation; PMO, Prime Minister's Office

[11] See, "The Rajiv Generation," *The New York Times*, April 2, 1986.

with capitalist ideas and ties to multinational corporations (MNCs) and international organizations (IOs). The names suggest a certain bureaucratic continuity in India from 1980 until today. Some had served under Indira, and some continued on after Rajiv's assassination. Before 1980, some individuals (such as T. N. Srinivasan and Jagdish Bhagwati) with foreign training and work experience also returned to India but found little acceptance of their policy ideas. Disillusioned, they emigrated to the United States and became influential policy advisors and academics there. Their experience suggests that diasporas' contribution needs domestic preconditions and opportunities.

Among Rajiv's top advisers, the "two Aruns" were particularly influential. Both were connected with domestic businesses and foreign MNCs operating in India (Merchant 1991). Arun Nehru was the President of Jenson and Nicholson, a Calcutta-based multinational paint corporation. Formerly an ally of Sanjay, Nehru partnered with Rajiv after Sanjay's death. He led the Ministry of Energy from 1985 on. Another Calcutta-based multinational executive, Arun Singh, followed Nehru into Rajiv's camp. Singh, a childhood friend of Rajiv's, was a committed careerist and had been the Marketing Controller for the Calcutta-based MNC Reckitt and Coleman. He was a well-liked figure in Calcutta's club circle, which included business executives, retired army officers, and young entrepreneurs.

Apart from the "two Aruns," a host of others with similar backgrounds and values joined Rajiv's government (Merchant 1991, 109). As seen in Table 5.3, Montek Singh Ahluwalia, a Rhodes scholar and Oxford economics doctorate, first worked for the World Bank and served in Indian government in various capacities. In the mid-1980s, he was appointed special secretary to Rajiv Gandhi. Bimal Jalan, another Oxford economist, served as the banking secretary. Manmohan Singh, also from Oxford, served as the chairman of the Planning Commission under Rajiv Gandhi. All these individuals continued to influence India's economic liberalization in the 1990s and beyond. Jayanta Roy, Shankar Acharya, Vijay Kelkar, Jairam Ramesh, Nitin Desai, and Madhur Srinivas, who served as advisors to the planning commission of the Prime Minister's Office (PMO), all had American educations and work experience in the United States, mostly with the IMF or the World Bank.

With these outward-looking advisors and bureaucrats, the Rajiv administration embodied different economic ideas than its predecessors. As a young PM, Rajiv had an unprecedentedly high electoral mandate, with a vast four-fifths majority in Parliament. The election mandate gave Rajiv a window of opportunity to pursue a liberalization program. He was determined to break from the past, instilling a "sense of hope and optimism in India" (Hardgrave 1985, 131).

Rajiv had developed cordial relations with representatives from several MNCs and was keen to stimulate growth and change in India by removing barriers to the import of technology from Japan and the West (Manor 1987, 39). He also fostered more agreeable foreign relations with Western countries and developed personal contacts with world leaders in Washington, London, Paris, and Tokyo. During his extensive foreign tours, business leaders, both in India and abroad, contacted him to explore opportunities (Narain 1986, 266).

The professional diasporas and external networks to foreign countries, MNCs, and IOs, however, were relatively weak in terms of domestic reach and material transfers and ultimately could not help Rajiv Gandhi to overcome domestic resistance. Specifically, Rajiv's external networks had few ties beyond the PM's inner circles, making idea transfers to broader domestic groups unlikely. Furthermore, as professionals, the returned diasporas failed to provide material resources to produce quick economic success. Economic indicators were difficult to assess under Rajiv Gandhi; the external sectors especially looked precarious, undermining domestic support for FDI liberalization.

The Commencement and Limitation of Rajiv Gandhi's Reform

When Rajiv came to power, he was profoundly unhappy with the country's economic conditions and was eager to change policy direction. In 1984, for example, the government's deficit reached 7.5 percent of GDP, an unsustainable rate for any country (Ahluwalia 2002). The government's annual interest payments represented about 30 percent of net borrowing, and its capacity to repay its loans was quickly diminishing. Worse yet, the country's trade deficit increased rapidly from 1983 to 1985 (Frankel 2005, 586). It was only through substantial NRI remittances, the so-called invisible earnings, that India's account balance was preserved (Hardgrave 1984, 137). Short of major changes, India was on a dangerous course to national default. The new prime minister was determined to avoid this by making India globally competitive in technology. His first budget was ambitious and designed to promote domestic industry, as well as international trade and investment.

The 1985 budget reduced income, corporate, and wealth taxes; cut import duties on capital goods; provided tax breaks to exporters; and largely eliminated licensing restrictions on investments in twenty-five main industries.[12] The idea was to help the private sector and to hold the growth in public sector expenditures to its lowest level in many years. The budget was exalted as marking the inception of a new economic regime.[13] Rajiv Gandhi was commended as an example of state autonomy rarely seen in India (Rubin 1985; Kohli 2006). In the young prime minister's words, his liberalization agenda was to involve a "judicious combination of deregulation, import liberalization, and easier access to foreign technology."[14]

Rajiv's popularity rating in 1985 was the highest ever for any prime minister in Indian history. He had the support of nearly 80 percent of Indians before the

[12] "India Plans Relaxation of Industry Control Law," *The Globe and Mail* (Canada), March 28, 1985.

[13] *Economic and Political Weekly*, March 7, 1987; *The Economist*, March 23, 1985.

[14] *Times of India*, January 6, 1986.

December 1984 general election and more than 85 percent after it. Rajiv's promise – "change with continuity" – attracted professionals from every walk of life to public service (Merchant 1991). Specific measures in the budget attested to the pro-liberalization inclination in Rajiv Gandhi's cabinet. In addition to exempting twenty-five industries from licensing, it also encouraged big business houses, previously regulated heavily by the Anti-Monopoly Act and Foreign Exchange Regulation Act, to participate in a number of high-technology industries. It also raised the cap on foreign exchange for importing raw materials and introduced tax concessions for the corporate and urban upper middle classes (Frankel 2005; Panagariya 2008).

Rajiv Gandhi's ambitious reform soon met domestic resistance. The public sector was the first to oppose it because Rajiv's reform policies explicitly capped investment in the public sector. In 1986, Finance Minister V. P. Singh presented the revised budget and claimed that the public sector remained a priority for the new government. This backpedaling led many observers to question whether Rajiv Gandhi truly represented change and whether liberalization since 1985 had been "real."[15] The 1987 budget indeed returned to an earlier focus on the construction of socialism and to strengthening the public sector. Rajiv Gandhi took a cautious approach, making piecemeal policy changes while insisting that his government was continuing the traditional Congress Party's program of a "mixed economy," with the public sector as its "commanding heights" (Nayar 1989).

With these reversals to socialist rhetoric, the essence of Rajiv's reform program did not change: the support for the private economy and foreign technology remained. Foreign investment liberalization was not a feasible option at the time. Domestic businesses in particular voiced their displeasure with measures regarding foreign goods and investment. They made the case that foreign MNCs and goods were creating undue pressure on indigenous companies. Lacking domestic support groups, Rajiv's cabinet abandoned those measures that would potentially introduce more market competition from external investors and goods. In the automobile industry, for example, established manufacturers feared a glut of overproduction and competition from new and likely better-made products and pressured the government to limit the access of foreigners.[16] As the *Economic Times* later observed, "The pace of domestic liberalization has not been slackened ... external liberalization [however] was not really an objective of the [overall] policy."[17]

In May 1987, Rajiv publicized a new industrial policy that detailed measures to promote private business and gradually reduce state regulation of the market.[18] It was clear that private business interests would be protected, despite

[15] "Rajiv's Charm Begins to Fade," *The Economist*, March 8, 1986; "Halfway House in India," *The Economist*, June 28, 1986.
[16] *Economic Times*, February 2, 1986.
[17] *Economic Times*, February 24, 1986.
[18] The summary measures are suggested in Frankel (2005).

strong criticism from public sector representatives and leftist political voices. The more controversial part of reform – opening to foreign goods and investment – was less emphasized, despite having been highlighted in the 1985 budget. The government continued to promote private business, including tax concessions, deregulation, and privatization.

RAJIV'S SOCIAL NETWORKS: WHY FDI LIBERALIZATION FAILED TO STAY

Why did Rajiv Gandhi fail to open India to FDI when he clearly sought MNCs' contributions? Current explanations focus on the inexperience of individual leaders or the incapacity of the state. In both political frameworks, society is viewed as resisting change, and it is up to the state leadership to overcome societal resistance. Social network analysis, by contrast, stresses different social groups, some pro-change and others anti-change, with dominant social groups supporting some changes while opposing others. During Rajiv Gandhi's term, external networks (diaspora professionals) were not strong enough to overcome domestic resistance or to produce compelling early success, and thus the pro-FDI agenda failed to incorporate sufficient domestic support. Absent resourceful diaspora networks, a Deng Xiaoping-like politician could not succeed in India. Indeed, while facing opposition, Deng Xiaoping twice recanted his support for FDI liberalization in the 1980s (see Chapter 3).

Internal Networks: Domestic Resistance to FDI

Industrial opposition under Rajiv's rule was mainly responsible for the failed FDI liberalization, and it is thus important to examine indigenous industries and their stances on liberalization. Indigenous businesses, however, were not static in their positions. Ideas and incentives of domestic business evolved, and therefore their stances on FDI changed, as demonstrated in 1990s India (see Chapter 6 in Part III). In comparing 1980s India and China, we find several common anti-FDI groups: socialists, the public sector, and nationalists. The Chinese government shielded these from direct competition, while diaspora entrepreneurs offered incentives for cooperation. Nevertheless, Chinese conservatives managed to challenge FDI liberalization on several occasions. In India, the government's response was similar: conceding to these interests and delaying a contentious opening to FDI. Indian professional diasporas were unable to transform incentives or produce the multilevel persuasion that was seen in China.

Other than ideology-based opposition, India's domestic resistance consisted mostly of private industries. China, however, had no private companies when reform began. The previous chapter offers cases of Chinese private enterprises emerging in the 1980s and how they relied on and drew upon diaspora connections. Conversely, in India, private capital was allowed to operate in many sectors upon independence and grew significantly under license-raj. This was the dominant business network of policy makers at the time.[19] Indigenous businesses welcomed and promoted pro-business policy shifts during Indira's return to power in 1980–1984. Although supporting Rajiv's domestic liberalization agenda, they resisted external opening. In the late 1980s, private businesses opposed openness to foreign goods and capital. They launched their opposition through predominant business associations, which expanded their roles and policy advocacy as a result of growing business influence in India.

The Associated Chambers of Commerce and Industry of India (ASSOCHAM) originated as an association of British industries in the preindependence period, and after 1947, it maintained its representation of companies with a large share of foreign investment, foreign management, or both. In the three decades after independence, these companies reaped handsome gains from India's protectionism and maintained strong interests in continuing such protectionism. In the mid-1980s, ASSOCHAM was reorganized after it drew in a significant number of private business members, and its agenda correspondingly shifted. Crucially, ASSOCHAM also began to represent India's large business houses in this period.

The Federation of Indian Chambers of Commerce and Industry (FICCI) was formed in 1927 by Calcutta industrialist B. M. Birla and was the largest, richest, and best managed interest group in the country by the mid-1990s, according to Dennis Kochanek (1996, 532). In the late 1970s, the emergence of West and South Indian industries changed FICCI's internal power structure to favor Mumbai businessmen, and the organization became even more powerful. By the 1980s, FICCI was the most significant voice of Indian business and represented indigenous capitalists. During each reform episode, FICCI welcomed policies to promote domestic industry and opposed efforts to introduce foreign competition. In the mid-1980s, ASSOCHAM was transformed into a "mirror image" of FICCI, although the two associations drew their memberships from different geographic areas (Kochanek 1995).

A third apex business association, the Confederation of Indian Industry (CII), also rose to prominence in the 1980s. The CII grew out of the merger of the Indian Engineering Association and the Engineering Association of India and was originally named the Association of Indian Engineering Industry (AIEI), with a membership of 2,000 companies. It received a major boost from Rajiv Gandhi in 1985, when the PM spoke at the organization's annual meeting. AIEI leaders also accompanied Rajiv on his trip to the Soviet Union. In 1986, AIEI changed its name to the Confederation of Engineering Industry, and finally settled on the Confederation of Indian Industry in 1992. Although CII appeared different from the other two associations in that it promoted Indian exports, its position on FDI liberalization in the 1980s was similar to those of its peers.

[19] CMIE, *Public Sector in the Indian Economy*. Bombay: CMIE, 1983, pp. 14–15.

Because CII adopted a proactive approach to influencing government policy, its impact on India's liberalization has been significant.

Although there were some clear differences among the industrial associations, the business community as a whole decided that it was not ready to cope with serious external opening. In the words of the head of FICCI: "After three decades of highly protective industrialization, liberalization cannot be taken up simultaneously on all fronts – it has to be phased in. The first stage has to be to allow domestic competitiveness. Only then, should we open up to outside forces" (Kohli 1989, 317).

Beyond these business associations, rivalry among business groups further obstructed Rajiv's reform agenda. From 1984 to 1986, domestic business as a whole favored change. However, the prime minister's apparently close ties to corporate conglomerate Reliance antagonized Nusli Wadia, the chairman of Bombay Dyeing, which was on a collision course with Reliance. Nusli's competition with Reliance bred animosity toward Rajiv Gandhi and brought Nusli's close friend, Ramnath Goenka, owner of *Indian Express*, to lead the charge against Rajiv's administration.[20] In discrediting Rajiv and his liberalization agenda, the national press, led by the *Indian Express*, played a part in rallying domestic resistance (Merchant 1991, 230).

Rajiv Gandhi's favoritism toward domestic business groups also angered Swraj Paul, the UK-based diaspora tycoon with close ties to Indira Gandhi. Paul held shares in two Indian companies, Escorts and DCM, which, in order to prevent Paul from selling the stock, refused to register their shares. Despite a court ruling in favor of Paul, the NRI tycoon decided to abandon his challenge to Escorts and DCM – reportedly due to pressure from Rajiv Gandhi.[21] Disappointed, Paul refrained from investing in India until the late 1990s, after FDI liberalization had been under way for almost a decade.

Furthermore, business support for economic reform faded when the government attempted to collect taxes. The late 1985 arrest of Kapal Mehra, Chairman of Orkay Silk Mills, during the government's tax raid placed the prime minister under the scrutiny of media. Finance Minister V. P. Singh's pursuit of large business houses for tax evasion, including the Kirloskars, the Bajajs, and the Thapars, further alienated the government from business leaders. Faced with a serious blowback from private industry, Rajiv removed Singh from the Finance Ministry, in turn rousing criticism from left-leaning intellectuals who increasingly viewed Rajiv as pro-rich. The media crusade against Rajiv Gandhi had serious repercussions for the performance of the Congress Party in the mid-term elections. Under such circumstances, Rajiv Gandhi returned to a more

[20] Goenka's opposition to Rajiv was mainly driven by his grievance with the Gandhi's family for the emergency rule in 1975–1977.

[21] See "Paul Plans Indian Share Sale," *The Times*, April 26, 1986; and "Ex-fertilizer Minister Scoffs at Swraj Paul's Claims," *The Statesman*, April 17, 1998.

constrained rhetoric of economic change for India and spent more time attempting to appease the opposition.

Rajiv's complex relationships with private business, inherent in a country with well-entrenched politicians and business sectors (and yet absent in China), undermined the prime minister's popularity in the late 1980s. Equally troublesome were the relatively weak external networks that India possessed – especially compared to its strong domestic resistance. The strength of a network is measured on three components: ideas and resources flowing within the network and the ties among individual nodes. Compared to China, India's diaspora networks provided ideas but failed to offer sufficient resources to co-opt the opposition or to produce early success for FDI liberalization. Their domestic access did not go below or beyond the national government. That perhaps explains the general insignificance of local governments in India's economic liberalization in the 1980s, with the exception of a few states.[22]

Professional Diasporas: Lots of Ideas, Few Resources, and Limited Ties

Rajiv Gandhi's diaspora networks consisted of those Indians who were posted abroad and exposed to successful experiences with development in other countries. These diasporas were extremely influential in Rajiv's economic reform. Abid Hussain, for example, served as a member of the Planning Commission from 1985 to 1990, as well as Ambassador to the United States during the debt crisis of 1990–1992. He admitted that the understanding he gained regarding the economic experiences of the East Asian countries while serving at the UN Economic and Social Commission in Asia and the Pacific (UNESCAP) program was crucial to his support for economic change when he joined Rajiv.[23] Lateral entrants into the government included specialized Indians who received their educations in the United States and/or worked at the World Bank and thus had a reasonably good grasp of late development elsewhere. Connected by these diaspora professionals, international organizations and Western MNCs had stronger voices during Rajiv's term than ever before. The World Bank, IMF, UN, Japanese Suzuki, and America-based Texas Instruments, for example, all came more readily to India during this era (Narain 1986; Narain and Dutta 1987; Wariavwalla 1988, 1989).

In the 1980s, diaspora professionals conveyed important ideas to India and shaped Rajiv Gandhi's reform agenda. Yet these diasporas did not have independent material resources, nor did their ties extend beyond national-level bureaucrats. The weakness of India's diaspora networks at the time was clear when they were juxtaposed with Chinese diaspora entrepreneurs, who provided capitalist ideas, substantial capital, and ties to broader domestic actors. In the

[22] Starting the 1990s, however, local governments became more influential in regional economic policies and development (Rudolph and Rudolph 2001). For regional variations, see Kohli (2012).

[23] Interview with Abid Hussain, Washington DC, July 18, 1991, in Shastri (1997).

1980s, a small number of MNCs also came to China, but the dynamic of nonethnic external networks was similar in China and India: rife with contention and mistrust. Within joint ventures (JVs) with Western MNCs, Chinese partners pushed for localization in an attempt to reduce foreign influence, whereas foreign investors were distrustful and wanted to keep the core technology outside the JV operation.[24] Many JV projects ended with dissatisfaction on both sides. In India, the reception of IOs was divided. There existed a suspicion that IOs represented American interests and likely infringed on Indian independence.[25]

More damning to Rajiv's efforts, however, was the fact that the macroeconomic state was not improving in India despite the presence of external ideas and top-level commitment to reform, In 1985–1986, when Rajiv Gandhi's first industrial policy went into effect, India experienced an unprecedented trade deficit. This led many in India to seriously question the soundness of external opening.[26] Without early success, a sense of "disillusionment with the national leadership" developed rapidly and was "particularly damaging politically" (Kohli 1990, 323). The pro-liberalization coalition narrowed in the late 1980s.

A comparison between China and India reveals that access, the third component of network strength, varied between the two countries' external networks. In India, with professional diasporas serving in New Delhi, Western IOs and MNCs were able to build ties to top politicians and national bureaucrats. However, these nonethnic foreigners had fewer ties to locally elected parliament members, on-the-ground chiefs overseeing local economies, and small-scale industrialists – those who comprised the majority of economic actors in India. These lower level actors constituted an important political force in India, and their knowledge of liberalization was critical to successful implementation of reform policies on the ground. Excluding them would make any reform difficult.

Democratic channels allowed these indigenous actors to express their opinions and oppose FDI liberalization. Due to the lack of ideational and resources inflows beyond the national level, India's local politicians and small-scale economic entities generally viewed FDI and foreign goods as harmful. By contrast, in China (see Chapter 3), diasporas had strong ties at the top and provincial governments levels and eased the initiation of FDI liberalization. They rapidly developed ties at societal levels, including with grassroots governments and local entrepreneurs, and such ties were critical to quick returns at the local level, and they expanded and expedited the diffusion process of FDI liberalization.

[24] See cases in *Zhongguo duiwai jingji tongji daquan 1979–1991 [China's External Economic Statistics Overview 1979–1991]*. Beijing: Zhongguo tongji xinxi zixun fuwu zhongxin chubanshe, 1992, pp. 296–356.

[25] When Mrs. Gandhi's government went to the IMF in 1981, opposition parties criticized her. See *Sunday*, December 31, 1981.

[26] "Halfway House in India," *The Economist*, June 28, 1986.

QUIET CHANGE IN INDIA'S GOVERNMENT–BUSINESS RELATIONS

Social network theory (SNT) argues that limited and incremental policy change can lead to a paradigm shift in a country's grand economic outlook and industrial strategy, as seen in the Chinese case. In India, the limited change in the 1980s critically affected what took place after the 1991 crisis. The preceding sections affirm the importance of internal business networks to India's reform – yet the ideas and interests of business networks shifted as they engaged with external actors more deeply. Liberalization in the 1980s enabled domestic business to acquire access to external networks and gradually change its stance toward FDI.

Diaspora connections have taken on new significance since the 1980s, with upper class families developing increasing ties to entrepreneurial relatives in America. Such transnational diaspora exchange and circulation of immigrants to the homeland have resulted in marked changes in the social basis of India's democratic regime (Kapur 2010). Although political institutions remain largely intact, the politics of India's economic reform has shifted, and a "pro-business" trend in policy making has surely intensified, as Kohli (2012) explains. Such trends and new social networks have become more evident since the 1990s, and Chapter 6 explicates the makeup of this social basis.

Back to India's interim governments from 1989 to 1991, reform continued. V. P. Singh held a personal grudge against the Gandhi family, but when he rose to power in 1989, he continued the liberalization measures started by the Indira and Rajiv administrations.[27] Singh also retained key supporters of reform, including Ajit Singh and Montek Singh Ahluwalia. These personnel provided continuity in economic policies. Ahluwalia, for example, advocated foreign investment and argued that FDI could play a key role in industrial modernization by providing access to technology, links to global markets, and ideas for new management styles (Bhusan 1990). Other important players included A. N. Verma and Ganesan, both of whom served in Rajiv Gandhi's government. Verma moved from the post of commerce secretary to become the principal secretary to the prime minister in 1991.

Chandra Shekhar's coalition government replaced V. P. Singh's minority rule in 1990. He continued to retain the above-mentioned "lateral entrants" and pursued economic liberalism at a more strident pace than before. Chandra Shekhar, previously a vocal critic of reform, said at a meeting with top economic bureaucrats: "Ignore the debate that we [politicians] are engaged in. You all carry on your work."[28] The interim period, marked by frequent government change, suggests that economic liberalism had persistent appeal among political

[27] Government of India, Prime Minister's Inaugural Address to the National Development Council (Press Information Bureau, June 18, 1990), p. 15.

[28] Interview with one of the economic advisors present at this meeting, in Shastri (1997).

elites in New Delhi after the 1980s reform and that liberal ideas flowing in from external networks were there to stay beyond individual policy makers.

The two-part reform of the 1980s also brought on a "quiet revolution" among Indian industrialists (Pedersen 2000, 276), with growing new industries, new technologies, and new personnel (such as Western-trained MBAs). The growth of new industries relied mainly on external linkages. These new industries, such as telecom, pharmaceuticals, and software, also claimed to be ready to compete globally. This was in stark contrast to the fear of external competition pervasive among traditional industries. Their emergence diluted industrial opposition to openness. The superior economic performance of new industries, as compared to that of traditional sectors, provided an alternative economic model within India and weakened the appeal of protectionism. Although yet uncommon, business houses and traditional industries underwent a quiet change in the 1980s. With foreign collaboration, indigenous producers increased their efforts to export products to the international market and transfer technology to improve productivity. Growth in international transactions moderated these industries' earlier resistance to FDI.

In contrast to what Dennis Kochanek (1986) viewed as a powerful antiliberalization business coalition without a pro-liberalization counterpart in the mid-1980s, there emerged a mix of anti- and pro-liberalization coalitions. At both ideational and material levels, the balance of external networks and domestic resistance slightly shifted. Thus, when the debt crisis occurred, India's domestic politics was already on the verge of change. The crisis strengthened the reform-oriented state and ushered in a period of FDI liberalization. Postcrisis policy consolidation, however, was challenged by domestic resistance, which ultimately eased due to the globalization of leading indigenous companies in the country.

CONCLUSION

The key questions in this chapter are how India pursued reforms in the 1980s and why FDI was not embraced. Earlier publications have stressed the effects of individual leaders' political calculations, as well as political factors like democratic institutions and interest group politics. They do not contradict SNT, which confirms that domestic private business shaped India's liberalization in the 1980s. Rather, SNT adds three points to the literature: first, indigenous business was a promoter of liberalization, albeit limited to domestic deregulation. Second, domestic interests can change; with external networks, their opposition can be overcome and even co-opted into a pro-liberalization coalition. Finally, SNT emphasizes the weakness of India's external networks, namely the lack of material resources and broader internal access of professional diasporas compared to Chinese entrepreneurial diasporas.

In the late 1980s and early 1990s, China's and India's reforms were highly comparable. Both countries experienced political crises in 1989. Reform was put on hold in China but continued in India despite political volatility. Both countries then had a top-down push for opening. Chinese leaders mobilized local support and refueled FDI liberalization; Indian policy makers capitalized on the debt crisis and pursued deeper opening. Foreign direct investment liberalization continued to diverge. Strong indigenous business, compared to relatively weak external networks, continued to constrain the diffusion of FDI liberalization in India in the 1990s; substantial inflows of diaspora entrepreneurs in China influenced homeland opening even more significantly, thanks to a pro-FDI ideational shift building up since the previous decade. In the 1990s, India still conformed to a slower and more limited liberalization pathway as described in Chapter 2, and its progress depended on the transformation of indigenous industry, helped by the emergence and circulation of new entrepreneurial diasporas in the United States.

PART III

REFORM STAGE II

FDI Expedited in China
FDI Resisted in India

5

Deepening Diffusion: "Zone Fever" and SOE Reform in China

In Part II, Chapter 3 explained the swift diffusion of foreign direct investment (FDI) liberalization in China from 1979 to 1992. After that period, China's pro-FDI policies further expanded during the "zone fever" period (1992–1994) and implementation of state-owned enterprise (SOE) reforms (1995–1998). The growth of annual FDI inflows in China was rapid: in 1991, FDI in the People's Republic of China (PRC) was $4.4 billion; in 1992, it increased to $11 billion; in 1993, $27.5 billion; in 1994, $33.8 billion; in 1995, $37.5 billion; in 1996, $41.7 billion; and in 1997, $45.6 billion. After that, it stagnated slightly due to the Asian financial crisis. Foreign direct investment inflows in China recovered to $47 billion in 2001 and $53 billion in 2002, surpassing the United States to become the world's largest recipient of FDI in those years.

Previous works have examined why FDI increased so rapidly in the PRC. Barry Weingast (1995), Dali Yang (1997), and Aseema Sinha (2005a) stress local governments that offered competing incentives to foreign investors, using frameworks such as "market-preserving federalism," "competitive regionalism," and "winners coalition." Yasheng Huang (2003) explores the communist "economic pecking order" that placed inefficient SOEs at the top and private companies at the bottom, which allowed FDI to benefit and thrive – a phenomenon he calls "selling China." Cai and Treisman (2006) counter the role of local governments and stress top leadership that made liberal policies and incentivized local governments to implement them. The roles of diaspora networks continued to be missing from the literature.

This chapter applies the diffusion model to the process of zone fever and SOE reform and uncovers the critical impact of diaspora entrepreneurs and the growth of diaspora networks in the country. Diaspora networks' policy and development effects were more direct at the local level, yet their local impacts ultimately shaped national policies. In the zone fever period, local governments strongly relied on diasporas to establish development zones. During the SOE reform, once the national government sanctioned local governments to reform SOEs in order to strengthen the state sector as a whole, local officials drew on diaspora networks and conducted SOE reform as de facto FDI liberalization. As two separate policy programs, zone fever and SOE reforms both deepened FDI liberalization in China in the 1990s.

As in the 1980s, the Chinese government was not monolithic, and FDI liberalization also encountered opposition. Rising nationalism, along with the emergence of the New Left – groups that argued for strong public sectors and challenged the government's globalization agenda (Fewsmith 2001). Halfway through the decade, for example, nationalist intellectuals argued that globalization contributed to the failing of SOEs. And in the late 1990s, when Sino-American relations deteriorated (due to incidents like the United States' accidental bombing of the Chinese embassy in Yugoslavia), anti-FDI nationalism heightened. The emergence of domestic private industries, which benefited from external ideas and resources, also lobbied against the preferential treatment given to foreign investors. The predominance of diaspora FDI and export orientation helped maintain China's liberalization trend in this period. In the intensified policy debate and confrontation between nationalism and globalization, however, the distinction between diaspora investment and FDI blurred, and the significance of diaspora contribution was left unexamined.

The next section introduces new trends in China's external networks, including the rapid growth of diaspora entrepreneurs and the arrival of nonethnic investors. I then document diasporas' contribution to the development of new economic zones in China. The last section focuses on the SOE reform: how local governments used diaspora capital to reform failing SOEs and, in the process, how diaspora entrepreneurs helped enlarge the pro-FDI coalition in China.

EXPANDING DIASPORA NETWORKS

As seen in the diffusion model illustrated in Figure 2.2, FDI liberalization reinforces the strength of external networks as more domestic actors are brought into interaction with external actors. In China, Western multinational corporations (MNCs) began to arrive in large numbers around the mid-1990s. More importantly, diaspora networks grew rapidly during the same period and had a greater impact on broader China.

Diaspora networks experienced three major developments in the early 1990s. First, they expanded beyond South China, spread across the Mainland, and contributed strongly to FDI liberalization in the central, northern, and interior regions of the country where Western capital rarely set foot.[1] Hong Kong

[1] The eastern region of the PRC refers to Beijing, Tianjin, Hebei, Shanghai, Jiangsu, Zhejiang, Fujian, Guangdong, and Hainan; the central region includes Shanxi, Anhui, Jiangxi, Henan, Hubei, Hunan; the northern region refers to Liaoning, Jilin, and Heilongjiang; and the western region comprises the remaining provinces. See *China Statistical Yearbook*, 2006 edition.

investors also expanded into inland cities like Chongqing and Wuhan. Second, diaspora entrepreneurs diversified their investment to include a broader set of industries, including intensified infrastructure development, while light manufacturing continued to attract substantial diaspora capital. Taiwanese investors involved themselves extensively in property development and services, as well as in manufacturing sectors ranging from footwear to computers. Third, the sources of diaspora networks became more diverse. In addition to those from Hong Kong, investors from Taiwan and Southeast Asia became more significant on the Mainland. Hong Kong began to serve as a model for China's various regulatory reforms.

Business families in Hong Kong, Macao, and Taiwan became more involved in China's economic development in the 1990s and developed more ties to policy-making circles on the Mainland. Assisted by political connections at the national and local levels, these diaspora conglomerates invested in infrastructure projects, modern seaports, container ports, railways, highways, commercial buildings, residential areas, department stores, telecommunications towers, and power plants. Corporations that successfully won their bids on large infrastructure projects include Lee Ka-shing's Cheung Kong Inc., Y. K. Pao's Dwarf, Inc., Hong Kong-based Kuok Group, and Thai-based Charoen Pokphand.

In 1993 alone, Wharf Ltd., managed by Y. K. Pao's son-in-law, launched simultaneous projects in Shenzhen, Shanghai, Ningbo, Wuhan, and Beijing. The company contracted to build a new village in Guangzhou, a container port in Wuhan, and a cable television station in Sichuan.[2] Lee Ka-shing's Cheung Kong Holdings also realigned its global investment strategy to center on the Mainland and was especially active in building container ports in South and Central China along the Yangtze River.[3] The Kuok Group launched major infrastructure projects in Fujian, including shopping plazas, luxury hotels, and high end residential areas.[4] Since 1994, Cheung Kong and Wharf have expanded aggressively in infrastructure development in northern China.[5]

In the 1990s, Taiwanese investment on the Mainland grew rapidly. Like Hong Kong, Taiwan had substantial entrepreneurship, investable capital, well-developed manufacturing skills, and extensive connections to global markets. Residents of Taiwan have strong ethnic ties to South and Southeastern China. Indeed, 71 percent of Taiwanese have traced their ancestry to Fujian and another 13 percent to Guangdong. The rest, called mainlanders [*waishengren*], primarily migrated from coastal China between 1945 and 1950. Zhejiang province is

[2] *Liao Wang* [*Outlook*], no. 12, 1994.
[3] *Macao Daily*, June 21, 1993.
[4] *Wen Hui Bao*, October 24, 1993.
[5] Hong Kong *Xin Bao*, July 3, 1994.

the largest source of these recent exiles, with 13 percent, followed by Fujian at 12.4 percent, Jiangsu at 12.2 percent, Shandong at 11 percent, Guangdong at 10.5 percent, and Shanghai at 1.8 percent.[6] All of these places attracted substantial investment from Taiwan in the 1990s and beyond. Several prominent business figures in Taiwan had close ties to these localities: Xu Youyang, Wu Shunwen, and Jiang Jingyi were from Jiangsu. Wen Daming, Yin Zhihao, Zhang Minyu, Xu Zhifeng, and Zu Zhiqin, were from Zhejiang. The well-known Chairman of Thompson Inc., Tang Jun-nian, was born in Shanghai. Business opportunities and ethnic affiliation worked in tandem.

As we shall see later, Taiwanese investment helped to build Pudong (in Shanghai) and other high-tech development zones in coastal China. Small- and medium-sized Taiwanese firms played a role in the development of Eastern China comparable to that of Hong Kong investors in South China. In Shanghai, for example, the number of Taiwanese-run business ranged from 10,000 to 20,000 by the end of 1990s.

Taiwan in the 1990s was home to some of the world's largest manufacturers of computer hardware. By mid-decade, many of the manufacturers began to shift production to the Mainland. In response, local officials in Shanghai, Zhejiang, and Jiangsu built additional business infrastructure with input and resources from these investors to accommodate their needs. Singaporean corporations were also proactive in the PRC, helped by close personal relationship between Lee Kwan-Yew and Deng Xiaoping. Singaporean investors, however, were initially inept at exploring local connections, and Singapore's largest investment project in the 1990s, Singapore-Suzhou Industrial Park, was not successful. The local government, which was not involved in the collaboration, sabotaged the park. Yet, copying the model of the Singapore-invested industrial park, Suzhou's FDI-led industrialization and exports progressed profoundly. Other local governments became eager to invite Singaporean investors to help spur new models of development – for example, the Tianjin Eco-City.

Diaspora investment paved the way for the entry of Western FDI into the Chinese market. Since the 1990s, Japanese and Western investors increased their presence in China, concentrated in coastal areas that had hosted considerable diaspora investment. Toyota set up its first joint venture (JV) in China in 1992. Nissan followed suit in 1993, as did Honda in 1998. Japanese electronics giants, such as Panasonic, National, and Sony, all began investing in China during this decade. Such FDI, unlike diaspora investment, was attracted primarily by domestic markets, as China was becoming the world's "must-win" site by Western multinationals (Fernandez and Underwood 2006).

The influx of nonethnic FDI had two contradictory effects. On the positive side, the arrival of more MNCs enabled the formation of larger external networks operating in China. On the negative side, their market penetration, which in some

[6] See *Census on Taiwan*, 1956 edition.

cases wiped out domestic brands, intensified antiglobalist forces within China. Antiglobalization sentiments, coupled with failing state sectors, led to the resurgence of domestic resistance to FDI in the mid-1990s.

There are more recent groups of diaspora networks that have had impacts on China's current development, yet these are not included in the entrepreneurial diasporas that we emphasize here. These are emigrants from Mainland China during reform and their ongoing circulation back to homeland. The first group was the second-generation of political elites, sometimes dubbed "princeling," who received education at prominent schools in advanced societies. Their return in the late 1990s has revamped China's financial sector in the past decade. The second group were graduates of Chinese top schools that continued advanced studies in the West. After acquiring scientific credentials, they have come back to homeland and are key forces in China's scientific communities. In the FDI liberalization studied here, entrepreneurial diasporas in Hong Kong, Taiwan, and Southeast Asia have played earlier and more profound roles than the recently returned "princelings" or professionals.

DIASPORA INVESTMENT AND "ZONE FEVER"

In the 1990s, high-tech development zones sprang up in many parts of China, competing to offer favorable policies to foreign investors. From 1991 to the end of 1992, special zones increased more than fifteen times, from 117 to more than 1,800 (Zheng 2009). Although the national government tried to rein in this zone fever after 1994, various special zones continued to expand. By July 2004, there were 6,899 special zones of different types around the country, covering a total area of 38,600 square kilometers.[7] These zones became the centers of China's FDI liberalization and attracted substantial FDI inflows. In the most recent decade, these zones' shares of FDI inflows declined as places outside the zones were able to offer comparable conditions to foreign investors.

In the early 1990s, diaspora investors were early entrants in newly opened development zones and represented the largest source of external funds. Because diaspora investors had preexisting export channels to global markets, they helped to make stellar export success in China early on. Early success served as the basis for rapid diffusion of zone fever throughout the country. Western MNCs also had global export linkages, but their contribution to China's export economy was indirect: diaspora entrepreneurs exported their Mainland-made products, notably to the United States. Western companies in China primarily

[7] There are five types of special zones in China. Five SEZs include Shenzhen, Zhuhai, Shantou, Xiamen, and Hainan. Most zones during the zone fever belong to either Economic and Technological Development Areas (ETDAs) or High-tech Industry Development Areas (HIDAs). In practice, differences between ETDA and HIDA are minimal. Free Trade Zones (FTZs, or tariff-free zones) and Export Processing Zones (EPZs) are much smaller and typically are located in other special zones. Pudong New Development Area, for example, is an ETDA, but in it there are FTZs and EPZs.

TABLE 5.1. *Foreign Direct Investment (FDI) in China's Regions by Source (%, 1993)*

Sources	*Shenzhen (southern)*	*Pudong (eastern)*	*Wuhan (central)*	*Changchun (northern)*
Hong Kong & Macao	65	65	82	65
Taiwan	3	12	8	7
Japan	15	8	1	2
United States	10	14	19	11

Source: Zhongguo jingji tequ yu yanhai jingji jishu kaifaqu nianjian [The Chinese Statistical Yearbook on Economic and High-tech Special Zones], 1993, pp. 364–365, Beijing: Reform Publisher; *Wuhan Statistics Yearbook*, 1996, pp. 359–360; *Pudong Statistics Yearbook*, 1994, p. 139; *Changchun Statistics Yearbook*, 1994, p. 283

vied for domestic market shares and often used diaspora professionals to execute their operations in China.[8]

Table 5.1 demonstrates that diaspora investment accounted for the lion's share of FDI in China's development zones, including the initial special economic zones (SEZs) and newly established high-tech areas. Shenzhen, the first SEZ in China, was opened to FDI for more than a decade. Yet it still received the vast majority of its FDI from Hong Kong and Macao – 65 percent in 1993. Japan and the United States provided 15 percent and 10 percent, respectively. Using the number of foreign-invested firms (FIFs), more than 90 percent of FIFs in Shenzhen were owned by investors from Hong Kong and Macao, whereas Japanese and American investors each held less than 2 percent of FIFs.[9] Shanghai's Pudong, which was most famous for its openness to Western MNCs, drew 65 percent of its FDI from Hong Kong and Macao and 12 percent from Taiwan. In contrast, only 8 percent of investment originated in Japan and 14 percent in the United States.[10]

As indicated in Table 5.1, in Wuhan in Central China, investors from Hong Kong and Macao provided 82 percent of FDI, whereas the United States provided an impressive 19 percent and Japan supplied just 1 percent. In Changchun, a city in northeastern China far from Hong Kong, Macao, or Taiwan (although near Japan), diaspora investment from these three sources provided 72 percent

[8] Many diaspora managers of Western companies reported this in the 1990s.

[9] *Zhongguo jingji tequ yu yanhai jingji jishu kaifaqu nianjian*, 1993, pp. 364–365, Beijing: Reform Publisher.

[10] Japanese and American investments via their Hong Kong subsidiaries were counted as Japanese and American FDI, not Hong Kong FDI. The importance of Hong Kong was somewhat undervalued in statistics because the city often provided facilitative roles in helping execute Western investments.

of total FDI, whereas Japanese FDI accounted for only 2 percent and American FDI 11 percent. Wuhan's and Changchun's heavier concentration of diaspora investment compared to Shenzhen and Pudong suggests that diaspora investors tended to be early entrants in newly available zones and likely improved infrastructure and institutions to facilitate the entry of other FDI – a pattern similar to SEZs in the 1980s.

Pudong: China's Dragon Head [Longtou]

Pudong, an area approximately 522^2 kilometers east of old Shanghai, was annexed as a district of Shanghai in 1990 for the purpose of attracting investment for development. Mayor Zhu Rongji (who went on to become Chinese Premier in 1998) hoped to develop Pudong into "a socialist Hong Kong." In 1993, the national government designated Pudong as a New Economic Development Zone and began to prioritize its construction. Since then, Pudong has been a development marvel, criticism notwithstanding.[11] With large SOEs and Western MNCs, Pudong may seem a counterexample of the diaspora-led story told here. Beneath the surface, however, diaspora investors have also contributed strongly to Pudong's development in its formative years and beyond. Zhao Qizheng, the famous "master" of Pudong New Development Area who is known in China as "Mr. Pudong," reflected in his memoirs that Hong Kong-led openness in SEZs in the 1980s was crucial to devising Pudong's development policies (Zhao 2008, 290).

When the Shanghai municipality published *Twenty Years of Reform in Shanghai, Pudong* in 1999, the volume opened with these remarks: "Pudong, an attractive place for foreign capital, a perfect marriage of international economic giants from Japan, America, Europe, and the best of Chinese companies [referring to Shanghai Volkswagen and Motorola]."[12] Investment statistics from Pudong's early years yield a different picture, however. As shown in Figure 5.1, among FDI projects valued at more than $5 million in 1993, more than three-quarters were from Hong Kong, Macao, and Taiwan. These statistics suggest that diaspora FDI constituted the largest share of major investment projects, apart from accounting for the absolute majority in smaller projects. Many of these big projects were infrastructure investments that required substantial funds, technology, and long-term commitments. Taiwan's Thompson Group, for example, invested more than $450 million in 1993 alone. By contrast, Japan and the United States together accounted for less than 14 percent

[11] One criticism of Shanghai's development strategy with regards to Pudong is that the city systematically privileged state and Western capital over the local, private economy (Huang 2008).

[12] *Shanghai gaige kaifang ershi nian: Pudong* [*Twenty Years of Reform in Shanghai: Pudong*], Huadong Publisher, 1999, p. 216.

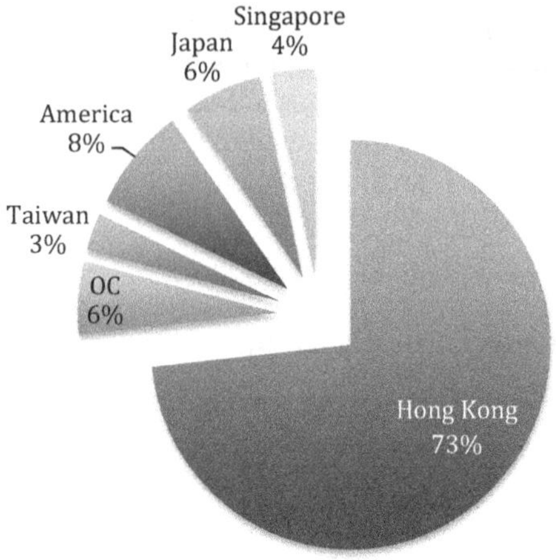

FIGURE 5.1. Sources of Major Foreign Direct Investment (FDI) Projects in Pudong, 1993. OC refers to overseas Chinese from areas other than Hong Kong, Macao, Taiwan, and Southeast Asia. These FDI projects were valued at more than $5 million each. Hong Kong's share included many projects from Taiwan. Thompson's $450 million investment was reported as of Hong Kong origin.
Source: Pudong tongji nianjian [*Pudong Statistical Yearbook*] 1994, pp. 143–146.

of the large investment projects,[13] whereas other diaspora investment made up additional 6 percent.[14]

Records show that the first industrial land-lease in Shanghai was made to a Taiwanese investor, Jiang Bingxin, in 1990. Jiang was born in Shanghai. When the ban on cross-strait travel between Taiwan and the Mainland was lifted, he visited Shanghai to search for business opportunities but found few manufacturing buildings available for rent. He invested over $8 million and built a 42,700 square meter industrial city that drew in many more Taiwanese manufacturers and traders.[15] Tang Junnian, the owner of Taiwan's Thompson Group, visited Shanghai in 1991, and within one year had invested billions of dollars in twelve projects. Tang was born in Pudong and became the largest investor there in the early 1990s (Zhao 2008). He claimed that "business potential in Shanghai [was] huge," creating a positive effect on Taiwan's business world.[16] In 1993, with $450 million, Thompson simultaneously launched

[13] *Pudong tongji nianjian [Pudong Statistical Yearbook]*, 1994, pp. 143–146.
[14] Disguised in the statistics is the fact that diaspora Chinese orchestrated the investments of many Western MNCs in China, a fact only apparent after reading the detailed project descriptions. Round-tripping – Chinese domestic capital disguised as Hong Kong investment – was not prevalent in these major projects, however. See *Pudong tongji nianjian [Pudong Statistical Yearbook]*, 1994.
[15] Hong Kong *Lian He Bao*, July 16, 1993.
[16] *Liao Wang* [*Outlook*], no. 12, 1994, p. 38.

a Financial Center in Shanghai's hottest financial district, a Trade Center near the Customs Office, a commercial center in downtown, 230 luxury houses in Shanghai's green zones, massive factories, residential buildings, and the first five-star hotel in Pudong. Hong Kong media suggested that Tang's hometown bias played a key role in Thompson's investment drive in Shanghai.[17] In the mid-1990s, Thompson pumped an additional $1.5 billion into Pudong.[18]

The Jinqiao Export Processing Zone in Pudong was approved by the national government in 1990 to attract Western investment and global markets. The actual configuration of FDI in the zone was similar to that in other zones, with a significant (albeit smaller) contribution by diaspora investors. In 1993, Hong Kong supplied 34 percent ($228 million) of contracted FDI in Jinqiao, while Taiwan provided $26 million. As Jinqiao's infrastructure and global networks expanded over the following decade, the shares of Western MNCs increased. Meanwhile, Taiwanese and Hong Kong manufacturers and exporters moved to rural and suburban areas near Shanghai, where production costs were significantly lower. Thus, although Taiwanese investors remained important in Pudong and Shanghai, their penetration into Shanghai's environs became more significant (Lin 2000, 57). Dialectic linkages helped; Taiwanese businesses blended into the local economy and helped to improve the economy in these rural localities.

In downtown Shanghai, the presence of diaspora entrepreneurs was notable, mainly in the services sectors. The Taiwanese, first arriving in large numbers in 1992, owned an estimated 10,000 to 20,000 businesses in Shanghai in 2000, including restaurants, fast-food chains, cafés, tea houses, fashion boutiques, interior design and photography studios, wedding services, and beauty salons. They also bought property in Shanghai. At the end of 2000, estimates of the number of settled Taiwanese in Shanghai ranged from 200,000 to 900,000 (Lin 2000, 57). Taiwanese shop owners revamped old Shanghai and breathed an air of modern style into this dilapidated "oriental jewel," making it more accessible to Western visitors.

Indeed, according to historian Jeffrey Wasserstrom, an expert on Shanghai, "the real Shanghai is where the East meets the East, and the Chinese meet the Chinese."[19] A 2010 Taiwanese study estimates that roughly 300,000 full-time professionals from Taiwan were working at Shanghai's Western-style hotels, intellectual property law firms, accounting firms, investment consultancies, and other agencies and institutions.[20] Hong Kong-based Li & Fung was the

[17] Hong Kong *Lian He Bao*, July 16, 1993. Shanghai municipal government appealed to Tang Junnian's ancestral linkage and arranged Tang's tour in Shanghai in 1991.

[18] *Shanghai gaige kaifang ershi nian: Pudong* [*Twenty Years of Reform in Shanghai: Pudong*], 1998, pp. 232–237.

[19] Jeffrey Wasserstrom, "Shanghai: the Myths and the Reality," speech at the Fairbank Center, Harvard University, March 23, 2010.

[20] See, "Qicheng taiqing zhuizhu shanghai jingyan" [70 percent Taiwanese youngsters Pursue Dreams in Shanghai], *Tianxia [Common World]*, no. 148, March 24–April 6, 2010, pp. 112–115.

real owner of the two Toys R Us superstores in Shanghai, and the company "Asianized" the American brand to fit the taste of Chinese customers.[21]

The massive movements of people from diaspora regions to Mainland China has not only driven investment flows and influenced China's FDI liberalization, as studied here, but also encouraged widespread intermarriage and cross-education that result in new social structures connecting China and its neighboring regions. The new social structures have facilitated Mainland–Taiwan relations in recent years (Calder and Ye 2010). The Economic Cooperation Framework Agreement (ECFA), for example, recognizes the newly emerging social reality and provides conditions that allow for cross-Taiwan straits families to interact more smoothly. Longer term, more profound impacts on society and state in China and the diaspora regions are still unfolding.

Back to FDI in Shanghai, the vast majority of the first external collaborations during reform were with diaspora businessmen, according to Shanghai's Economic Reform Council's 2008 compilation of new developments during reform. In Table 5.2, Hong Kong's largest textile manufacturer, Tang Xiangqian in 1980, invested the first JV in textiles. The first Economic and Technology

TABLE 5.2. *Shanghai's First Foreign Collaborations during the Reform Era [*Shanghai diyi*]*

Project	Diaspora FDI	Diaspora Connection*
First JV in textiles (1980)	Yes	Yes
First high-tech JV (1983)	Belgium	
First ETDZ development (1986)	Yes	Yes
First land sales (1988)	Japanese Diaspora	Yes
First old city renovation (1989)	Yes	Yes
First JV in retails (1990)	Yes	Yes
First industrial land lease (1990)	Yes	Yes
First five-star hotel in Pudong (1991)	Yes	Yes
First SOE overseas listing (1993)	Yes	Yes
First tariff-free zone (1993)	Japanese	
First JV in electricity generation (1995)	America	
First urban credit union (1995)	Yes	Yes
First bank with FDI (2001)	Yes	Yes
First share-holding bank (2004)	Yes	Yes

* Diaspora connection refers to technological assistance and other services provided by Hong Kong investors or other diasporas during the formation of the collaborations. ETDZ, Economic and Technology Development Zone; JV, joint venture; SOE, state-owned enterprise

Source: Compiled from raw materials in Zhou Bo (ed.), *Gan Wei Tianxia Xian* [*To Be the First*], Shanghai: People's Publisher, 2008 and author's own archival materials.

[21] *Xianggang lifeng jituan de shijian [The Operation of Hong Kong's Li & Fung]*, Beijing: People's University Press, 2009, pp. 274–281.

Development Zone, Hongqiao, was invested in by Hong Kong business in 1986. The same was true of the 1989 first old city renovation project, the first SOE overseas listings, the first retail JV in 1993, and various financial reforms since the late 1990s that were facilitated by Hong Kong capital and expertise. Coming from Taiwan, Jiang Bingxin leased the first industrial land in Shanghai in 1990, and Tang Junnian built the first five-star hotel in Pudong in 1991.

Shanghai's diaspora-driven investment also demonstrates the importance of home state. Tang Xiangqian, the first diaspora investor in Shanghai, had strong personal connections there. He was born there, and his parents stayed in Shanghai after 1949. When economic reform began in 1978, the Chinese government made unusual efforts to enhance Tang's connection with China's development. They appointed Tang's father vice chairman of Shanghai's Chinese People's Political Consultative Conference (CPPCC), a provincial branch of national CPPCC chaired by Deng Xiaoping. Shanghai's CPPCC was closely involved in devising economic policies in the 1980s.[22] In the early 1990s, the Taiwanese company Thompson's substantial investment in Shanghai was also drawn in by the proactive Shanghai government. In 1991, while Thompson's chairman Tang Junnian visited Beijing as a tourist, Shanghai's senior officials traveled there to meet him and persuaded Tang to tour his birthplace. When Tang was in Shanghai, he was offered the highest hospitality and most open policies. In short, governments can play decisive roles in building diaspora networks and enhancing diaspora contributions. This is clear in Shanghai and also clear in FDI liberalization in Kunshan.

Kunshan: A Small City with Global Business, Thanks to the Taiwanese

An hour's drive from Shanghai is Kunshan, another 1990s development marvel. Although it is just a county-level municipality (below city, provincial, and national administrative units), Kunshan's success has encouraged higher levels of government (especially those in its vicinity) to emulate it. Ranked as the most successful county-level economy in China each year from 2005 to 2008 (the latest data available), Kunshan had a gross domestic product (GDP) of RMB 150 billion (equivalent to $22 billion) in 2008 and a GDP per capita of RMB 120,882 ($17,687) – significantly higher than that of Shanghai, at $12,529. Moreover, Kunshan's economic success has been attributed to its openness to FDI.

Like Shanghai's Pudong, official accounts of Kunshan emphasize Western MNCs' importance. When President Jiang Zemin toured Kunshan in 1994, the media focused on investment by Western MNCs and overlooked the more

[22] Tang was also among the first group of investors in Shenzhen and later became the first investor in Urumqi. He had interactions with Deng Xiaoping and served in the CPPCC starting in the mid-1980s. See Wu (1999).

important contribution by diaspora entrepreneurs.[23] In 2000, the local government continued its misinformation concerning FDI in its report to Beijing. Their report said that openness was the first driver of growth [*kaifang shi fazhan de diye tuidongli*], and it emphasized that twenty or so *Fortune 500* companies from the United States, Japan, and Europe had invested in Kunshan, making it a part of global production networks.[24] Unmentioned in the report was the crucial bridging role played by Taiwanese investors. Indeed, Western MNCs mostly did business with Kunshan subsidiaries like Foxconn, Compal, and other Taiwan-based companies.

In Kunshan's FDI, local governments drew decisive help from diaspora networks. Kunshan was neither an SEZ nor an OCC in the 1980s. Yet as early as 1984, Kunshan's local government began to attract foreign investment. In that year, it signed its first investment contract for a project amounting to less than $1 million. In 1988, FDI inflows had already increased to $4.2 million. In 1991, just before Deng Xiaoping's 1992 Southern Tour, Kunshan attracted more than $56 million in FDI. Its success then caught the attention of its superior government, the Jiangsu provincial government. Jiangsu designated Kunshan as a provincial-level development zone in that year. A year later, in response to Kunshan's request, the State Council authorized the city to become a national-level zone,[25] followed by a visit by Chinese President and Jiangsu native Jiang Zemin.

Kunshan far exceeded the parameters set for it by the national government.[26] It offered preferential policies to foreign investors, reducing their tax obligations. Tax exemptions were even greater for companies designated as "high-tech." Kunshan eliminated export-import (exim) duties for foreign companies categorized as exporting enterprises.[27] The city gave the zone management committee the authority to approve investment projects of less than $30 million, and the committee then set up a consultancy company to help with projects of more than $30 million. It was common to have diaspora investment larger than $30 million broken into smaller projects to avoid higher level scrutiny.

23 See, for example, "Oumei qiye qinglai kunshan kaifaqu" [European and American Companies Like to Invest in Kunshan Special Zone], *Renmin Ribao* [*People's Daily*], April 30, 1994; "Shijie mingrencheng zai kunshan shoujian" [World Luminary City to Be Built in Kunshan], *Renmin Ribao* [*People's Daily*], September 13, 1994; "Kunshan zai dakaifangzhong zaizhu huihuang" [Remaking Economic Miracle through Openness], *Qunzhong [Masses]*, 1994, no 3; "Kunshan kaifa jianshe de chenggong jingyan" [Successful Experience in Development through Openness in Kunshan], *Shanghai Companies* [*Shanghai qiye*], 1993, no. 12; "Kunshan chengbi huoju kaifaqu yinlai zongduo waishan" [Torch Open Area in Kunshan Attract many Foreign Investors], *Renmin Ribao* [*People's Daily*], December 9, 1992.

24 "Kunshan: gaosu zengzhang conghe lai?" [What Was Driving Kunshan's Rapid Growth?], *Jingji cankao bao* [*Economic Reference Paper*], November 2, 2000.

25 See *Kunshan nianjian* [*Kunshan Yearbook*] (1988–1993).

26 Ibid.

27 Ibid, pp. 16–17.

TABLE 5.3. *Major Foreign Investments in Kunshan (1992–3)*

Investor's Country of Origin	Founding Time	Amount ($Mi)	Sector	Export ratio
Paraguay OC	1.1992	$12.4	Textiles	70%
Taiwan	7.1992.	$29	Electronics	N/A
Taiwan	7.1992	$10	Apparel	Majority
Taiwan + Japan	9.1992	$23	Auto parts	100
Taiwan	9.1992	$29.5	Sports equipment	Majority
Japan	10.1992	$30	Sporting equipment components	50
Taiwan	11. 1992	$12	Electronics	Majority
Hong Kong	12.1992	$12.5	Packaging materials	N/A
Hong Kong	1. 1993	$10	Electronics	60%
Hong Kong	4. 1993	$10	Real estate	N/A
Hong Kong	4.1993	$25	Food	N/A
Taiwan	7.1993	$12	Textiles	70
Hong Kong	7.1993	$30	Auto parts	50
Japan	11.1993	$30	Electronics parts and components	N/A
Hong Kong	12.1993	$15	Parts and components	N/A

Source: Kunshan tongji nianjian [*Kunshan Statistical Yearbook*], and *Kunshan nianjian* [*Kunshan Yearbook*], 1991–1994. *Kunshan Yearbook, 1988–1993*.

Diaspora investment played crucial roles in Kunshan's development success. As indicated in Table 5.3, diaspora investors dominated Kunshan's large FDI projects in 1992–1993.[28] Of the fifteen largest contracted investment projects, twelve were solely financed by overseas Chinese, six by Hong Kong investors, five by Taiwanese investors, and one by Paraguayan Chinese. Japanese companies contracted two wholly owned FDI projects and one joint project with a Taiwanese partner.Table 5.3 also shows that FDI tended to be concentrated in textiles, electronics, and parts and components, and had high export orientation. The diaspora investment contracts pledged to abide by "minimum export ratios" ranging from 50 to 100 percent, although some did not specify precise exports ratios.

The implementation of Kunshan's development zones was remarkably successful. From 1988 to 1993, foreign trade growth in Kunshan averaged more than 70 percent annually, coupled with impressive gains in GDP per capita. With growing diaspora investment, Kunshan's growth trajectory in the 1990s remained resilient and sped up even more impressively later in the decade when

[28] Kunshan nianjian [Kunshan Yearbook] listed all the FDI projects with more than $10 million.

Taiwan's computer manufacturers began to relocate to Kunshan, making this small town a globally consequential computer export hub.[29]

During Kunshan's economic takeoff, the importance of Taiwanese-based diasporas cannot be overemphasized. More than 60 percent of hotel guests in Kunshan in the 1990s were from Taiwan (Lin 2000). The local government also consciously modeled its development strategy after the Hsinchu and Southern Taiwan Science Parks and established the first high-tech export-processing zone in China in 1997 without permission from Beijing. Within two years, the export zone had contracted $1.2 billion in FDI, mainly in the electronics sector.[30] Beijing finally authorized the zone in 2000. Also learning from Taiwan, Kunshan set up a special zone for returnee Chinese in 1998.

With these efforts, Kunshan became an attractive site for Taiwanese capital, especially in the electronics manufacturing industry. In 2000, when the Kunshan export-processing zone was approved by Beijing, more than 760 Taiwanese-invested firms already existed in Kunshan. By 2005, Kunshan had received one-tenth of Taiwanese investment in all of China. Based on Taiwanese investment, Kunshan emerged as a critical manufacturing site in the global production network of computer hardware.[31]

Kunshan's success in attracting FDI and promoting exports had a significant impact on preexisting local development projects. The "Torch Plan"-inspired technology park serves as an example.[32] Work on the park began in 1992 as the national government pushed to develop indigenous technology. In 1999, the local operation of this park was similar to that in other special zones, striving to attract as much FDI as possible. Of the park's total $1.8 billion in contracted investment, $1.2 billion was FDI – most of which was contributed by Taiwanese investors. The park's 265 FIFs accounted for more than 70 percent of the local economy.[33] In broader Kunshan, FIFs contributed more than 50 percent of revenue, more than 60 percent of taxes, more than 70 percent of industrial sales, more than 80 percent of investment in fixed assets, and more than 90 percent of exports.[34]

Without specifying the sources of foreign investment or making a distinction between diaspora investment and FDI, the lesson for other localities has been clear: FDI created Kunshan's developmental marvel. Local officials in Kunshan, boasting about their open FDI policies, proudly proclaimed that a sound strategy should promote a policy to "never say no to foreign investors."[35] This

[29] *Kunshan tongji nianjian* [*Kunshan Statistical Yearbook*] *1998*, pp. 36–38.

[30] *Kunshan nianjian 2000* [*Kunshan Yearbook, 2000*], pp. 107–108.

[31] "Kunshan chengwei taishan touzi redian qu" [Kunshan Became a Hot Area for Taiwanese Investment], *Guangming Ribao* [*Enlightenment Daily*], April 11, 2000.

[32] The Torch Plan was China's industrial policy to develop indigenous technology started in 1988.

[33] "Kunshan chengwei taishan touzi redian qu [Kunshan Became a Hot Area for Taiwanese Investment]," *Kunshan nianjian 2000* p. 108.

[34] Ibid.

[35] "Kunshan yinjin waizi bijin baiyi meiyuan [Kunshan Attracted Ten Billions USD]," *Jiefang Ribao* [Liberation Daily], November 13, 2000.

policy was followed elsewhere in China. Yet applying the same policies does not always bring similar results. The crucial connections between diaspora entrepreneurs and local governments in Shanghai and Kunshan were not closely followed by local officials elsewhere.

Wenzhou: A Failure in FDI

In 1990s China, local and national governments promoted FDI as a superior development policy, and all local governments strove to attract FDI. In such an atmosphere, Wenzhou – an economy dominated by indigenous private capital – was viewed by its superior government as a failure.[36] The FDI-led development mentality was so pervasive that officials in Wenzhou made efforts to build special zones for foreign investors. During the peak of zone fever in 1992–1993, Wenzhou developed plans for five development zones and received necessary approvals from higher levels of government. By 1997, all the zones were in operation and complete with policies to attract foreign investors.[37]

Despite the Wenzhou government's efforts to welcome foreigners, FDI has contributed little to the local economy. In 2006, after a decade of running development zones, FIFs accounted for only 6 percent of total firms in Wenzhou, and SOEs accounted for only 4 percent, with indigenous firms accounting for the remainder of firms. In all five development zones, FDI was minimal. The largest zone in the city, for example, had only 1 percent of capital supplied by foreign investors in 2006.[38]

Wenzhou's failure to generate FDI inflows was not due to its lack of diaspora population; the city has substantial numbers of emigrants in Taiwan, Europe, and the United States. And a large number of these are entrepreneurs and have helped the city's dazzling exports to global markets – Wenzhou-produced cigarette lighters, for example, hold 80 percent of the world's market shares. Wenzhou diasporas' investment lag behind those in Shanghai and Kunshan is derived from two main factors. One, on the supply side, Wenzhou diasporas were more recent immigrants, most of them emigrated during reform, and their businesses in their host societies were generally small-scale and not equipped for large development projects or major manufacturing sectors, as seen in diaspora business in Hong Kong and Taiwan.

The second factor is demand-side. The Wenzhou government is generally weak and cannot secure preferential policies for diasporas from superior governments or mobilize diaspora entrepreneurs effectively. The government's proposal to set up a diaspora bank in Wenzhou, based on diaspora networks' push and influence, was repeatedly rejected by superior governments. Even recently,

[36] See the discussion in Yeung and Hu (1992, 172–198).

[37] Those policies were not as well spelled out as those in Kunshan. See *Wenzhou nianjian* [Wenzhou Yearbook],1998.

[38] *Wenzhou tongji nianjian [Wenzhou Statistical Yearbook]* 2007, p. 113.

after the Chinese State Council designated Wenzhou as an experimental site for new financial reforms, particularly in creating private banks in China, a hopeful proposal from Wenzhou diaspora representatives to establish a diaspora bank was again denied, without explanation.

The 1990s zone fever period demonstrates a national–local disjuncture: local officials appeared more decisive in driving zone fever, irrespective of the winds and tides in Beijing. Thus, although China's national FDI regime may be similar to those in other countries, local practice made China's FDI liberalization profoundly favorable to foreign capital. The diffusion analysis supports that diaspora networks influenced the ideas and incentives of local governments on FDI, as seen in Pudong and Kunshan. Diaspora investors helped to generate economic success in particular localities; that success in turn broadened domestic support for FDI. Over time, FDI liberalization became the predominant developmental ideology. State-owned enterprise reform since the mid-1990s additionally reveals the disjuncture between national and local policy preferences and the ultimate victory of local interests.

SOE REFORM DEEPENED FDI LIBERALIZATION

Consolidated FDI liberalization does not mean the end of domestic resistance or rule out the possibility of policy modification. Domestic resistance can still generate formidable forces against FDI, although in a consolidated liberal economy a complete reversal is unlikely. In China, despite economic success, many intellectuals and political elites (known as neoconservatives) rose to resist FDI liberalization in the 1990s (Fewsmith 2001). One of the key issues for the new conservatives was the failing of SOEs, which they attributed to FDI liberalization. These opinions came to be held by various groups in the government and resulted in some efforts to reduce FDI. In saving SOEs, the national government resorted to the Japanese and Korean models of economic planning; interest in industrial policy was revived.[39] The involvement of diaspora entrepreneurs in SOE reforms in the decade helped to sustain and even deepen FDI liberalization at the local level and finally influenced the national guidelines on SOE reforms.

Diasporas' influence on SOE reform was inseparable from broader pro-FDI ideas and incentives at the local level, mounting since the early success in SEZs and further development marvels during the zone fever period. Compared to vibrant and profitable companies in open areas, SOEs with chronic losses and growing debts were a burden to local governments. When the national government authorized local officials to reform smaller state companies, local officials

[39] According to internal sources, advocates for the developmental state model argued strongly to political leaders about the advantage and the fit of the model. See, "Jiejian riben zhengfu guanli chanye de jingyan kan woguo hangye guanli jigou gaige de fanxiang" [Using Japanese Industrial Policy to Direct our Industrial Management Reform], *Jingji cankao* [*Economic References*], Z4, 1992.

were eager to dispose of them by selling them to any buyer, domestic or foreign. Diaspora entrepreneurs made the early and successful international buyouts that expanded the practice of using FDI to reform SOEs, and more foreign buyers also entered the market.[40] SOE reform thus deepened FDI liberalization.

Domestic Resistance Mounted in 1993–1995

Policy debates persisted. Just as FDI liberalization was becoming a national strategy, some central bureaucrats and scholars criticized FDI because they felt that FDI did not promote indigenous technology, despite the fact that China's initial rationale for allowing FDI was "yielding market to exchange for technology" [*yi shichang huan jishu*]. In the mid-1990s, these critics were again attracted to the Japanese model, which built globally competitive business conglomerates while maintaining the country's own institutions (Fu 1992). Korea's model also had strong appeal, considering its success in protecting domestic markets, developing indigenous industry, and strategically placing itself in the global system. Many argued that if China were to achieve globally competitive industry, it must emulate the state-led industrialization model (Ye 2009).

The new conservatives explicitly criticized FDI. The *Internal Reports on Reform* [*Gaige neican*], for example, presented ardent arguments against "too much" FDI in China and criticized that China's FDI policies were too liberal and conceded too much domestic market space to foreign producers (Ye 2009). Chen Yuan, an influential economist and the son of the conservative leader Chen Yun, organized a group called the Beijing Young Economists' Association [*Beijing qingnian jingji gongzuozhe xiehui*] to help formulate China's development strategy and advocate "new centralization." Chen repeatedly maintained that a strong state was indispensable to late industrialization (Chen 1991).

Hu Angang and Wang Shaoguang, two influential advocates of a strong national government in China, took issue with the SEZ policy (Hu and Wang 1995). Their outspoken criticism of the policy inspired the widely circulated *Economic Daily* [*jingji ribao*] to publish a series of articles under the title, "How Will the Special Zones Continue to Be Special?" Even the traditionally pro-FDI magazine, *Foreign Investment in China* [*zhongguo waizi*], published an editorial arguing that China's priority should be to encourage top domestic companies to go abroad and compete with MNCs internationally.[41] Official policies were modified; the 1994 National Party Congress drew considerable attention to

[40] The precise period of SOE reform is not well defined in China. There were some efforts to reform SOEs before 1993, and many SOEs in various regions were yet to be reformed after 1998. 1993–1998 was the most intensive and extensive period of SOE reform, involving policy debates, central decision-making, and implementation. See Ye (2009).

[41] "Chuangjian yipi daxin kuaguo qiye" [Construct a Group of Large Multinational Corporations], *Zhongguo waizi* [*Foreign Investment in China*], no. 2, 1995.

regional inequalities, and President Jiang Zemin explicitly called for reducing regional gaps in his speech to the Fifth Plenum in September 1995.[42] These steps were seen as a victory for domestic resistance because the opposition groups succeeded in connecting FDI to growing regional inequalities.

The idea of establishing a strong national state appealed to a range of political and economic elites in Beijing. The ever-increasing connections between diaspora networks and local governments, however, continued to influence policy implementation. National bureaucrats, for example, wanted to prop up the SOEs through reform, but local governments arranged foreign buy-outs. Diaspora investors orchestrated SOE bailouts early on and indeed transformed many failing SOEs into profitable ventures. These early successes enhanced the appeal of using FDI to reform SOEs at the local level and later shaped national guidelines on SOE reforms.

Diaspora contributions eased the daunting task of SOE reform in China in two important ways. First, during the fifteen years of FDI liberalization before SOE reform, local governments, SOE managers, and motivated workers came to view FDI more desirable than SOEs and voluntarily changed their preferences from SOEs to FIFs.[43] Second, when SOE reform began, diasporas' capital, expertise, and global connections offered incentives to large numbers of domestic actors to privatize SOEs and meanwhile helped to transform loss-making SOEs into profits in southern and eastern China. Absent diaspora contributions, SOE reform in northern China incurred enormous dislocation and social protest, and in the western region, SOE reform was completed much later than in the rest of the country.

Diaspora Networks' Involvement in the SOE Reform

Before 1995, the national government did not provide a clear guideline for SOE reform, and some local governments took the initiative to reform loss-making SOEs under their jurisdictions.[44] Local governments in South China delved into privatizing SOEs as early as the mid-1980s and turned these SOEs over to diaspora investors. Both sides claimed success in such collaborations.[45]

[42] Pro-FDI groups also refuted Hu's views. The *Shenzhen Special Zone* newspaper [*shenzhen tequ bao*] responded with a series of highly vitriolic personal attacks on Hu. *The Enlightenment Daily* [*Guangming Ribao*] ran an article arguing that the zones should be made even more "special" (see *Guangming Ribao*, October 7, 1994). To show support for these groups, Jiang Zemin visited Shenzhen in June 1994.

[43] Mary Gallagher (2005) uses "contagious capitalism" to account for the ideational shift and change from socialist labor policy to capitalist practice, thanks to FDI.

[44] The vague principle of "grasping the big and letting go the small" [*zhuada fangxiao*] was announced only in late 1995.

[45] See, The Study Group on SOEs Using Grafted FDI in Fujian Province, "Fujian SOEs Using Grafted FDI," *Jingjixue dongtai [Trends in the Study of Economics]*, no. 10, 1994, pp. 26–30.

Diasporas further influenced SOE reforms in the 1990s, and this practice – using diaspora buyouts to dissolve failing SOEs – became quite popular. In Quanzhou (Fujian province) in 1993, the municipal government conducted the so-called Whole Package Joint Ventures Program [*yilanzi hezi*]: in one agreement, Quanzhou sold 90 percent of its local SOEs to China Strategy Investment Co. [*Zhongce*] and transferred most SOE responsibilities to the diaspora buyer (Xi and Shan 1996). *Zhongce* transformed the newly purchased SOEs and listed them on Hong Kong Stock Exchange. Both sides were happy with this result.[46]

By the mid-1990s, the appeal of FDI – that from diasporas and Western MNCs included – had expanded to local governments outside Guangdong and Fujian. Local officials in eastern China observed how FDI had transformed once-backward South China into the most prosperous part of the nation and believed that their localities could benefit just as much, if not more, from FDI liberalization (Ye 2009). When they were charged with reforming SOEs, these officials devised various schemes to partner SOEs with foreign investors and offered the latter controlling shares of these ventures. The SOE reform thus became an opportunity for local officials in eastern China to draw in FDI.

Systematic data on FDI's involvement in SOE reform are lacking, but a survey done by the National Development and Research Council in 1993 showed that 81 percent of contracted FDI in Shanghai was used to reform SOEs; in Fujian, 32 percent of JV projects were involved in SOE reform, and 53 percent of existing SOEs used FDI for self-transformation.[47] Furthermore, 22 percent of FDI projects in Qingdao and 44 percent in Yantai (both in Shandong province) were contracted to reform SOEs. Dalian also transferred substantial FDI to reform its SOEs (Ye 2009). Tianjin municipality explicitly preferred using FDI to reform existing SOEs: by 1994, it had contracted $1.8 billion FDI specifically for SOE reforms, covering 421 projects, and in 1994 alone, the city contracted $500 million to transform 124 existing SOE operations (Liu 1994). Even Dandong, bordering North Korea, contracted more than 50 percent of FDI to reform SOEs.

Although neoconservatives managed to influence debates on FDI at the national level, local governments remained proactive in involving foreign capital in SOE reform.[48] Pan Huanyou, a local official in Zhejiang province, took to the airwaves in 1995 to discuss the topic, using specific examples of SOEs in Zhejiang that used FDI to transform themselves from loss-making companies to globally competitive corporations. He used these companies' growing export

[46] China Strategy Investment Co. later broke the diversely composed JV and formed different JVs with other diaspora investors and foreign partners, often giving the controlling share to the other parties. The company subsequently sold its majority share to Indonesia-based Farlim Group.

[47] These data are from the Development Research Center of the State Council, *Zhongguo jingji nianjian 1996 [Almanac of China's Economy 1996]*. Beijing: zhongguo jingji nianjianshe, pp. 26–27.

[48] Taiwan, *Jingji shibao* [Economics Daily], July 7, 1998.

figures as evidence for his claims (Pan 1995). His arguments were affirmed by local officials in other areas and influenced debates in Beijing. Echoing local interests, reformists in the national government defended FDI liberalization, and successful local practice strengthened their policy stance against the conservatives. In the policy debates between reformers and conservatives, however, diaspora networks were left out.

Liao Wang [Outlook], a popular journal, published a long treatise that defended China's FDI-led industrialization in 1996. The article's main argument was that global business strategies had changed, and benefits of globalization accrued to nations attractive to MNCs.[49] Researcher Sun Xiaohua at the Research Institute of the Ministry of Foreign Economics and Trade applauded the success of China Strategy Investment's partnership with Chinese SOEs in various locations. He argued that using FDI to reform SOEs solved the major challenges of improving capital, technology, and management all at one time (Sun 1994). In defending FDI liberalization, a group of economists at Beijing University studied the impact of Coca Cola on China and found a single yuan worth of investment in cola production produced 2.66 yuan in demand for other sectors. The authors showed that, in 1998, Coca Cola paid RMB 160 million in taxes and contributed RMB 260 million to related sectors, in addition to creating 400,000 new jobs in China.[50] The study was printed in *Internal Reports on Reform*, a publication explicitly serving policy makers.

Anticipating material gains, many economic bureaus in Beijing supported FDI liberalization as well. In 1995, *Liao Wang* conducted an extensive survey of various top bureaucrats regarding FDI.[51] The survey revealed a strong message: "China's door should be further opened" [*Zhongguo guomen jingyibu changkai*]. The Ministry of Railways [*Tiedao bu*] announced in 1994 that it was cautiously yet proactively seeking FDI. The Ministry of Electricity [*dianli bu*] also declared that it "welcomed FDI." Apart from development loans, the Ministry encouraged foreign companies to invest directly in electricity plants and hoped to receive $12.6 billion in FDI by 2000. The Ministry of Aviation [*Hangkong bu*] opened itself to a variety of foreign collaborations and, in 1994, had already utilized $1.6 billion in FDI. The Ministry of Foreign Trade and Economic Cooperation (MOFTEC), a traditionally more liberal ministry, highlighted the importance of legal provisions in taxation, finance, foreign exchange, foreign trade, and investment to facilitate FDI. Foreign Economics and Trade Minister Wu Yi also argued for deepening institutional reform to facilitate international trade and foreign investment.

These pro-FDI advocates, eager to defend globalization, did not do justice to the role of diaspora entrepreneurs. The discourse on FDI, openness, and

[49] *Liao Wang*, 1996, no. 41, p. 23.

[50] "Waiqi dui woguo de jingji fazhan youshenme zuoyong" [Role of Foreign Invested Firms in China's National Economy], *Gaige neican* [*Internal Reports on Reform*], 2000, No. 13.

[51] *Liao Wang*, 1995, no.11.

globalization in China made little distinction between diasporas and other foreigners and instead focused on the entry of Western MNCs and the country's pending World Trade Organization (WTO) membership. This trend was in line with what Barry Naughton (2007) described as an "institutional-based" reform that aimed to build a regulatory state under the influence of global practices and institutions. An unintended consequence, however, was that positions on reform were sharply divided into either liberal or conservative, defined as pro-West or anti-West, respectively. Chinese successes were ascribed to globalization, but failures were also blamed on globalization. Over time, neither policy debates nor development studies came to note the importance of diaspora entrepreneurs to China's FDI-led industrialization and export economy. Diaspora contributions, if mentioned at all, were treated as a residual effect of China's reform.

Returning to the subject of SOE reform, diaspora entrepreneurs were the early foreign buyers of bankrupt SOEs, and their success persuaded other investors to follow suit. *Zhongce*, after acquiring almost all SOEs in Quanzhou, set up JVs with more than 100 other SOEs. Taiwanese entrepreneurs also came to China to buy out SOEs. Tai Fook bought many SOEs in 1997 and successfully turned them into profitable companies, creating ripple effects throughout the Mainland.[52] Headquartered in Tianjin, Tai Fook purchased all state-owned paper mills in northern China and, by 1998, had built the largest chain of paper mills in the country. Successful cases like those of *Zhongce* and Tai Fook drew more diaspora capital to SOE privatization.[53]

The reform of large SOEs followed a different path from the locally led process. The national government's official policy was to "grasp the big and let go the small," and it retained authority over the reform of large SOEs. In practice, individual SOEs had tremendous leeway for self-restructuring. These SOEs had relatively more advanced technology, better facilities, more skilled labor, and better connected managers than did the smaller firms. Reconstruction of many such SOEs drew heavily on China's connection to Hong Kong. For example, after restructuring, many large SOEs listed themselves with the Hong Kong Stock Exchange. By 1997, more than thirty major SOEs had overseas listings. Others established joint ventures, cooperative operations, or strategic alliances with foreign capitalists, while retaining some management control.

For medium-sized SOEs, a combination of restructuring, mergers, and joint ventures customarily constituted the reform process. Shanghai municipality, for example, simultaneously suspended one-third of textiles factories, reorganized home appliance producers, and promoted mergers among major SOEs in heavy industries. They then relocated many factories to surrounding rural areas where production costs were lower. In this process, foreign capital was solicited for JVs, collaborative ventures, equity shares, mergers, and acquisitions.[54]

[52] Singapore, *Lianhe Zaobao*, March 22, 1997.

[53] Hong Kong, *Da Gong Bao*, February 7, 1998.

[54] *Liao Wang* [Outlook], 22, 1997, pp. 12–17.

Following coastal China's example, the country's central region implemented SOE reform in the late 1990s and also drew on FDI. The region, although not a pioneer in FDI liberalization, was the largest source of migrant workers for diaspora-invested companies in the coastal area. From 1997 to 2001, approximately half of the region's SOEs were dissolved. Chongqing, the industrial hub in central China, reformed 76 percent of its SOEs in 1997 and became an attractive site for FDI starting in this period. In western and northern provinces, due to the lack of diaspora connections, SOE reform followed a different path: only 13 percent of SOEs used JVs in the course of restructuring, whereas the rest were done through employee shareholding (19 percent), internal restructuring (18 percent), merger (14 percent), leasing (14 percent), bankruptcy (11 percent), and open sales (11 percent) (Garnaut, Song, Tenev, and Yao 2005). The social cost of layoffs in the northern region, where FDI was relatively scarce and SOEs dominated local economy, was horrendous, but contained within the region. In China, thanks to prior FDI liberalization, there was no nation-wide opposition to SOE reforms in the 1990s.

The zone fever and SOE reforms drove substantial inflows of FDI in China from 1993 to 1997. In 1993, China had about $28 billion in FDI, but this figure increased to more than $50 billion in 1997. The share of diaspora capital from Hong Kong, Taiwan, and Southeast Asia combined was enormous: FDI from diaspora communities constituted 55 to 80 percent of total FDI in those years, surpassing the combined shares of American, Japanese, and European investment by large margins.

Figure 5.2 provides a historical diagram of diaspora investment's share of FDI inflows in China. There was a spike in the 1990s, although diaspora investment

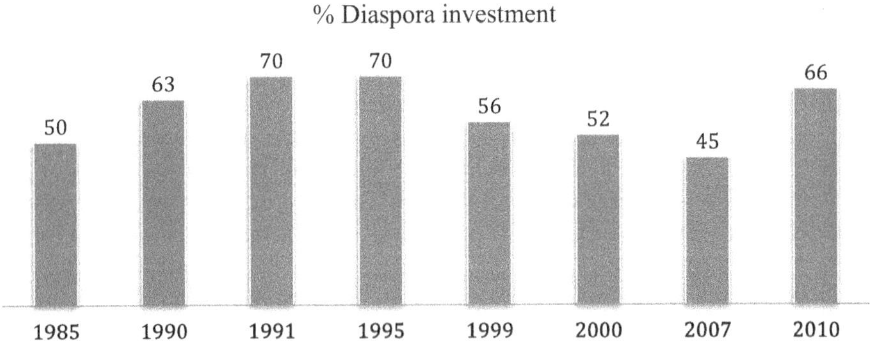

FIGURE 5.2. Diasporas' Contribution to China's Foreign Direct Investment (FDI), selected years (%). Diaspora investment is the sum of FDI from Hong Kong, Macao, Taiwan, and nations in Southeast Asia where Chinese immigrants are concentrated. In the case of Hong Kong, companies headquartered in other countries, such as the United States or Japan, were excluded from such statistical counting.
Source: Zhongguo tongji nianjian, 1979–2011 [*China Statistical Yearbook*, 1979–2011].

always hovered above 50 percent throughout reform. The shares of diaspora investment had a relative decline after the 1997–8 Asian financial crisis, but recovered to become majority shares in recent years. In 2007, for example, diaspora investment's share was 45 percent, but surpassed 50 percent in 2008. In 2010, the share of diaspora investment in China was 66 percent.

The social network analysis finds that the importance of diaspora investment lies not only in the size of capital, but also in the timing. The early entry and ability to generate early success in the process of China's economic reform were pivotal to the construction and expansion of pro-FDI coalitions in the country. Chapter 5 thus needs to be read sequentially with Chapter 3. Together, these two China chapters establish the decisive role that diaspora networks played in the speedy diffusion model hypothesized in SNT.

CONCLUSION

In China and beyond, discourse on FDI liberalization – either pro-FDI or anti-FDI – has downplayed the contribution of diasporas and instead emphasized the "foreignness" of external funds in the country. This chapter, following Chapter 3, establishes that diaspora entrepreneurs contributed to the pro-FDI zone fever and transformed the national state-motivated SOE reform into FDI liberalization – two key liberalization episodes in the 1990s – by transferring ideas, technology, and capital to Chinese actors at both the central and local levels. Diasporas were the main and early entrants in newly constructed development zones in the early 1990s. They then helped to overcome new domestic resistance to FDI later in the decade. With cooperation from local governments in South China, diaspora entrepreneurs pioneered using FDI to reform SOEs, the success of which expanded this practice in the country and shaped the national policy of SOE reform.

The two China chapters in this book (3 and 5) also affirm the importance of leadership, decentralization, and local governments. These constitute the inseparable domestic politics that enabled diaspora entrepreneurs to play such transformative roles in China's late development. To begin with, Deng Xiaoping, although he did not design FDI policies, was remarkably open to and supportive of diaspora influence. When he recognized the effectiveness of FDI in China's late industrialization, he threw his weight behind openness. Decentralization allowed local governments to experiment with various economic practices, and local cadres were quick to discard unhelpful policies and embrace FDI. Indeed, persuasion went both ways. From the top down, the proactive and pragmatic state convinced diaspora entrepreneurs to come and to invest their wealth in China's future. While helping homeland development, diasporas enhanced their global competitiveness and emerged as even stronger transnational business forces in the world.

India's reform was more complex: rapid liberalization in the early 1990s, heightened opposition in mid-decade and a narrowing of liberal policies at the end of the decade. Chapter 6 shows that three conditions in India were similar to China: the national state's drive for liberalization, a general consensus on economic priorities, and a growing interest from and influx of Western MNCs. A crucial difference persists between the two Asian giants, however: that is, the two types of capitalist networks. In China, diaspora entrepreneurs played very important roles in the 1990s, whereas Indian indigenous industry was more influential. These capitalist networks each exploited existing political institutions to their own advantage and influenced the pace and direction of economic reform in their respective countries.

6

Indian Indigenous Industry and FDI

India's foreign direct investment (FDI) liberalization started in 1991. Moving quickly at first, it soon experienced setbacks. On India's post-1991 reform, scholars' views are divided. On the one hand, Atul Kohli and Dani Rodrik remain skeptical of "real change." They highlight the obstructionist stances of domestic interest groups and constraining democratic institutions. On the other, Rob Jenkins (1999) explains that despite democratic institutions and opposing interest groups, politicians have used "camouflage" to circumvent opposition and implement significant reforms. Economists have generally been positive in appraising post-1991 changes (Panagariya 2008). This chapter compares policy liberalization in the 1990s with developments of the previous decade and demonstrates that the country has made considerable progress with foreign trade and investment. Yet the process tracing and policy oscillation demonstrate that domestic resistance to FDI was influential and only abated with the globalization of indigenous companies in the new millennium, often helped by diaspora professionals at Western corporations.

Indian diaspora professionals have overall become much more important in the country since the 1990s. Jagdish Bhagwati and T. N. Srinivasan, for example, served in the Indian government in the 1960s and faced an uphill battle in advocating liberalization. Yet, Bhagwati's college roommate Manmohan Singh (with whom he shares important economic views) became India's finance minister in 1991 and prime minister in 2004. During reform, a host of Western-trained liberal economists returned to influence economic policy making. In the recent period, diaspora professionals emerged as an influential globalization force connecting Indian indigenous business and global corporations. While working at Western companies, diaspora professionals proposed, executed, and managed their companies' investments in India. In sectors such as software services, entrepreneurial diasporas also emerged and directly invested in the growth of these new services sectors in the homeland.

There are three sections in this chapter. The first covers India's continual divergence from China in terms of FDI. The second section examines India's FDI liberalization in the 1990s: the initial liberalization in the aftermath of the 1991 crisis, followed by domestic opposition in mid-decade, and policy vacillation in the late 1990s. The third section centers on the new social basis surrounding India's liberalization in the current period, including growing Western multinational corporations (MNCs), globalized Indian companies, and strengthened local states, and the new diaspora networks that are increasingly connecting these three forces in India.

CONTINUAL DIVERGENCE IN FDI BETWEEN CHINA AND INDIA

In the new millennium, India's formal FDI policies became similar to China's in some important ways. The national government, despite varied bureaucratic interests, generally pursued openness to foreign investment and implemented measures to facilitate foreign investors' entry. Policy makers began to see China's economic success more clearly, coming to believe that what worked for a comparably populous, agrarian, and underdeveloped pre-reform China ought to have some relevance for India. A visit by Commerce Minister Murasoli Maran to China in 2000 resulted in an earnest push for liberalization and a comprehensive special economic zone (SEZ) policy in India, complete with favorable tax codes, flexible labor practices, and generally more open trade and investment rules in such zones (Jenkins 2011). The same policy, however, has yet to achieve visible gains in investment inflows.

The implementation and results of India's FDI liberalization continue to diverge from China's. Openness to FDI has existed alongside protection for domestic industry. A wide gap developed between formal policy liberalization and actual implementation. Contrary to China, where local implementation of new policies was typically more liberal than what was officially sanctioned by the national government, the implementation of new policies in India was more constrained than what was nationally authorized (with the exception of the software services industry). The developmental effects of the two countries' FDI liberalization seem to differ: in China, FDI helped to create development miracles along the coast, whereas, conversely in India, the results were less clear. Domestic resistance, strengthened by the lack of compelling success, was able to influence the Indian government to pass laws to restrain FDI. As a whole, FDI's direct impact on India's economic structure and external sectors remained small.

The divergence between China's and India's FDI inflows grew greater in the 1990s and remained wide in the new millennium, although both countries gained considerably from global capital inflows. As indicated in Figure 6.1, India had $75 million in FDI in 1991; China had $4.4 billion in FDI that same year. As both countries pushed for openness over the next two years, China

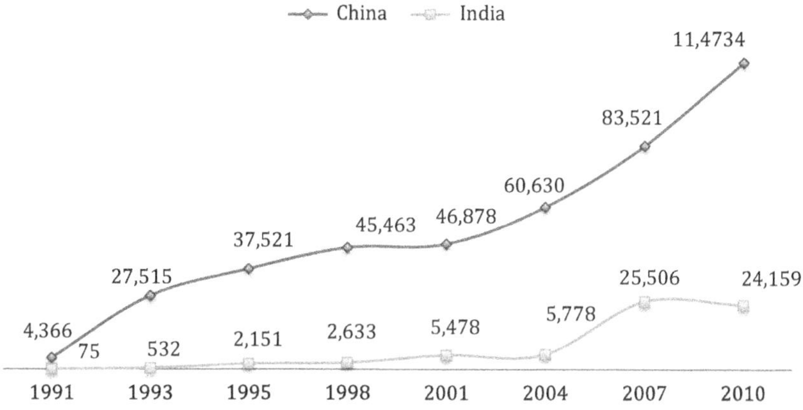

FIGURE 6.1. Continual Gap: Foreign Direct Investment (FDI) in China and India ($Mi)
Sources: Compiled from raw data in UNCTAD, UNCTADstat.

received more than $27.5 billion in FDI in 1993, whereas India managed to get more than $500 million. In the following five years, India's FDI inflows increased fivefold, whereas China's rose almost seventeen times. China's FDI has continued to increase steadily ever since, with just a minor aberration after the Asian financial crisis. India's FDI, on the other hand, picked up more rapidly after 2005. In 2011, as the most recent data reveal, India's FDI inflows reached an impressive $24 billion – still almost five times less than Chinese FDI, which came in at $115 billion.

The two countries' divergence in exports was also significant. China's export economy took off, whereas India's exports have been growing more slowly. Their different types of FDI caused the export differentials: in China, FDI was largely export-oriented, whereas FDI in India was much less so. Furthermore, the Chinese private manufacturers growing in alliance with diaspora entrepreneurs were also export-oriented and inherited global markets for textiles, sporting goods, footwear, toys, and the like from diaspora entrepreneurs, who moved to more value-added high-tech industries and services.[1]

CRISIS, REFORM, AND BLOWBACK IN INDIA

The 1991 crisis was a watershed event in India's economic reform. It ushered in two decades of FDI liberalization. Policy makers and scholars in Delhi observed that the crisis itself was not the cause of India's liberalization: the groundwork

[1] The Chinese tax and foreign exchange policies also helped China's exporters. Yet Bergsten (2006) has proved that foreign exchange policy was not the driver of China's export success; instead, it was due to Asian manufacturers relocating production sites to the Mainland. The diaspora investment highlighted here was precisely the driver of manufacturing relocation.

for a reformist state was laid in the 1980s. Chapter 4 has confirmed that important shifts in policy priorities, bureaucratic personnel, and industrial composition occurred in the 1980s, serving to spur liberalization in the later decades. The 1991 crisis played an important part because it was so grave and imminent and in part because it transformed the policy landscape, rendering difficult liberalization feasible in its aftermath. The crisis also strengthened the effects of international organizations such as the International Monetary Fund (IMF) and World Bank. The 1991 industrial policy and subsequent liberalization was thus a product of three interactive factors: the crisis, external actors, and the state.

In June 1991, the Congress Party returned to power. Narasimha Rao was elected prime minister, and he appointed Manmohan Singh finance minister, barely in time to confront a raging financial crisis. India's current account had been low for many years, and the depletion of remittances from immigrants in the Gulf made the country's financial state unsustainable. The country had only enough foreign exchange to import two weeks' worth of supplies needed to continue the country's industrial production. Without quick and substantial external assistance, India would be forced to declare a national default that would entail massive layoffs and widespread cutbacks in industrial output. Former finance secretary Bimal Jalan reflected that the 1990–91 period was "among the cruelest in India's Post-Independence economic history" (Jalan 1991, 1).

The worst was narrowly averted thanks to massive financial injections from the IMF, World Bank, and Asian Development Bank (ADB). Yet those loans came with specific conditions for structural reforms, and "a long list of changes" was presented to the Indian government (Bajpai 1992, 210–211). At the heart of these reforms was the abolition of existing controls on the flow of foreign goods and capital. The Indian government complied and exceeded these requested changes, implementing whole-scale reform.

The government's response to external pressure marked a clear departure from the past, when it normally resisted external pressure after crises (e.g., the 1960s and 1970s). Insiders even claimed that the IMF loans were already approved to India without conditionality because the United States needed landing rights in India.[2] It was clear that the Congress government used the crisis to implement reforms long deemed essential to the country. I. G. Patel, the long-term governor of the Reserve Bank of India, confirmed that India's post-1991 liberalization reflected a consensus among ruling elites that it was necessary to move away from trade and investment controls – a consensus that had been building since Indira Gandhi's last term (Patel 1997; 2002).

The June 1991 budget laid out the basic elements of an integrated strategy for trade, tax, and foreign exchange reforms. This was followed by the July 1991 industrial policy, which detailed measures to reduce the public sector, promote private industry, and encourage external trade and foreign

[2] Confirmed by interviews with Indian policy makers and scholars in New Delhi.

TABLE 6.1. *India's Foreign Direct Investment (FDI) Liberalization, 1991–1994*

	By 1991	1994
FDI Equity Cap	Case-by-case approval <40%	Automatic approval <51%
Qualitative Restrictions	91% of tradable goods	Greatly reduced
Import licensing	26 separate lists	One single negative list
Maximum tariff	400%	85%
Other restrictions	Government permission to produce, expand, relocate, and remit required	No explicit permission required

Source: Compiled from raw data in *Economic Survey*, 1991–1994 volumes.

investment. Foreign-invested firms (FIF) were allowed in more sectors, and the automatic approval list was expanded. These firms were allowed to sell up to 25 percent of products they made on domestic markets. Policies governing nonresident Indians (NRI) were more favorable, allowing them to hold 100 percent of equity shares in selected sectors. In the export-oriented units and export-processing zones, the government employed tax breaks, concessionary duties, and other types of preferential treatment for foreign direct investors (Kundra 2010).

In 1991–1993, liberalization continued. As indicated in Table 6.1, the government eliminated import licenses for most capital goods, raw materials, and other intermediates and reduced the maximum tariff from 400 percent to 85 percent. Tariffs on machinery and capital goods imports were lowered to 55 percent and 30 percent, respectively. 1994 witnessed further liberalization of the FDI regime, increasing the foreign equity shares under automatic approval from 40 percent to 51 percent. Foreign shares above 51 percent were allowed in specific sectors and in the special zones. In these zones, India allowed tax holidays for foreign investors for up to five of the first eight years of operation. Under the schemes of software technology parks (STPs) and electronics hardware technology parks (EHTPs), foreigners could hold 100 percent equity and pay no import duties provided that the foreign exchange balance was maintained.

Policy liberalization in 1991–1994 led to the arrival of more foreign investors in India. Figure 6.2 compares increases in FDI inflows and portfolio investment. Foreign direct investment grew from $129 million in 1991 to $315 million in 1993 and further increased to $1.314 billion in 1995. Portfolio investment was almost nonexistent in 1991, but with the 1991 policy liberalization it increased to $244 million in 1992. By 1994, portfolio investment had reached $5 billion, more than four times the FDI in India. The increases in FDI and portfolio investment, however, did not generate significant gains in exports or improve national account balances. In the 1990s, the arrival of foreign investors created competitive pressure on domestic companies and heightened industrial

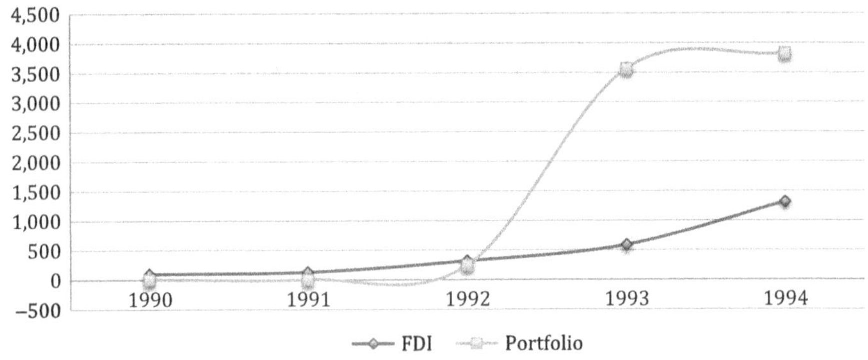

FIGURE 6.2. Foreign Capital in India: Foreign Direct Investment (FDI) versus Portfolio Investment ($mi)
Source: Raw data are from Ministry of Finance and Ministry of Commerce & Industry, Government of India.

resistance. Domestic companies' fear was later found to be exaggerated because Indian business gained substantially from partnerships with Western MNCs in the new millennium.

Different growth rates between FDI and portfolio investment, as indicated in Figure 6.2, are telling because these two forms of foreign capital have varied implications for foreign investors and domestic firms. Foreign direct investment entails establishing a physical presence in another country and is much harder for foreign investors. From a domestic perspective, FDI represents an intrusive form of foreign capital and results in immediate competition from foreign products. Portfolio investment refers to foreign investors putting money in another country's equity market without physically founding an operational site in that nation. This is much easier for foreigners to do. It is also easier for domestic companies to accept, because although domestic companies who receive portfolio investment are accountable to foreign shareholders, their corporate decisions and business plans are rarely subject to external interference. Portfolio investment also does not bring competing products and companies to domestic markets, and domestic manufacturers are thus less affected by the entry of such capital.

The contrast between FDI and portfolio investment thus demonstrates that whereas India no longer opposed foreign capital on an ideational level, arms-length portfolio investment increased more rapidly than FDI. This shows that foreign companies were interested in exploring commercial yields in India but not as willing to commit to physical operations there. Meanwhile, domestic companies welcomed the injection of foreign liquidity but opposed possible competition from FDI.

India's experience with SEZs contrasted with China's. Despite similar policies, foreign investors were not particularly responsive to India's calls for FDI, and the actual construction of SEZs lagged far behind the approval rates. In states such as Andhra Pradesh, Maharashtra, and New Delhi, local governments each approved more than a hundred SEZs, but only a handful had been completed by 2005. These patterns differed from China, where diaspora entrepreneurs were more responsive to the home government's call for investment and committed capital and technology in a major way, as suggested in the numerous investment projects in the development zones in China in the 1980s and 1990s.

Since 1991, external networks had become more important in India, driven by two developments: first, foreign-trained bureaucrats were more salient in economic policy making, and with them more diaspora professionals returned to influence policy; second, Western economic ideas received broader acceptance in India via newspapers and scholarly publications that elaborated on Western economic gatherings.[3] International organizations (IOs) appeared to play a bigger role through their connections to high-level Indian bureaucrats. In rescuing India's 1991 debt crisis, IMF loans amounted to $3.0 billion, the World Bank offered $500 million, and the ADB's loans amounted to $250 million. Each IO secured promises from India's policy makers that India would undergo liberalization (Bajpai 1992; Sengupta 2004). Domestic opposition later criticized India's liberalization, saying that it was driven by IOs' demands.[4]

The impact of the crisis, however, was short-lived. It did not change key domestic interests, but temporarily neutralized their resistance. Once the debt crisis was weathered, domestic resistance to FDI resurfaced and challenged the consolidation of FDI liberalization in India. Domestic resistance, embodied perhaps most clearly in the powerful anti-FDI business group known as the "Bombay Club" redefined India's liberalization in the late 1990s, with policies put in place to constrain foreign investors and enhance the gain for indigenous companies. Globalization of Indian business was achieved in this context and featured a two-pronged strategy of dominating domestic markets while forging global footholds.

[3] Shortly after the 1991 reform, Indian media followed closely the World Economic Forums in Davos. See "Economic Reforms to Continue: PM," *Times of India*, February 3, 1992; "Economic Reforms Will Accelerate," *Hindustan Times*, February 4, 1992; "Irreversibility of Reform," *Financial Times*, February 15, 1992.

[4] During June and July of 1991, *Hindustan Times* published the following titles: "Foreign Policy: How to make it work?" June 21, 1991, p. 11; "New Government to Present White Paper on Economy," June 21, 1991, p. 13; "IMF Suggests Many Reforms," June 28, 91, p. 18; "Agenda for Reform," July 3, 1991, pp. 1–2; "IMF Officials Hold Talks," July 5, 1991, p. 1; "U.S. Welcomes Reforms in India," July 6, 1991, p. 1; "IMF Ready to Support India," July 6, 1991, p. 12; "Reforms Based on World Bank Report," July 7, 1991, p. 24; "Pranab for Following IMF Prescription," July 12, 1991, p. 13; and "What to Choose – IMF or NRI?" July 18, 1991, p. 11.

Blowback: Domestic Resistance and FDI Policies Turned More Restrictive

The increase in FDI in India following the 1991 liberalization did not convince Indian industrial representatives that FDI was good for the country or beneficial to domestic companies. By the mid-1990s, they had repeatedly expressed displeasure with the direction of reform. K. K. Birla, for example, publicly announced that reform was not in the best interest of the country or its industry. Birla particularly objected to the automatic increase in the foreign-equity cap to 51 percent.[5] In 1991, the Bombay Club was founded, comprised of the members of several of India's most prominent business families. Rahul Bajaj, owner of Bajaj Motors, acted as its dynamic chairman and played an influential role in rallying domestic resistance to FDI. Domestic opposition succeeded in persuading the government to cap foreign equity in joint ventures (JVs) at 40 percent.

Domestic resistance to FDI liberalization consisted of business communities, nationalist forces, and Leftist parties. Whereas the business groups objected to FDI primarily out of protectionist interests, the latter two groups resisted FDI liberalization mainly due to ideology. Additionally, the Left parties opposed FDI because of their concerns with state sectors. Together, the Left and nationalist groups likened India's acceptance of conditional loans from the IMF and World Bank to allowing these IOs to rob India of its economic independence. In the words of senior Communist Party leader E. M. S. Namboodiripad (1991), the government was like "a thirsty man taking a cup of poison." The Left-leaning press became the primary source of criticism against the government for "succumbing to external pressure" (Bajpai 1992, 211). These multifold forces became increasingly powerful as the effects of the debt crisis wore off. The lackluster economic performance of FDI did not help liberalization either, as Bhagwati warned in 1993 that quick and visible improvements would be needed to sustain liberalization.

India's implementation of the post-1991 liberalization encountered many difficulties that strengthened domestic resistance. Compared to China, the lack of local-level diaspora networks was particularly damning to India's FDI liberalization. Lacking transfers of pro-FDI ideas and resources, on-the-ground policy implementers in India had limited incentives or expertise to carry out new policies. Early success, central to policy consolidation, was thus elusive. Finance Minister Manmohan Singh knew this well. He once remarked, "[r]eform does not mean announcing a few policies and sitting back but involves working out the nuts and bolts of wide-ranging political initiatives and examining the various alternative sectoral policies. In India, there were not enough people of the right type to do this" (Roy 1994, 201).

Recall that, in China, diaspora investment led to remarkable early success in SEZs and helped to expand support for FDI in the country. In Chapter 3, local

[5] *Times of India*, August 1, 1991.

officials in southern China benefited from their connections to entrepreneurial diaspora networks and were much more receptive and knowledgeable of FDI liberalization than were those in other parts of China. In Chapter 5, the diaspora-local government networks further drove "zone fever" and pushed SOE reforms toward deepening FDI liberalization. Comparing the Chinese state with the Indian one, it was at the local level that China appeared more engaging to FDI than India. Yet local governments' proclivity to embrace FDI was embedded in China's strong diaspora networks. In 1980, China was poor across all regions, and the country's technology and infrastructure were backward. Within four years, based on diaspora investment, southern areas achieved impressive gains in infrastructure, local revenues, and industrialization that surpassed even the most developed metropolis, Shanghai. We can only imagine the magnitude of ideational impact on local officials in the rest of China. Hsing (1998) confirms that labor, talent, and capital swarmed into South China from elsewhere and joined in the diaspora-invested industrialization there.

India's own reform history supports the importance of early success. Lackluster economic performance rendered Rajiv Gandhi's external liberalization unsustainable. The lack of visible success continued to slow India's liberalization in the 1990s. In the mid-decade, economic frustration was apparent in the country. A World Bank study characterized India as "moderately indebted" and "beyond investment grade."[6] Figure 6.3 shows that the 1990s liberalization did not improve India's general economic outlook. Foreign capital indeed grew, but

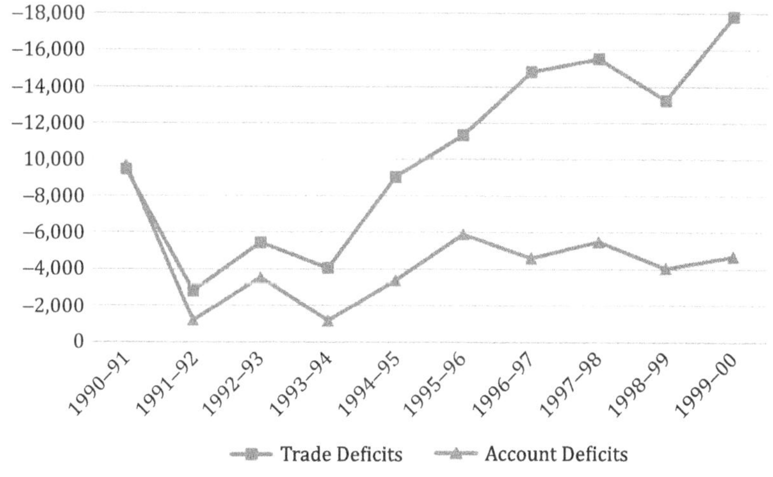

FIGURE 6.3. Economic State in Reformist India: Worsening Accounts ($mi)
Source: Raw data are from India BOP 1990–2000, Reserve Bank of India statistics

[6] World Bank, *India: Five Years of Stabilization and Reform and the Challenges Ahead*, Washington, DC: The World Bank Publications, 1996.

exports were not improving. The country's current account and trade balances both worsened. In 1991, as Figure 6.3 indicates, India managed to lower its current account deficit to a little over $1 billion. In 1994, after the most ambitious reform policies were introduced, the current account deficit swelled to $3.4 billion. The deficit further increased to $4.7 billion in 1999. Trade deficit also grew from $2.8 billion to $9 billion in 1994 and further to $18 billion in 1999.

The lack of persuasive success made many in India skeptical of the utility of FDI, causing them to join domestic resistance against FDI liberalization. The opposition reached a climax in the mid to late 1990s and influenced the government policy toward more restrictive to foreign investors. Domestic resistance then gradually eased as leading Indian companies ventured abroad. Nevertheless, skepticism toward FDI inflows remains strong in India, and many politicians and the public are not yet convinced of FDI's effectiveness in spurring India's late development. The lack of local-level diaspora networks perhaps accounts for the slow change in India's localities.

Deteriorating account deficits suggest that FDI in India was different from that in China. India's FDI came predominantly from Western MNCs, which targeted India's consumer markets for Western products – with the exception of the software services sector. It thus exerted competitive pressure on domestic producers of substitutable goods. Indian private companies were concerned about the threat of subordination or eventual acquisition by foreign MNCs and the prospect of being squeezed out of business by them. Setting aside their internal differences, the corporate world concluded that their interests differed significantly from those of foreign MNCs (Nayar 2001, 168) and requested "internal liberalization" before "external opening" and demanded the government offer a grace period and strengthen indigenous companies.[7]

By contrast, in China, diaspora entrepreneurs helped develop infrastructure and exports. Local governments and companies either benefited from or were shielded from FDI. In India, domestic companies, although many supported the 1991 liberalization, tasted pain before gain and changed their positions in the mid-1990s. A leading industrialist confessed, "I am afraid many of us, who were for liberalization, did not understand the full ramifications."[8] L. M. Thapar, chairman of the Ballarpur Group, admitted, "We did not realize how quickly we would need funds to face the competition that was around the corner."[9] Ravi Ruia, Essar Gujarat's managing director also acknowledged in 1993, "I think the true implications of liberalization are only now gripping people, and they are realizing the problems."[10] Referring to traditional business houses, Great Eastern Shipping Director, Ravi Sheth, stated: "Let's face it. In his or her heart

[7] "Changing Structure of Corporate India," *Hindu*, Nov 11, 1998.
[8] *The Statesman*, October 11, 1993.
[9] *Business India*, November 22–December 5, 1993, p. 54.
[10] *Business World*, October 20–November 2, 1993, p. 24.

of hearts nobody wanted liberalization. It sounded nice, so everyone cheered. Now that it begins pinching you, you cry foul."[11]

Under these circumstances, the Bombay Club, formed in 1991 to represent private industrial interests, gained salience in the mid-1990s. At the Club's 1993 convention, participants expressed their discontent with competition from foreign goods and capital allowed to enter the market since the 1991 liberalization. They unanimously called for a "leveling of the playing field" before any further reduction in tariffs or increase in foreign equity caps.[12] Rahul Bajaj, chairman of the Bombay Club, used mass media and news outlets to further the group's anti-FDI campaign. In mid-1996, when joint ventures between Indian partners and foreign MNCs went sour, statements from disillusioned business representatives were hostile to foreign capital.[13] EID Parry's Managing Director, M. V. Subbiah, complained, "The multinationals have a stronger financial power. They are gradually killing us." Another important industrialist, S. K. Birla of the VXL Group, affirmed, "If the multinationals are allowed to hold a majority stake in the Indian joint ventures in an unfettered way, Indians will be second-class citizens in their own country."[14]

The three industrial associations – the Federation of Indian Chambers of Commerce and Industry (FICCI), the Confederation of Indian Industry (CII), and the Associated Chambers of Commerce and Industry of India (ASSOCHAM) – launched an anti-FDI lobby that involved politicians, business elites, and intellectuals. Despite internal competition among them, the associations aligned to ask the government to implement protectionist measures, which they argued would be critical to ameliorate the threats from foreign goods and investment. The associations used their annual executive meetings, public speeches, official lobbying venues, and other occasions to meet with governmental officials, either in public or private, to advance their protectionist requests. Their core interest was in securing a "level playing field" for domestic industry (Nayar 2001). They requested that the government halt any further reduction in import duties, and they proposed additional duties on specific items to compensate for potential losses to local business.

Representing the interests of big business families, FICCI argued that Indian companies should play a dominant role in infrastructure building, as well as a leadership role in exports (Nayar 2001, 176). ASSOCHAM President H. Somany also strongly conveyed his own distaste for what he regarded as the government's pro-MNC policies. The CII, generally friendly to MNCs, was similarly wary of the threat posed by FDI. Although it stressed its image as representing new business elite in India, CII adopted a position on FDI similar to

11 *Business World*, October 20–November 2, 1993, p. 25.

12 "Industries and Globalization," *New Times*, August 13, 1993; "Industries Cry Wolf," *Deccan Herald*, December 12, 1993; and "Industries Divided over Reform," *Times of India*, May 8, 1995.

13 "Lows after the Early Highs," *India Today*, August 15, 1996, pp. 87–89.

14 *Economic Times*, March 24 and April 18, 1996.

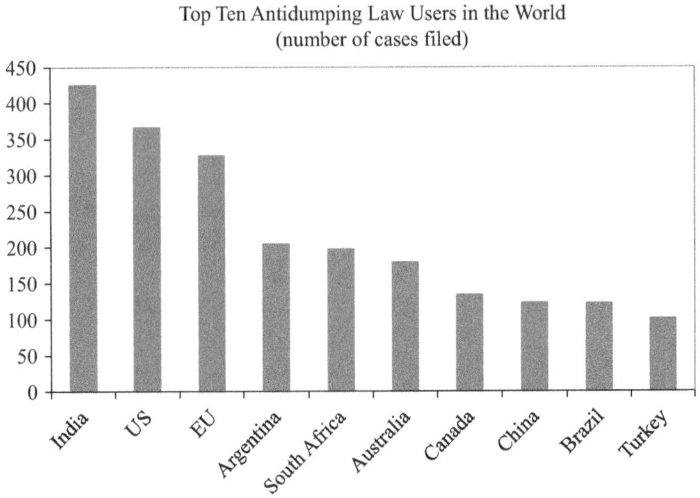

FIGURE 6.4. Protectionism in India: Use of the Antidumping Clause (1993–2001)
Source: Original data from Aradna Aggarwal, "Anti-dumping Law and Practice: An Indian Perspective," ICRIER Working Paper 85, 2002.

the other two industrial associations. Indeed, the main participants in the Bombay Club were also influential members of CII (Sinha 2005b). In March 1996, CII Secretary-General Tarun Das issued a formal criticism of the ways in which MNCs were allowed to behave toward their Indian partners.[15] Tarun Das sharply attacked the MNCs' "cowboy" approach and uneven distribution of benefits between foreign investors and domestic enterprises.[16] Charges against MNCs also included the transfer of obsolete technology, the MNCs' majority share in JV partnerships, and unfair profit sharing.[17]

India's protectionism in the 1990s was clear from the number of antidumping cases that the country filed. As demonstrated in Figure 6.4, India logged the world's largest number of antidumping cases in the 1990s, many more than the United States. It filed a total of 425 cases from 1993 to 2001, and requested punitive duties on the disputed import items. India's ranking in overall antidumping cases was remarkable given its modest share of global imports. In 2003, India's share of world imports was less than 1 percent, in contrast to the United States with 17 percent and China with 5.3 percent (Kowalski 2008).

After the Bombay Club's period of influence, domestic resistance continued and used India's mediocre growth indicators and controversies in existing JVs to strengthen their arguments in the late 1990s. In January 1998, FICCI

[15] *Financial Times*, December 4–5, 1993, and April 26, 1994; and Kochanek (1996).

[16] *Economic Times*, March 20, 1996.

[17] "MNCs: India Strategy Needs Rethink," New Delhi: Confederation of Indian Industries, 1996, pp. 3–5.

President, K. K. Modi, recommended that foreign MNCs be barred from establishing wholly owned subsidiaries.[18] His predecessor, Deepak Banker, suggested that MNCs should be required to divest after a predetermined period.[19] Ideological arguments against FDI also gained ground during this time. The Rashtriya Swayamsevak Sangh (RSS, National Volunteers Organization), a nationalist member party of the BJP coalition government, questioned the effectiveness of liberalization.[20] The Swadeshi Jagaran Manch (SJM), formed in 1991, likened India's liberalization to externally imposed economic imperialism. A statement by Murli Manohar Joshi, Minister of Human Resources Development, captures how widely such thinking permeated the government: "I am favorable to U.S. investment, which helps to make a decent living for my people, but if there is a negative effect on small-scale industries, then no." Joshi pointed out, "India will negotiate from case to case, industry to industry."[21]

Domestic resistance shaped government policies at the end of the decade. The national government conceded, popularizing the phrase "calibrated globalization" to demonstrate India's resolve to guard against negative impacts of liberalization. Foreign investment beneficial to Indian business would be supported, whereas projects with potential negative effects would be opposed.[22] On May 2, 1998, Prime Minister Vajpayee officially adopted a "carefully calibrated approach" to globalization. In December 1998, the BJP government passed a referendum, Press Note No. 18 of 1998, requiring that foreign firms wishing to set up a new Indian operation obtain a "no-objection" certificate from all Indian partners. In practice, pressure was brought on foreign investors to team with domestic companies if they wished to produce for Indian markets.

Moderate diffusion of FDI liberalization, however, has occurred in India since 1991. Limited openness to FDI, the entry of MNCs, and domestic companies' overseas ventures helped to transform the political environment around FDI liberalization in India. In 1994, the government backed STPs and EHTPs with additional policies that allowed duty-free imports and 100 percent foreign equity shares. More such parks were approved in the decade. In the late 1990s, the government set up new bureaucratic agencies and rules to facilitate FDI's entry, including the Foreign Investment Promotion Board, the Foreign Investment Promotion Council, the Foreign Exchange Management Act, and the Foreign Investment Implementation Authority. Finally, the national government opened more sectors and lowered tariffs to attract foreign investors.

India's two-pronged FDI liberalization, which protected indigenous companies while inviting foreign investors, had two consequences that shaped corporate networks surrounding the state, the effects of which became apparent in the

[18] *Hindu*, January 8, 1998.
[19] *Economic Times*, October 11, 1997.
[20] For details, see Frankel (2005, pp. 728–729).
[21] Interview with Murli Manohar Joshi, August 15, 1998, cited in Frankel (2005).
[22] News archive research in India, August, 2006.

recent decade. First, more foreign actors came to India; second, foreign investors were pressured to form domestic partnerships. The result of these factors was the emergence of many globalized domestic companies that became part of external networks in India. With their emergence, India's FDI liberalization has deepened at a rate comfortable for domestic actors.

Meanwhile, there were important new developments in the country's diaspora networks in the current era. As highly educated Indians made inroads in the American corporate world, they bridged Indian business more closely with global capital and markets and intensified the globalization of leading Indian businesses. In many services sectors, entrepreneurial diasporas also came back to India and, with their ideas, resources, and market access, led the emergence of new services industries in the home country. Chapter 8 elaborates on these developments in the informatics sector.

THE EVOLVING NEW SOCIAL BASIS OF INDIA'S FDI LIBERALIZATION

In the 1990s, India experienced crisis, economic liberalization, and intensified opposition politics. In the muddled process just described, key changes took place in the social basis of the state that influenced new liberal policies and economic development in India in the current era. Helped by Indian diasporas, foreign companies are an important business force and have reasonable representation in business associations and policy debates in the country. More importantly, the arrival of foreigners and diasporas, the formation of external networks, and an expansion in the global market have resulted in the transformation of indigenous corporate communities. Large and successful businesses have benefited from diaspora networks and collaboration with Western MNCs, and their stances on liberalization have thereafter softened. Such globalized businesses are currently advocates for FDI, although the pro-FDI advocacy remains limited to specific cases and subsectors. Local governments have meanwhile experienced modest, pro-liberalization change, with some regions being profoundly more liberal than others.

Foreign Investors in India: A New Business Force

Foreign direct investment liberalization in the early 1990s led to the arrival of more foreign investors in India, although this trend was slightly reversed in the late 1990s. In 1991, there were 750 foreign collaboration projects in India. Three years later, the number reached 1,855; it grew to 2,326 in 1997. In 2000, there were an additional 1,834 new foreign collaboration projects. Table 6.2, focusing on the auto and electronics industries, demonstrates how foreign collaborations grew in the 1990s. In the auto sector, there were thirty-four foreign collaborations between 1991 and 1994. Foreign equity shares

TABLE 6.2. *Foreign Collaborations in India: Automobiles and Electronics*

	Automobiles		Electronics	
	Number of Projects	Foreign Equity* (%)	Number of Projects	Foreign Equity* (%)
1991–1994	34	39.6	40	24.3
1995–1997	87	52.4	91	62.7
1998–2000	75	6.3	143	54.6

Note: * Foreign equity share is an average of all the projects in each period.
Source: Compiled from data on India's foreign collaborations, 1991–2000, Ministry of Commerce and Industry, Government of India.

across the projects averaged 39.6 percent. In the following three years, from 1994 to 1997, eighty-seven foreign collaborations occurred, with majority shares held by foreign partners in a number of projects. Thus, in this period, the average foreign equity share was 52.4 percent. In the third period, from 1998 to 2000, another seventy-five foreign collaborations were signed. However, the equity shares between domestic and foreign partners suggested a clear advantage to domestic partners. Average foreign equity fell to a mere 6.3 percent.

The patterns represented in the auto industry share some similarities to those in the electronics industry but also display clear differences. In electronics, there were 274 total foreign collaboration projects in the 1990s. In the first four years (1991–1994), only forty projects were contracted, and most of them were majority domestic-owned, with the average foreign share around 24 percent. In the following three years (1994–1997), there were ninety-one foreign collaborations, and most involved majority foreign ownership. Many even had sole foreign ownership. The average foreign equity share for these projects reached 62 percent. There were clearly more foreign collaboration projects in electronics (143) than in automobiles (75) in the third period (1998–2000). Foreign equity shares declined slightly from the mid-1990s. Yet, overall, the average foreign shares hovered around 55 percent, giving foreigners majority ownership. The FDI pattern in electronics differed from that in automobiles.

The arrival of large numbers of foreign investors nevertheless changed the dynamics of policy networks in New Delhi. When foreign MNCs set up subsidiaries in India, these subsidiaries joined Indian industrial associations. In the CII, for example, the membership of multinational affiliates increased from a few dozen to a few hundred in the 1990s. Industrial associations, although conventionally a venue for advocating traditional business interests, have since become venues for social networking between domestic companies and foreign MNCs. Although business representatives continued to express their reservations about FDI, increasingly more were eager to form ties with foreigners. These internal divisions prevented the formation of a consistent and potent industrial opposition strong enough to forestall India's external opening.[23] In aggregate, the policy agendas of these industrial associations shifted. Especially among industrial associations, the ability to draw membership from foreign MNCs was a strong selling point in recruiting domestic corporate members. Thus, in the new millennium, the incentives of business associations were somewhat different.

India's post-1991 liberalization offered foreign investors opportunities to enter and operate in India, but whether they succeeded in the country depended on working through domestic state and societal actors. Korean automaker Hyundai, for example, proactively worked with its domestic advocates and overcame investment barriers in the country. The company entered in 1996 and was intent on building a wholly owned auto subsidiary there. To circumvent India's formal ban against 100 percent foreign equity, Hyundai utilized lobbying networks in Delhi, which were able to persuade incumbent bureaucrats to allow the corporation to establish the first wholly foreign-owned automobile company in India.[24] These lobbies, called "circles of networks," consisted of retired officials and politicians who used their former connections in the government to form consulting companies that helped foreign companies operate in India.[25]

Thanks again to domestic networks, Hyundai constructed an automobile assembly plant in only seventeen months – a miracle in India's slow-moving bureaucracy. Within six months of operations, Hyundai became the number two automaker in India measured by the quantity of automobiles manufactured. In 1998, Hyundai introduced a new model, the Santro, which became the best selling car within two years. In 2005, Hyundai built a new plant in Chennai, and within a year, the company exported 30 percent of its Indian production to the global market (Barnett, Kim, and Rhee, 2008).

American company Enron was a high-profile investor in India in the 1990s but failed miserably. In 1992, as part of the Indian national government's liberalization drive, Enron was invited to bid on a major power plant in Maharashtra. The company used its resourceful political connections in the national and state governments to push the project through within weeks. The construction of the power plant was severely delayed, and when grassroots protest rose against the plant, the liability of Western MNCs began to show – Enron became a rallying

[23] *Business Standard*, March 10, 1994; "Exporting, Cabinet Secretary Style" (editorial), *Economic Times*, November 2, 1997.

[24] The case description is based on interviews at NASSCOM and is supplemented with news archives available in India and the West. To cite a few: "Dynamic Companies to Benefit from Indian Reforms," *the Australian*, January 31, 1994; "India Needed a Clear-Cut Gov't Agenda for Maruti," *Business Line*, December 29, 1997; "India: Auto Industry Drives in Lower Gear in 1997," *AAP Newsfeed*, December 27, 1997; and "FDI Inflows: The Southern Drift," *Business Line*, December 22, 2000.

[25] According to interviews with retired officials.

point for India's societal backlashes against Western-imposed globalization in the country.[26]

The lack of early success in the Enron project worsened the situation facing the Western company. Not only was the power plant slow to produce electricity, but also the cost of its electricity was way above affordable rates in the state. The local government decided not to pay for the continued production of the power plant, and politicians in New Delhi and Maharashtra abandoned the Enron project as circumstances evolved.[27] After spending more than ten years and accumulating a $1 billion loss, Enron pulled out of the project, and the state of Maharashtra continued to suffer from a severe shortage of electricity.

The relative absence of entrepreneurial diasporas and the liability of Western investors prefigured that India's reform would be driven by different corporate networks. Indigenous companies that grow and benefit from global partnerships provide countermeasures to domestic opposition: economic losers, public sectors, and nationalist intellectuals. Indigenous industries' fundamental interests in protecting domestic markets constrain their support for FDI, however.

Transforming Indian Business: Diaspora Professionals and Global Business

Powerful internal networks shape India's FDI liberalization, but interests that constitute internal networks are neither static nor uniform. Domestic businesses, once ardent opponents of FDI liberalization, became accepting and even welcomed foreign investors after their own companies went through internationalization. At the end of the 1990s, the incentives of Indian companies changed and stances on FDI shifted.[28] A clear example is Bajaj Motor. Rahul Bajaj was the chairman of the antiliberalization Bombay Club and led the charge against FDI in the mid-1990s. At the turn of the century, Bajaj Motor began to export to Africa, Latin America, and North America. Rahul Bajaj became more open to foreign capital as a result. In 1999–2000, he served as the president of CII, the leading industrial association active in developing external business networks.

Many other traditional Indian companies experienced similar growth and transformation during reform, especially as a new generation of Western-trained successors took over these companies. Reliance Group, India's largest private company, increased its profits more than fourteen times from 1991 to 1996 and has since diversified into strategic sectors such as oil refining and exploration. With its stock being listed in India and abroad, Reliance has acquired immense

[26] Interviews with Mohan Guruswamy, president, Center for Policy Alternatives, August 10, 2006; "India's Economic Reforms – II," *Times of India*, September 27, 1996.

[27] "Enron in India: The Giant's First Fall," Alternet.org. See www.alternet.org/story/12375; and "Enron's Eight-Year Power Struggle in India," *Asian Times*, January 18, 2001.

[28] "Changing Structure of Corporate India," *The Hindu*, November 11, 1998.

international perspectives and interests. Arvind Mills, a company owned by another business family, grew eight times between 1986 and 1996. TVS Group, A. V. Birla Group, LML, and the Burman Family experienced similarly remarkable growth in the 1990s.

Leading companies such as Ranbaxy Laboratories, Escorts, RPG, and Mahindra and Mahindra (M&M), all came under new leadership with substantial Western experiences in the 1990s. Ranbaxy became a major multinational player in pharmaceuticals in the 1990s under the leadership of Parvinder Singh, who was trained in the United States. The Escorts empire passed from Nada to his sons, Rajan and Anil, in the 1990s and also flourished. The RPG group achieved dazzling growth after passing from father Rama Prasad Goenka to sons Harsh and Sanjiv. M&M experienced a renaissance in the 1990s, with Wharton-trained Keshub Mahindra and nephew Anand Mahindra, a Harvard Business School graduate, at the helm.

The new generation of leaders of traditional families helped to transform Indian business communities. Versed in Western economic ideas and business practices, they viewed foreign investment more as opportunity than threat. Although inheriting traditional business networks in India, such business leaders have built their own external ties, fostered through educational, professional, and personal experiences in the West.[29] Concurrent with Western-trained business leaders, many more diaspora professionals working at Western companies emerged as an influential economic force connecting India and Western markets and technology.

In the following section, I examine Tata (a traditional business house), Infosys (a reform-era IT firm), and Bharti (a recent IT manufacturer and service provider). Although these firms differ in size and history, they have all benefited from internationalization and diaspora connections. As part of India's global corporate networks, these companies represent the foundation of India's FDI liberalization. The limitation of such indigenous corporate-led liberalization is also clear. On the one hand, the successful Indian companies compete with foreign investors in the domestic market, which limits how far they can go in terms of FDI liberalization. On the other, numerous small businesses are not included in the globalization process described here. Small business remains wary of FDI in India.

Tata's Global Footholds as a Means to Renaissance

The Tata Group, established in 1868, has been India's leading business house since the country's independence. Tata expanded from thirteen subsidiary companies in 1938 to more than 300 in 1991. Its leader, J. R. D. Tata, had strong connections with the national government and the Gandhi family. Yet in 1991, the outlook for Tata Group appeared gloomy. Facing not only its traditional competitors within India but also newly arrived MNCs, Tata's performance was sliding, and its component companies, like Tata Steel and Tata Motors, as well

[29] "Successful Successors," *India Today*, July 7, 1997.

as its hotels and retail outlet, were performing especially poorly. Liberalization in the 1990s provided opportunities for Tata Group to "go global" (Khanna, Palepu, and Bullock, 2009).

Within Tata Group, Tata Consultancy Services (TCS), the group's information technology division, was the first division of the company to benefit. TCS hired Indian immigrants in the United States to develop its business in America starting in the early 1970s. Its post-1980 growth relied nearly entirely on exports to America. In 2006–2007, TCS derived more than 90 percent of its revenues from outside India. It emerged as the most dynamic and fastest growing component within the Tata Group, accounting for $28 billion of Tata's collective $60 billion market capitalization in 2007 (Khanna, Palepu, and Bullock 2009, 5). More importantly, TCS influenced Tata Group's general outlook on international markets, encouraging it to abandon its traditional focus on serving domestic markets to proactively expand its "global footprint."

Tata Tea, another subsidiary of Tata Group, faced dwindling domestic market shares in the 1990s. It became a success after launching an ambitious takeover of the UK tea brand Tetley in 2000. This overseas acquisition was Tata's first and also the largest by any Indian company at the time, worth £271 million. At the time of the acquisition, Tetley was three times the size of Tata Tea. Following suit, Tata Steel remade itself by acquiring Singapore-based NatSteel Asia in 2005 and Thailand's Millennium Steel in 2006. Through these acquisitions, it expanded into the Asian Pacific market, including Australia, China, and Southeast Asia. In 2007, Tata Steel made another major acquisition, taking over Netherlands-based Corus with a $12.1 billion bid. Tata Motors likewise acquired Land Rover and Jaguar in 2007 in an effort to expand its exports to South Africa, the Middle East, and South Korea.

Growing exports and overseas acquisitions propelled Tata Group to global fame. Yet Tata's renaissance drew heavily on the influx of Western MNCs in India. Both due to policy requirements and practical needs, many Western companies came to India and sought partnership with Tata. As mentioned earlier, the government required foreign companies to pair with domestic companies in the 1990s. As the country's leading company, Tata teamed with global giants such as AT&T, Mercedes-Benz, IBM, Silicon Graphics, Cummins Engine, and Honeywell. Via these partnerships, Tata maintained an advantage in domestic markets because foreign partners were required to obtain a letter of consent from Tata before launching any new projects in India. Meanwhile, the partnerships helped Tata's subsidiaries to compete in the global marketplace.

During Tata's internationalization, the company employed corporate leaders with connections to and experience with Western MNCs and governments. In 2003, the Group hired Alan Rosling, who had served as an executive in several leading Western MNCs and as an advisor to British Prime Minister John Major, to coordinate the group's global strategy. Under Rosling, Tata Group established offices in the United States, the United Kingdom, South Africa, Bangladesh, and China to coordinate government and media relations.

TABLE 6.3. *Shareholding Structure of Tata Group (%, 2007)*

	Tata Group	Mutual Funds in India	Government Companies, Banks, Insurance Companies	Foreign Institutional Investors	NRIs, Foreign Companies	Others
TCS	82	2.00	2.88	7.06	0.18	6.23
Tata Steel	31	4.52	17.38	17.42	NA	30.16
Tata Tea	32	10.7	19.07	12.94	0.46	24.49
Indian Hotels	28	7.58	16.06	24.07	1.19	22.82

Source: Data compiled from Tata's corporate documents; also cited in Khanna et al. (2009).

In addition to foreign talent, Tata used global financing for its expansion.[30] Tata's acquisition of Tetley, for example, was executed by a UK-based financial agency and was financed entirely with external funds. Although the deal was worth £271 million in total, Tata Tea only committed £70 million in equity, of which £45 million was raised through a global depositary receipt (a financial scheme used by American and European investment banks to raise money globally), and £25 million was funded through nonrecourse debt financing, a less risky financing scheme that prevents creditors from seeking repayment from assets other than the project for which the money was loaned.

Globalization has made Tata Group a multiownership entity, as Table 6.3 demonstrates. Tata Group held less than a third of the equity in all its major subsidiary companies: 31 percent in Tata Steel, 32 percent in Tata Tea, and 28 percent in Tata Hotels, except for TCS, the most lucrative member of the group, in which Tata held 82 percent. The other shareholders include mutual funds in India, government units, and foreign institutional investors and foreign companies, including diaspora ones. None of those equity holders challenges Tata's control of its business empire.

Succeeding in the world market has shifted Tata's stance on FDI. In recent years, Tata has led the "India Shining" program to promote Indian influence in the world by sponsoring investment fairs and cultural events in major U.S. cities and at global business gatherings such as the World Economic Forum. Like the other companies examined here, globalized Indian companies have made liberalization a likely irreversible path in India. However, these companies have carefully watched their domestic market shares and corporate interests and used international forces strategically. TCS, for example, is ambitious in exporting to global markets but also stringent in issuing shares to outside investors. Such a two-pronged strategy continues to define India's FDI liberalization.

[30] Private external flows to Indian companies and government entities from bonds, equities, and loans increased from $2.2 billion in 2000 to $19.3 billion in 2005 (Sekhar 2006).

Infosys: An Entrepreneurial Legend

Tata is among India's most preeminent business families, and it had little difficulty developing global partnerships with the best Western companies. For smaller and newer companies, whether they could develop diaspora networks and, via such networks, grow their international business, was critical to their emergence at the top of India's corporate world. Infosys and Bharti, examined here, confirm the strategic roles that diaspora networks play in revamping India's corporate map by selecting the most competitive Indian enterprises, channeling Western funds to them, and facilitating their growth in India and abroad.

Infosys, presently the largest information technology (IT) services company in India, was founded in 1981 by seven engineers in Pune and had a humble beginning (Martinez-Jerez, Kaplan, and Miller, 2009). The company started as an IT "body-shop" – a firm that deployed skilled IT labor to work abroad, on a contract basis, at a client's facility.[31] More prominent companies, such as HCL, typically refused to provide these services. Body shopping, however, provided revenue for Infosys in the late 1990s, thanks to American companies' need to deal with the Y2K (Year 2000) problem. Body shopping also helped Infosys to build networks with American companies and entrepreneurial diasporas in the United States. In the early 2000s, Infosys expanded its services to business process outsourcing (BPO).

Table 6.4 demonstrates that Infosys' revenue grew more than 26 times in the period from 1999 to 2007, from $121 million to $3.1 billion – almost entirely derived from international markets, with overseas branch offices increasing from five to twenty-three in the same period.

Infosys is an influential company in India, attracting the country's most aspiring talent. Yet, as indicated in Table 6.4, the domestic market represents

TABLE 6.4. *Infosys's Revenues by Area*

	1999	2001	2003	2005	2007
Total Revenue ($mi)	121.0	413.9	754	1592	3090
% by regions					
North America	82	73	73	65	63
Europe	9	19	18	22	26
Rest of the World	6.9	6.3	7.3	10.6	8.7
India	1.7	1.4	2.1	1.9	1.6
Countries with branch offices	5	13	17	16	23

Source: Infosys Annual Reports 1999, 2001, 2002, 2003, 2005, 2007, and Infosys Investor Presentation, http://www.infosys.com/investors/pdfs/IR-Presentation.pdf. Cited in Martinez-Jerez, Kaplan, and Miller 2009.

[31] For a description of the labor side of this story, see Xiang (2006).

minimal shares of its revenue, constituting less than 2 percent. America has been its largest market. In 1999, North America (mainly the United States) accounted for 82 percent of Infosys' total revenue, whereas Europe contributed 9 percent. In 2007, North American revenues continued to dominate at 63 percent and Europe's share climbed to 26 percent, whereas domestic market accounted for only 1.6 percent. Globalization of Infosys has deepened since 2007. As of 2010, Infosys set up an additional five branch offices abroad, bringing the total number to twenty-eight. In the United States, where the bulk of its business is concentrated, it has sixteen sales offices. Infosys has increased its presence in China and thus far established two sales offices, in Beijing and Shanghai, respectively.

Based on its role in the international market, Infosys has become a corporate giant within India. Its leaders are inspiring young Indians to get into software engineering and entrepreneurship and also influencing India's public debate over liberalization policies. Although not necessarily pro-FDI, Infosys leaders have opposed unexamined domestic attacks on liberalization, and their views carry weight in the country.

Bharti: Walking on Two Legs

Bharti, a cellular provider now diversified into many sectors, emerged in the 1990s. By 2000, it had become the largest cell phone provider in India, with its business expanding to retail, insurance, investment, services, real estate, and infrastructure development. This young company illustrates how India's new corporate elites successfully expand abroad while capturing burgeoning domestic market and how foreign collaboration, with the help of diaspora professionals, undergirds both endeavors. Bharti's founder, Sunil Bharti Mittal (hereafter referred to as Sunil), represented the new hybrid business elite in India and had extensive internal and external political-economic networks. Sunil was a graduate of Harvard Business School, a leading member of FICCI, a one-time president of CII, and the co-chairman of the Indo-U.S. Joint Business Council. Before Bharti's cellular business, Sunil had founded several ventures in the 1980s.

Bharti's phenomenal growth since the late 1990s benefited from two factors. One, the 1999 New Telecom Policy that liberalized the sector to private players. And two, the availability of Western ideas and resources to Indian companies. With passage of the telecom policy, ideas and investment from the New York-based private equity investment company Warburg Pincus provided major boosts to Bharti's growth. The equity company's involvement in Bharti, however, was proposed and materialized by two diaspora professionals working there: Pulak Prasad (an associate) and Dalip Pathak (a managing director). More importantly, after Warburg Pincus injected funds into Bharti, Prasad and Pathak worked closely with Bharti's management team and provided them with vision and a blueprint to "go big."[32] Warburg Pincus's financial input to Bharti was by far the

[32] www.insead.edu/facultyresearch/faculty/personal/lfang/cv/documents/bhartitele-ventures.pdf. Accessed on January 10, 2013.

largest venture capital investment in India and led to the rapid globalization of Bharti in the new millennium.

In 2000, Bharti formed a JV with SingTel, which provided $400 million in funds and more advanced technology in exchange for a share of India's burgeoning cellular market. In the same year, Bharti received an additional $460 million in equity investments from Asian Infrastructure Funds, International Finance Corporation, and New York Life, which the company used to establish new mobile telecom ventures, develop projects involving national long-distance operations, fund foreign acquisitions, and expand services.

In 2002, Warburg Pincus orchestrated Bharti's global debut, again with the help of Indian diasporas working there. Bharti made its initial public offering (IPO) on the New York Stock Exchange.[33] Building on the IPO, Bharti expanded its cellular business, and, within a year, it added 300,000 new cellular customers in India; within two years, its total customer base reached 10 million. With such a strong market share, Bharti set the standard for corporations operating in India's telecom sector.[34] In 2004, Bharti formed another alliance with Nokia, a world market leader in cellular technology, thus further expanding Bharti's coverage in India. A year later, Bharti recruited Kurt Hellstrom, the former President and Chief Executive of Ericsson, as the newest member of its board of directors.

Using India's rapidly growing cellular market as backing, Bharti delved into IT manufacturing via foreign partnerships: with Atlinks (a Thompson subsidiary) in 2004, and with Vodafone and UK-based Alpha Data in 2005.[35] In that year, Bharti moved into the life insurance business by teaming up with France-based financial company AXA. Two years later, it teamed up with the London-based GSMA Association to tap into the business of diaspora remittances to India. In 2008, Bharti teamed with retail giant Walmart to explore business opportunities in India. Although foreign retail chains were officially forbidden at the time, Bharti and Walmart created the Best Price Modern Whole chain, a 50–50 venture, and began to sell products to Indian middle class shoppers in that year.[36]

The corporate transformation, as represented by Bharti, Infosys, and Tata, has changed the interests of domestic business. These cases demonstrate that Indian companies thrived on linkages to foreign markets, financing, technology, and talents. Diaspora professionals who migrated from India's upper class families, received advanced studies in Western countries, and succeeded in the corporate world in the United States, have played critical, bridging roles in the process. The

[33] JM Morgan Stanley and DSP Merrill Lynch were the running managers for the IPO. See "Bharti Tele-Ventures Announces Rs.45 as the Floor Price for its IPO," Bharti media center, January 23, 2002, http://www.bharti.com

[34] "Bharti Heralds the Beginning of a Unified Era in the Indian Telecom Industry," Bharti media center, September 15, 2004, http://www.bharti.com

[35] "Strategic Tie-up with Thompson Arm, Atlinks," *The Business Line*, February 21, 2004; "Vodafone Buys into India's Bharti," *BBC News*, October 28, 2005.

[36] "Walmart in India Fact Sheet," www.walmartstores.com.

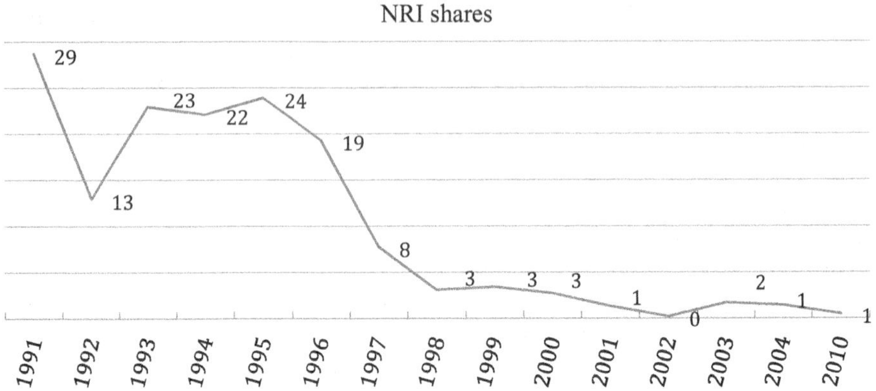

FIGURE 6.5. The Shares of Diaspora Investment in India (%)
Source: For NRI investment, see Lok Sabha Unstarred Question No. 390, dated February 3, 2005; for non-NRI FDI, see Economic Editor's Conference, November 17–18, 2004, Ministry of Finance and Ministry of Commerce & Industry, Government of India.

above-mentioned companies' success has shifted domestic industry's stance on globalization and moderately reduced fear of foreign competition in India. Such successful companies, however, represent only a small number of indigenous firms in India. For the less successful players, concerns about foreign competition remained and served to slow the domestic diffusion of FDI liberalization.

In India's FDI, the shares of diaspora investment were far smaller than in China and had been getting smaller since the mid-1990s. In Figure 6.5, in 1991, when India formally initiated FDI liberalization, Indian diasporas constituted 29 percent of FDI inflows. Starting the mid-1990s, diaspora shares quickly eroded. In 1998, diaspora inflows dropped to only 3 percent. In the new millennium, diaspora investments' shares in total FDI were reduced to an average of just 1 percent.

In short, although diaspora professionals have a thriving role in India, diaspora investment has been declining. There are two main reasons. On the one hand, the investment capacity of professional immigrants was much smaller than overseas Chinese entrepreneurs who amassed capital, manufacturing technology, and international trade during the high-growth era in East Asia. Thus, Indian diasporas could not keep up with growing investment from Western companies in India. On the other hand, diaspora investment shares were reduced by state policies. In the early 1990s, the government set preferential provisions for NRI investment, but in the recent decade no diaspora schemes have been announced, despite gestures such as offering dual citizenship and voting rights to Indian immigrants. Underlying the state policy was the salience of indigenous industrialists – the bigger ones built partnerships with diaspora professionals and Western companies, and the smaller ones opposed FDI in general. Within India, domestic calls for embracing diaspora investment are lacking.[37]

Local Dynamics in India's FDI

Local governments in China have played a critical role in the country's FDI liberalization, as seen in the process tracing of SEZs, zone fever, and SOE reforms in Chapters 3 and 5. A local–national disjuncture has worked to the advantage of diaspora networks and deepened FDI liberalization at the local level, and the diffusion of FDI liberalization across localities has been typically faster and more profound than national policy making.

Like China, India is a large country with significant subnational diversity. On FDI liberalization, however, the role of India's local governments has been much more limited than in China. With diaspora professionals returning to apex bureaucracies in New Delhi, FDI policy making in the national government was rather favorable, but local implementation has been narrow and lacking. The salience of indigenous business also prevented local governments from pursuing foreign investors in the 1980s and 1990s. Even in development-prone states such as Gujarat and Maharashtra, the local governments privileged private business without liberalizing policies for FDI. Mirroring the post-2000 liberalization trend at the national level, but slower in coming, Indian local states gradually began to welcome FDI, but only as large indigenous business became globalized and as ideas and interests surrounding economic policies were slowly transformed.

There are substantial local variations in FDI, however. In Map 2, FDI concentration diverges across Indian states and has primarily gone to five destinations: Mumbai (Maharashtra), New Delhi (Delhi and Haryana), Bangalore (Karnataka), Ahmedabad (Gujarat), and Chennai (Tamil Nadu). In 2011, these five states together accounted for 69 percent of FDI inflows in India. All these localities are well-to-do states in the country and had reasonably strong indigenous business before liberalization. Their attraction to foreign investors during reform demonstrates that FDI in India takes place via partnership with domestic private companies.

Liberalization in the 1990s has meanwhile led to the emergence of a federal market economy in which decision-making powers are shared between the center and local states, and local governments have become the principal arena for private investment. Lloyd Rudolph and Susanne Rudolph (2001, 1541) observe, "By the end of the 1990s, state chief ministers became the marquee players in India's federal market economy." Aseema Sinha confirms the new, entrepreneurial

[37] The current Indian government appears more interested in attracting diaspora investment. See Aarti Dhar, "Manmohan Singh Tells Diaspora to Help Build New India," *The Hindu*, January 8, 2007.

role of chief ministers in Tamil Nadu and Gujarat. In these states, traditional business networks and new social relations, such as returning diasporas and the arrival of foreign investors, have some real impacts on FDI inflows, distribution, and development at the subnational level.

Like Tamil Nadu and Gujarat, Andhra Pradesh (AP) is one of the fastest growing local states during reform. It embraced FDI and developed infrastructure for software services in the capital city, Hyderabad. From a middling state to the best performer in the country, Bibek Debroy, Laveesh Bhandari, and Swaminathan Aiyar (2011) ranked AP the number one state in the economic freedom score in 2009. Diaspora connections and entrepreneurial local governments are both important factors to AP's development. As a state with substantial out-migration to the United States, AP was blessed with resourceful diaspora communities abroad, and, for years, the state's ruling party Telegu Desam made sustained engagement efforts toward such bodies while improving local conditions for diasporas' return. The synergy was remarkable and led to the rapid development of software service industries in the state (see Chapter 8).

CONCLUSION

When we read the two chapters in this Part together, the comparative experiences of China's and India's reforms in the 1990s and beyond are revealing. When the two are juxtaposed, three conclusions can be made. First, regime-dichotomous views need to be modified. Leaders of democracies and autocracies strive for economic growth and have the capacity to pursue economic change forcefully. Narasimha Rao and Manmohan Singh seized the 1991 crisis as an opportunity and launched a dramatic opening in the early 1990s. Even their rival party, the BJP government, expedited reform in the new millennium. Second, in autocracies and democracies, powerful antireform forces exist. In the mid-1990s, both China and India experienced domestic resistance to FDI, and national government in China was divided. The assumption that interest groups are unimportant in an autocracy also needs to be revised. Finally, policy change needs early success to be sustainable. Only when Indian companies achieved great success abroad was resistance to FDI moderated. Such corporate success, however, makes FDI liberalization in the Chinese style unlikely in India: if domestic companies are as successful or more successful than foreign companies, why apply more favorable policies to foreign investors?

The liberalization process in India supports that incremental yet transformative social changes are taking place. As the country has opened to Western MNCs, particularly when substantial diasporas returned to the homeland, prevailing economic ideas are surely changing, indigenous business interests are evolving, and local governments are becoming more prone to support FDI liberalization. All these trends are unfolding, and countertrends still remain in the country, yet one thing is clear: the mid-1990s business blowback and anti-FDI policy reversal are unlikely in India's future liberalization. Thirty years of economic liberalization have made the country a more fertile ground for foreign investors, although protectionist indigenous interests and limited entrepreneurial diasporas, two key obstacles to FDI, are here to stay.

PART IV

FOREIGN DIRECT INVESTMENT IN SECTORS

7

China's Electronics and Automobiles

Part II and Part III compare the processes of foreign direct investment (FDI) liberalization in China and India from 1980 to the present. They demonstrate the importance of social networks to the adoption and diffusion of new policies in each country. Two types of capitalist networks have influenced the specific policies and the speed of diffusion in these two Asian giants. In China, the emergence of diaspora entrepreneurial networks at the central and local levels led to the early initiation of FDI liberalization, rapid industrialization, and the development of an export economy based on FDI. India's private business sector built robust networks with the government and precipitated the country's domestic deregulation – yet it resisted FDI liberalization. Indian professional diasporas have had important roles, serving as advisors to policy makers and connecting domestic industries to the global market. In FDI, however, Indian diasporas were less significant investors than Chinese diaspora entrepreneurs.

The internal and external social networks of industrial sectors also vary in the two countries. Diasporas tend to have different sectoral strengths. Domestic industries also differ on the issue of external opening. This Part (Chapters 7 and 8) investigates how external networks and domestic resistance have shaped FDI liberalization across sectors within China and India. I focus on and compare two sectors in both countries: electronics and automobiles. Map 3 illustrates the main locations of FDI in electronics and automobiles in the two respective countries. The location of China's electronics FDI conforms to the country's general FDI pattern as revealed in Map 1. By contrast, in India, the auto industry's FDI resembles the national-level FDI pattern shown in Map 2, clustering near the sites of indigenous producers. The main task in this part is to explain how the combination of diaspora networks and domestic producers in these countries have interactively shaped their divergent FDI liberalization across sectors.

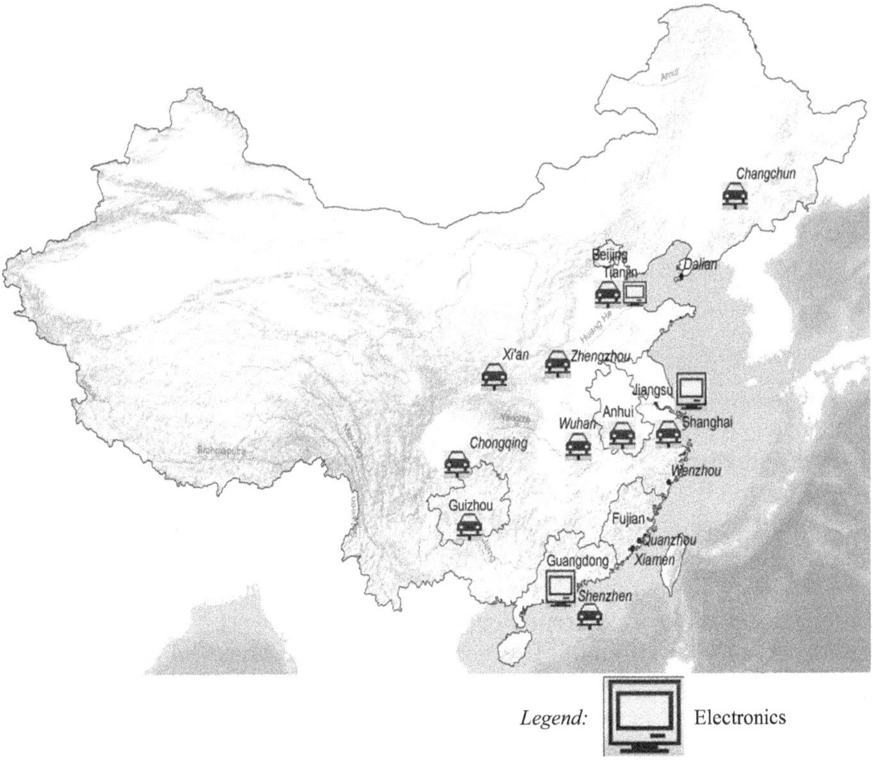

MAP 3. Foreign Direct Investment (FDI) in Automobiles and Electronics in China and India (2011)

Notes: (1) Foreign direct investment in the Chinese automobile sector followed the state automakers and concentrated in traditional industrial sites, whereas electronics FDI conformed to diaspora networks in the coastal region. (2) India's FDI inflows were led by domestic private companies: the two largest destinations are Mumbai and Bangalore, followed by Chennai, Calcutta, and New Delhi. All these places are either traditional centers of private business or new ones for private industries.

At the time of China's reform, electronics and automobiles existed under common political-economic conditions in the nation: an authoritarian political system, powerful yet individualistic leaders, overstretched economic bureaucrats, few financial resources, and backward technology. Furthermore, state preferences and industrial policies were similar in the initial years of reform: opening to foreign loans, licensing foreign technology, and supporting state-owned enterprises (SOEs) to produce for domestic markets. There were minor intrasector variations. Within electronics, appliances manufacturing was decentralized, and local governments played a bigger role in production. Yet a

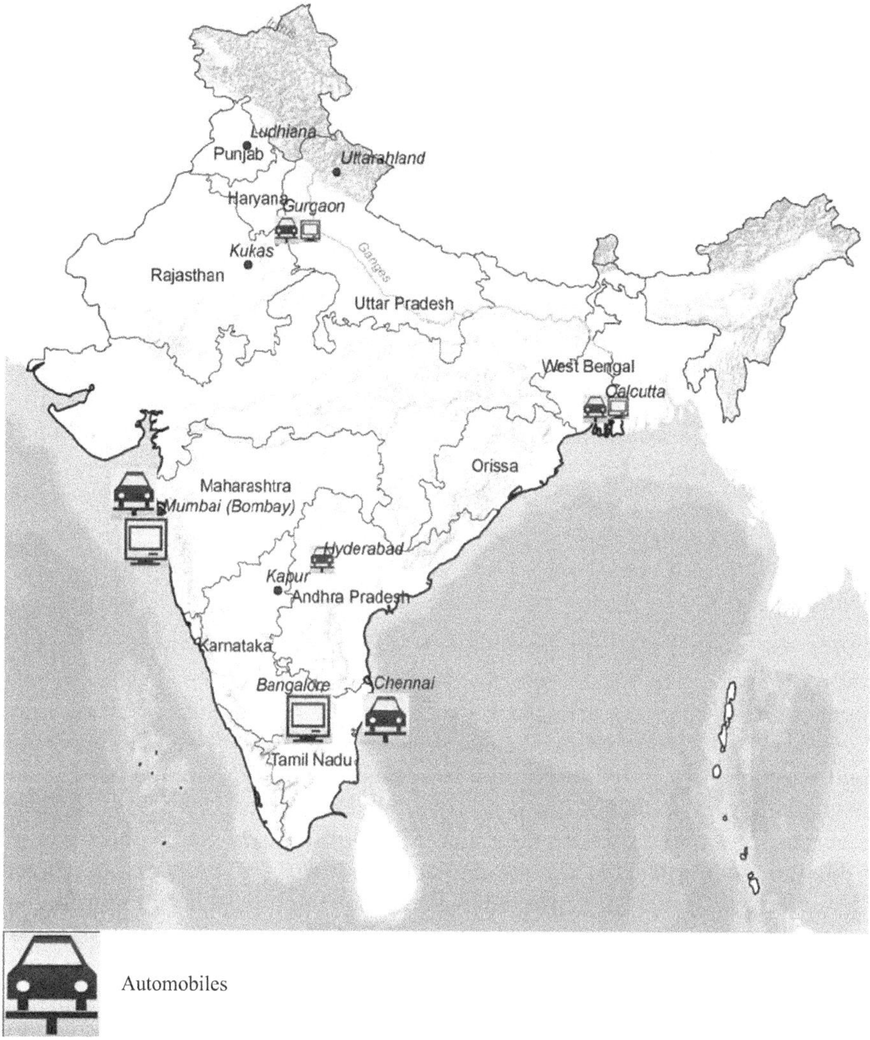

MAP 3. (cont.)

"socialist import-substituting industrialization" strategy (SISI) prevailed in all industries in China, including automobiles and electronics (Lardy 1992). Under this strategy, only state companies with government licenses had foreign exchange (and official channels) to purchase technology and equipment from abroad.

Although internal conditions and national policies were highly comparable, diaspora networks varied greatly between electronics and automobiles, and decentralization amplified the impact of diaspora networks at the local level. Chinese diasporas were global players in electronics manufacturing and exports. When China initiated its economic reforms, diaspora entrepreneurs were quickly engaged in electronics manufacturing in southern China, producing visible early success in electronics. This helped to deepen FDI liberalization in this sector. The initially preferred SISI model was outcompeted and dismantled in electronics.

Such a diffusion process did not take place in the auto industry. Diaspora entrepreneurs were unavailable in automaking, and the main players in China's auto liberalization were national bureaucracies, SOEs, and Western automakers. Such a mixture of external and internal networks in autos made FDI liberalization much slower to start and more difficult to proceed than in electronics. In the current period, Western dominance causes antiglobalization backlashes in the sector from time to time, and the Chinese auto exports face insurmountable problems in the world market.

THE ELECTRONICS INDUSTRY: FROM SEZS TO HIGH-TECH CLUSTERS

Table 7.1 summarizes the development history of the electronics sector and shows that the sector's pre-reform policies were similar to those in the auto industry (see Table 7.2): oriented toward military use, consumer electronics was ignored. When reform began, Beijing designated appliances as a light industry and selected a few SOEs to produce for domestic consumption. Local governments had more influence in the newly established electronics SOEs. With the construction of special economic zones (SEZs) in southern China and the entry of diaspora entrepreneurs into the appliances industry, two pathways developed in this sector. The first path was led by SOEs that had official licenses for foreign technology, foreign exchange, and domestic markets. On the other path, diasporas came to set up factories to manufacture for the global market and assisted new indigenous entrepreneurs at the local level. The second path ultimately won out and influenced the construction of high-tech development zones. In southern and eastern China in the 1990s, local governments embraced Taiwan's computer manufacturing companies and paved the way for China's rise as a major manufacturer and exporter of consumer electronics and computer hardware in the world.

Socialist Import-Substituting Industrialization and its Downfall

When China began reform, bureaucracies responsible for the electronics sector were in poor shape. The government streamlined new bureaucracies and SOEs to promote electronics production. In 1978, it centralized all electronics SOEs to the Fourth Ministry of Machine Building [*Siji bu*], and Deng Xiaoping personally

TABLE 7.1. *The Development History of the Electronics Industry in China*

Period	Main Actors and Main Policies
Pre-reform	The industry was developed for military use only; consumer electronics were ignored.
1980s	Two paths: (1) The state and state-owned enterprises (SOEs) transferred technology from advanced countries (2) The arrival of diaspora investment in special economic zones (SEZs) and the emergence of private producers.
1990s	Burgeoning high-tech development zones and dominance of diaspora investment in the zones
2000s	An open and competitive market emerged.

TABLE 7.2. *Development History of China's Auto Sector*

Period	Policy frameworks
Pre-reform	Military connections, weak passenger vehicles
1980s	High tariffs, aggressive technology transfer Restrictive joint venture policies
1990s	Massive losses, massive criticism Moderate protection, moderate control
2000s	Contentious liberalization, strong nationalism in indigenous production

urged all government agencies to use electronics as part of the four modernizations [*sige xiandaihua*]. A year later, the State Council established the National Computer Bureau. In the government work report to the second plenum of the Fifth National Party Congress in 1979, the state planner emphasized electronics as "the key industry of modernization [that] should be actively developed."[1]

In 1980, the government launched the Chinese Electronics Export and Import Company. Two years later, it inaugurated the Ministry of the Electronics Industry (MEI) as a super ministry, combining the Fourth Ministry of Machine Building, National Commission of Communication, Radio and Television Industries, and National Computer Bureau. The MEI was granted the authority to orchestrate the development of the electronics industry in China. Jiang Zemin, Chinese president from 1989 to 2002, became the Minister of MEI in 1983. Electronics was called a "pillar industry," and its development received

[1] *Zhongguo dianzi gongye nianjian [China Electronics Industry Yearbook]* 1986 edition, Beijing: dianzi gongye chubanshe, pp. 1–21.

strong government support. The conservative leader, Chen Yun, urged Jiang Zemin to "use all forces to develop the electronics industry."[2]

The national government's supportive policy, as well as high demand for consumer electronics, led to a rapid increase in the number of consumer electronics manufacturers. Local governments supported the establishment of state-owned appliance factories. Quickly, however, state appliance makers operated at a loss and became a growing financial burden on the government. Beijing Snowflake, Suzhou Refrigerator Factory, and Tianjin Refrigerator Factory, for example, were on the national government's priority list in the 1980s. By 1993, they had lost so much money that they were auctioned off.

State companies' earlier preeminence in the Chinese market and connections with national and local governments made them attractive targets of foreign acquisition when foreign firms began to enter the Chinese market in the 1990s. State-owned enterprise-multinational corporation (SOE-MNC) marriages followed: Whirlpool invested $17.7 million in Beijing Snowflake and acquired 60 percent of its stake in 1994. A year later, Samsung took over Suzhou Refrigerator Factory, and LG acquired Tianjin Refrigerator, both controlling 80 percent of their respective SOE. Other MNCs, such as Electrolux, Siemens, Sharp, National, and General Electric also formed joint ventures (JVs) as an entryway into China's consumer markets. Foreign investors then discarded the Chinese brands and marketed their own. By 1999, via acquisition of Chinese SOEs, foreign brands already held 21 percent of domestic market shares. The operation of MNC-SOE JVs was not smooth and was challenged by diaspora and private companies emerging on the second path of electronics development in China.

Diaspora Connections and Private Electronics Producers

A key difference between the Chinese electronics and auto industries was the presence of diaspora networks. The emergence of diaspora-driven electronics manufacturing in southern China triumphed over the state-led pathway just described. In Guangdong and Fujian, electronics manufacturing thrived on connections to Hong Kong. In Guangdong, annual growth in electronics production averaged 53 percent in the 1980s. Within the first five years of reform, Guangdong's electronics production increased eleven times, rising to become the third largest province to produce electronics in the country, a remarkable jump from the ninth position in 1979.[3]

Guangdong soon became the major hub for China's electronics exports. Hong Kong-invested Xia Hua Electronics was established in 1982 with fourteen

[2] Chen Yun, "Yao ba dianzi gongye gaoshang qu" [Should Develop the Electronics Industry], *Chen Yun wenxuan [Selected Works of Chen Yun]*, Vol. III, Beijing: zhongyang wenxian chubanshe [Central Compilation Publisher], 2005, pp. 533–534.

[3] *Zhongguo dianzi nianjian [China's Electronics Yearbook]*, 1987 edition.

divisions, several R&D centers, and four automatic assembly lines. Upon its establishment, the company had an annual production capacity of 480,000 units and export permits for the U.S. market (Zheng 2006, 109). Foshan, a small city in Guangdong, entered the electronics industry with a modest JV with Hong Kong's Yamei to process assembly orders. With the strength of its Hong Kong investors, Foshan grew to be one of the four largest electronics producers in Guangdong by 1984.

Fujian's electronics sector also relied on diaspora connections before reaching out to Japanese investment. From 1979 to 1980, there were twelve companies in Fujian processing for Hong Kong factories, and with Hong Kong connections, they also manufactured for the Japanese. In 1981, Fujian's local government formed a JV (Fu Ri) with Japanese investors, as well as a JV with Hitachi. The growth of Japanese investment was slower than that of diaspora investment. In August 1981, Hong Kong's Xin Li set up a JV, Xia Xin, with a group of electronics companies in Fujian. Within two years, Xia Xin, later renamed Xiamen Diaspora Electronics [*Huaqiao dianzi*], had launched an additional thirteen subsidiaries and produced a wide range of products for export. In 1984, Hong Kong's Ming Tai set up Yong Tai Electronics, the first wholly owned foreign company in Fujian. Yong Tai manufactured mobile telephones and exported its entire production to the United States. In 1985, Guangdong and Fujian's electronics production accounted for 12 percent of the national total – a major accomplishment given their humble beginnings. By 1995, these two provinces were already producing 30 percent of all electronics products in China (Naughton 1997).

Diaspora connections facilitated the growth of private entrepreneurs in southern China. Private capital was eradicated under Mao's rule. Along with FDI liberalization, private entrepreneurs revived. Among the largest electronics producers, private companies had higher representation than did state-owned companies. In 2003, three of the four Chinese firms in the top ten computer-net equipment producers were private. Two of the four Chinese home audiovisual equipment manufacturers were private. And all Chinese players in communications, mobile technology, integrated circuits, and home appliances were private.[4]

Specific cases reveal the critical role of Hong Kong as an intermediary of ideas, technology, and markets to newly emerging private companies. Lenovo and Great Wall, for example, both originated in Beijing in the mid-1980s and had access to human talent and government support there.[5] In the late 1980s, both moved their headquarters to Guangdong. Lenovo in particular established a number of additional subsidiaries and JVs in Hong Kong. In Hong Kong, Lenovo forged distribution agreements with AST and Compaq to market these

[4] *Zhongguo gongye tongji nianjian, 2003 [China's Industrial Statistical Yearbook, 2003].*

[5] Lenova, then called Legend, was a spin-off from the Chinese Academy of Sciences, and Great Wall was developed by MEI.

companies' products in China. By drawing on financing in Hong Kong, Lenovo prepared to dominate China's domestic market and acquire IBM's notebook division in 2004 (Ling 2005). The stories of Kelon, Konka, ZTE, Huawei, and more all had origins in diaspora networks.

Diasporas were important global players in electronics hardware manufacturing. Hong Kong was the "world market factory" of electronics products before the 1980s and had strong connections to American, Japanese, and European markets. Facing rising production costs, Hong Kong manufacturers relocated their factories to the Mainland after the establishment of SEZs. In 1986, a survey concluded that the majority of Hong Kong manufacturers had transferred their production to the Mainland.[6] Taiwan's electronics producers began to follow suit in the late 1980s. By the mid-1990s, the majority of Taiwanese producers had been operating in mainland China.

Diaspora investment came with export networks. Xiamen Diaspora Electronics and Shenzhen Kanka, both founded by Hong Kong investors, were among the top electronics exporters in the PRC throughout the 1980s.[7] By 1990, these companies were exporting more than $100 million worth of products annually.[8] Hong Kong was the Mainland's largest export market, predominantly in processing trade. The 1990 statistics suggest that Hong Kong was the destination for 62 percent of China's electronics exports, followed by the United States (6.23 percent) and the European Union (6.15 percent).

Concurrent with rising imports of finished electronics products from the Mainland, Hong Kong exported a growing number of components and equipment to the PRC. $1.9 billion was exported to the PRC in 1990 versus almost $17.5 billion in 1995, suggesting that processing trade dominated the two sides' economic relations in those years.[9] Electronics production on the Mainland climbed the technological ladder as diaspora manufacturers of increasingly sophisticated products relocated to China to take advantage of lower production costs. Driven by diaspora entrepreneurs, China improved labor skills training (evidenced in the growing programs at college and vocational schools teaching electronics) and infrastructure that suited high-end manufacturing and exports. With China becoming the main site for electronics production, Hong Kong shifted to support services, such as packaging, promotion, design, and technical assistance in the transfer of technology and management to China. In short, the development success of China's electronics industries was an outgrowth of industrial expansion within "Greater China," and coethnic and corporate ties undergirded such development.

[6] H. Lau and S. Green, "The Electronics Industry: Can Manufacturing Continue in Hong Kong?" *The World Economy*, 24(8), pp. 1075–1090.

[7] *Zhongguo jixie dianzi gongye nianjian (dianzi juan) [China Statistics Yearbook in Electronics and Machinery]*, Beijing: Dianzi gongye chubangshe, 1991, III-31, VI-3.

[8] Ibid., V-10.

[9] See *Zhongguo duiwai jingji tongji nianjian [China Foreign Economic Statistics]*, various years.

Newly Emerging Chinese Electronics Makers

The importance of diaspora entrepreneurs to China's electronics sector lay not only in investing in China but also in helping private entrepreneurs to grow. In the early 1980s, the government only gave licenses to SOEs for electronics manufacturing. Without such licenses, entry into the market would be difficult because control over foreign exchange and technology imports was thorough (Lardy 1992). In Guangdong, with the establishment of diaspora electronics firms and the availability of funds and technology via diaspora connections, fledgling private companies came into being – although sometimes wearing "red hats."[10] In the mid-late 1980s, aspiring private entrepreneurs from other places also moved to Guangdong to take advantage of the more liberal policies and connections to Hong Kong. In the growth of many private firms, diaspora entrepreneurs conveyed ideas, technology, capital, and links to export markets.

By contrast, in the auto industry, there were no diaspora entrepreneurs; neither Hong Kong nor Taiwan was strong in the auto industry. Western automakers did come, but only to collaborate with major state companies, and the collaboration was not smooth, as the latter section explains. Lacking technology and capital inputs, new private automakers did not arrive in China until the late 1990s. Even today, real private automakers are few and small. The first private auto manufacturer in China, Geely, was founded in 1998. Nevertheless, Geely's success demystified previous assumptions that only large SOEs could succeed in auto manufacturing. Geely's birth was somewhat similar to private electronics producers, except much later.

Lenovo was an official spin-off of CAS, but had humble beginnings. Its founders were technicians voluntarily laid off by CAS and provided with small starting funds. It operated as a de facto private company, subject to market competition and budget constraints. Then it moved to southern China and, capitalizing on diaspora connections, emerged at the top of the industry. The leading appliance makers in China were also either diaspora companies or private companies reliant on diaspora networks, all located in South China. Midea Enterprises, Galanz Corporation, Gree Electric Appliances, and Kelon were all founded in Guangdong.

Kelon's birth and growth was representative of other companies in the way it successfully used its Hong Kong connections to grow and advance. It began as a small factory in rural Guangdong that specialized in making cheap transistor radios for a Hong Kong company (Huang and Lane 2003). Wang Guoduan, the founder of Kelon, was an entrepreneurial technician. After observing the popularity of refrigerators as gifts from Hong Kong residents to their relatives in Guangdong, in 1984, he decided to produce refrigerators.

[10] Under SISI, private entrepreneurs had to find sponsorships with government-related agencies to promote the image that they were public companies.

Wang had relatives in Hong Kong who brought him two refrigerators. Wang disassembled the refrigerators to learn how they worked, a technique strikingly similar to that of Li Shufu, the founder of Geely who dismantled two Mercedes-Benzes to learn automaking. Via reverse engineering, Wang's company was able to make its own refrigerators. Driven by high demand in China, Kelon took off. By 1991, Kelon had become the largest refrigerator manufacturer in the country.

Kelon's growth in the 1990s drew on connections to Hong Kong, which served as a major source of financing. In 1996, Kelon became the first Chinese private company to list its stock in Hong Kong and raised enough funds to develop a national distribution base. The number of Kelon provincial sales offices rose from twelve to thirty-one.[11] In 1997, Kelon raised an additional HK$704.7 million ($93.8 million) through another listing in Hong Kong. These funds helped Kelon expand into the compressor industry and greatly enhanced Kelon's refrigerator business. Kelon's share of China's refrigerator market grew from 17 percent in 1996 to 25 percent in 2000.

Kelon's performance seems even more remarkable when compared to Beijing Snowflake, a 1980s privileged SOE licensed to make refrigerators. In 1994, after chronic losses, Snowflake was broke and sold itself to Whirlpool. The resultant JV was unsuccessful for both sides. Since Whirlpool held a majority share of the JV, it discarded the Snowflake brand and marketed its own products, raising intense criticism in China. Yet Whirlpool was ultimately unsuccessful: by 1997, it had lost more than $100 million and had to shut down its refrigerator and air conditioner plants in China. The company's microwave factory survived by subcontracting for Kelon: "A reversal of the usual hierarchy between Western and Chinese firms," according to the *Economist*.[12]

Connections to Taiwan and Computer Manufacturing

While appliance production was decentralized, the national government viewed computer manufacturing as crucial to national industrial strategy ("the foundation of four modernizations") – perhaps more so than automaking. Yet this subsector of the electronics industry experienced similar industrialization and export success based on diaspora networks. The difference was that such development occurred later, and the Taiwanese took the center stage. In 1988, Taiwanese authorities lifted the ban on investment in the Mainland. Simultaneously, the PRC applied especially favorable policies to Taiwanese investors. In July 1988, the State Council announced the Regulation on Encouraging Taiwanese Investment (the Twenty-Two Items) and detailed a wide range of preferential policies for Taiwanese. Taiwanese investors could receive a break on their income taxes, a 50 percent reduction in other types of

[11] "Kelon: China's Corporate Dragon," p. 6.

[12] "Infatuation's End," *The Economist*, September 25, 1999.

taxes, and free land use for the first five years. Local governments often provided even more attractive packages to Taiwanese investors than those specified in the central documents. Localities such as Shanghai, Guangdong, Fujian, Zhejiang, and Jiangsu, where Taiwanese had extensive ancestral lineages, were especially effective in attracting Taiwanese firms.

Like the Hong Kong diaspora, Taiwanese were responsive to China's policy opening. After Deng's Southern Tour, Taiwanese invested $393 million in Shanghai, $312 million in Xiamen (Fujian), $150 million in Fuzhou (Fujian), $108 million in Shenzhen, and $105 million in Ningbo (Zhejiang) in 1992 alone.[13] Due to Taiwan's strength in electronics, this sector attracted the largest amount of investment from Taiwan to the Mainland (Fu 2002, 28). Capital and technology from Taiwan were crucial to the establishment and success of New and High Technology Zones in the Guangdong and Shanghai areas. The operation ran as follows: (1) parts and components were ordered from Taiwan, (2) final products were assembled on the Mainland, (3) products were packaged in Hong Kong, and then (4) exported to the world (Fu 2002).

In the mid-1990s, Taiwan occupied 30 percent of the world market for notebook PCs and 70 percent of the market for computer motherboards (Callon 1995). It was the world's top producer of eight computer parts. The Mainland offered a much larger workforce and lower production costs; thus, Taiwan's companies increasingly relocated to the Mainland, driving the construction of high tech zones in China. By the late 1990s, 60 percent of Taiwan's computer-related production had relocated to the PRC. In 1999, 2,700 Taiwanese companies used Shenzhen as an export base for the global market.[14] In 2003, 55 percent of Taiwan's desktop computer production, 60 percent of motherboard production, and 71 percent of monitor production took place on the Mainland (Chen Yun 2005).

Taiwan's electronics investment was concentrated in the two growth centers – Guangdong and Shanghai – and propelled hardware manufacturing and exports in China. Taiwanese investment first arrived in Guangdong. Almost all of the computer-related manufacturers from Taiwan had facilities there. They then expanded to Shanghai proper, similarly concentrating on hardware manufacturing. Diaspora entrepreneurs also spurred the growth of private companies, which received supplies and technologies from these diaspora companies and then grew independently by relying on global markets. In Shanghai, Kunshan, Suzhou, and other locales, Chinese private companies grew alongside the diaspora entrepreneurs.

Taiwanese investment helped to build development marvels in coastal China. Dongguan, a fairly small city in Guangdong, had 2,800 computer manufacturers with substantial Taiwanese investments. Shunde, another small city in

13 *Zhongguo duiwai maoyi nianjian [China's External Trade and Investment Statistics]*, 1993 edition.

14 Taiwan, *Jingji shibao*, November 1, 1999.

Guangdong and also home to numerous Taiwan firms, had an annual production capacity of 1 million computers. Near Shanghai, computer hardware production grew rapidly in the 1990s. Chapter 5 examined Kunshan as an example of the role of diaspora investment in China's computer hardware manufacturing and exports, and several other cities (such as Suzhou, Ningbo, Yangzhou, and others) also built electronics manufacturing and exporting by embracing diaspora networks. By 2002, the region surrounding Shanghai was producing 60 percent of the world's mouses, 25 percent of motherboards, 18 percent of monitors, 15 percent of scanners, and 10 percent of keyboards. In the new millennium, the PRC became the world's largest production site for computer hardware.

The synergy between diaspora investment and the Mainland's opening also benefited diaspora firms that enhanced global competitiveness because of their relocation to the PRC. Taiwan's Foxconn, maker of 40 percent of the world's electronics components, is the largest exporter in Greater China and has been operating on the Mainland since 1988. Quanta Computer, which made roughly a third of the world's laptops, shifted 90 percent of its production to a facility in Shanghai, employing more than 20,000 Chinese workers (Luo 2000). Acer, the world's second largest PC maker, had three subsidiaries on the Mainland, including Acer Softech in Shanghai and Acer Information Products in Shenzhen and Zhongshan in 2000. In 2005, Acer set up another facility in the Beijing-Tianjin corridor. Asus, Taiwan's largest IT hardware manufacturer, which produces components for Sony, Apple, HP, Intel, and many others, had an enormous manufacturing facility in Suzhou that covered 540,000 square meters – roughly the size of eighty-two soccer fields (Calder and Ye 2010).

The electronics sector has many subsectors: home appliances, electronic machinery, integrated circuits, computers, information technology, and software. Foreign direct investment liberalization has varied across them. The strong role of diaspora entrepreneurs was most clearly seen in the home appliances and computer hardware industries, in which Chinese diasporas had great success prior to China's opening. The sector's history suggests that the government initially prioritized state-led industrial policy similar to that in automobiles: foreign funds and technologies were transferred to SOEs. Yet this growth model was slow to produce success because China's isolation in the previous decades rendered its expertise, technology, and market institutions extremely lacking. Clearly, SOEs were unable to export sufficiently, and in domestic markets, foreign and private producers challenged them. The superiority of openness was thus compelling, and local governments were more willing to attract foreign investment than to support SOEs. State appliance makers were forced to dissolve. And finally, diaspora companies' technology upgrading cascaded to the Mainland in the 1990s. Growing numbers of Taiwanese computer manufacturers came to the Mainland. Their pivotal position in global computing production networks helped China to build information technology clusters and rise to its position as the world's leading exporter of high tech manufacturing goods.[15]

A diffusion process was evident. First, diaspora entrepreneurs initiated investment in SEZs alongside SOEs manufacturing in China. Second, foreign firms' success compared with the failures of SOEs led the national government to reevaluate FDI and abandon socialist production. Finally, the ideas and incentives provided by diaspora entrepreneurs caused local governments' preferences to shift. Those places that previously supported SOEs, like Suzhou, began to embrace FDI eagerly. New indigenous electronics producers grew by relying on diaspora connections to access advanced technology, capital, and global markets. They were part of a growing pro-FDI coalition. In the process analysis, national policies, local governments, and private companies were all active players. Yet the force mobilizing them toward FDI liberalization was the strength of diaspora entrepreneurs who were the world's most competitive manufacturers and exporters prior to China's opening.

The auto sector, as the next section investigates, lacked diaspora networks. Hong Kong, Taiwan, and Southeast Asia had not developed strong auto sectors. They lacked even a large domestic market for automobiles. When China opened in 1979, the available sources of capital and technology for automobiles were MNCs in America, Europe, and Japan. The SOE-MNC JVs were difficult to establish and hard to maintain. In China's auto sector, a shift from socialism to FDI did not occur. Reform and development of the country's auto manufacturing industry has exhibited quite different policies and economic effects from reform in the electronics industry. Liberalization in the auto sector was expedited with China's negotiations to join the World Trade Organization (WTO) at the end of the 1990s, and Western MNCs entered China in a big way as the country emerged as one of the largest markets for passenger vehicles.

THE AUTO SECTOR: FROM PROTECTIONISM TO INDUSTRIAL POLICY

When reform began, China's initial policy on automaking was similar to its policy in electronics. The government allowed decentralization in the auto sector, but this decentralization entailed a shift in power from the supervising ministry to individual SOEs, in contrast to the case of the home appliances industry, where power shifted from the ministry to local governments. Individual SOEs, with the support of ministerial leaders, were encouraged to use external collaboration – foreign loans, technology, and even equity – to manufacture passenger vehicles to satisfy domestic demand. To minimize the import of vehicles, the government applied high tariffs and stringent licenses – a strategy that exemplified SISI.

[15] In 2005, of China's high-tech exports, 80 percent were contributed by foreign-invested firms. See *Zhongguo keji tongji nianjian [China Science and Technology Yearbook]*, 2006.

In the 1980s, high-level economic bureaucrats and SOEs were growth-oriented and open-minded. They visited Europe, America, and Japan to seek cooperation with the world's leading automakers (Thun 2006). They were generally encouraged by these automakers' willingness to transfer technology and export products to China. Foreign MNCs were more cautious in setting up JVs or developing assembly lines in the PRC. Upon China's requests to form JVs, Toyota declined China's request, but three Western companies agreed and this resulted in the negotiation of the first three JVs in automaking. The Chinese negotiators were careful not to sacrifice autonomy in JVs or their control over the Chinese market, whereas Western companies remained wary of technology sharing.

Wide differences in organizational norms and culture made the collaboration in the early JVs difficult to start. Nevertheless, formal openness to foreign collaboration that the national government allowed was unusually high and surpassed the latitude given to SOEs in electronics at the time. In electronics, for example, the government allowed only nationally licensed state producers to operate, and only with licenses could manufacturers transfer technologies from abroad or access foreign loans. Foreign equity sharing, allowed in autos, was not permitted in electronics. Only with the help of diaspora networks were entrepreneurs in electronics able to circumvent such a restrictive policy environment.

Divergence between the auto and electronics industries was clear starting in the mid-1980s. Diaspora entrepreneurs demonstrated the superiority of FDI in electronics, and the emergence of both diaspora and private manufacturers challenged SOEs' market dominance and resulted in the latter's reform. The two-pathway competition and the diffusion of FDI liberalization did not take place in the auto sector. The first three JVs in automaking encountered difficulties in the mid-1980s. Yet there was no competing model to replace the insufficient extant one. The national government stepped up its recentralization, assuming that firm-level decentralization was causing the lack of desired results. National planning agencies took more control of these JVs and urged the recentralization of auto manufacturing in China.

Recentralization was not effective either. In 1986, the government passed a comprehensive auto policy in which high tariffs and a licensing system were maintained, but specific conditions were also prescribed for foreign companies' entry. Driven by this policy and China's growing demand for passenger vehicles, foreign automakers began to enter more actively and pushed liberalization in the sector; intensified external networks and powerful domestic resistance coexisted.

Table 7.2 summarizes the development history and policy frameworks in the auto industry during the reform period. The first period continued restrictive SISI policies, although it did allow some JVs. In the mid-1980s, foreign auto investors withdrew from China, and auto manufacturing was recentralized. Then, in the 1990s, domestic pressure for openness in the auto sector built up as Chinese consumers demanded cheaper and better passenger vehicles. Growing demands also drew more foreign MNCs to the country, and collaboration between MNCs and SOEs intensified. Yet China's negotiation over WTO membership in the 1990s provided the biggest push for FDI liberalization in the auto industry. In sum, FDI liberalization in China's auto industry conforms to the second pathway outlined in Chapter 2: slow, limited, and contested. This pathway differs from that of electronics in China, but somewhat resembles our characterization of India's FDI liberalization.

The 1980s: Failed Socialist Joint Ventures and Enhanced State's Role

The auto sector had a comparatively uninterrupted and protected past under Mao's rule. Even during the Cultural Revolution, the auto industry was under the protection of the military. It was also a sector that had relatively well-trained technocrats via cooperation with the Soviet Union until the Sino-Soviet split in 1960. Thus, when reform began, technocrats in this sector were eager to rebuild China's auto industry. In the passenger vehicle division, they authorized the SOEs to involve foreign collaboration. Import and export companies were established in Tianjin, Beijing, Changchun, and Chongqing, where important state automakers were located. Joint ventures with Western automakers were approved as a means to access foreign technology.[16]

The first JV proposal came from Shanghai Auto Works in 1981; more JVs were proposed shortly thereafter, including Beijing Auto Works and American Motor Company (AMC) in 1983, Guangzhou Auto Works and French Peugeot, and Beijing Auto Industry Company and Japanese Isuzu in 1985–1986.[17] The first to launch, the Shanghai-Volkswagen JV, got off to a slow start and rolled out production only in 1988. In the other JVs, foreign partners withdrew shortly, only to return in the 1990s.

When it invited Western automakers to form JVs, the Chinese government outlined three conditions for such ventures to be approved. First, foreign equity shares were not to exceed 50 percent, and SOEs had to retain control of these JVs. Shanghai Volkswagen pushed the limit to a 50:50 equity split. Second, foreign partners were required to promote localization of their products. Rebates of tariffs and taxes were available only to investors with more than a 40 percent localization rate. Third, high tariffs were levied on imports of parts and whole cars. In the 1980s, tariffs on passenger vehicles ran as high as 220 percent.[18] These restrictions signaled the continuity in import-substituting industrialization in general and were common in many sectors.

The MNC-SOE ventures were controversial. Internal disputes, managerial disagreements, and other types of conflicts between Chinese and foreign partners were frequent. Chinese partners criticized foreigners for withholding core

[16] *Zhongguo qiche gongye tongji nianjian* [*China's Automobile Statistics Yearbook*], various issues.
[17] *Zhongguo qiche gongye tongji nianjian* [*China's Automobile Statistics Yearbook*], 1991.
[18] Ibid.

technology, monopolizing management, and disrespecting Chinese managers.[19] Meanwhile, MNC investors were discouraged from operating in China. AMC withdrew after it suffered losses. Other investors failed to fulfill their localization requirements and complained about administrative distortions in the market. Mistrust was clear in these early JVs, and these mutual complaints were similar to those heard in India's JVs in the 1990s (see Chapter 6). The policy results were also comparable for Chinese automobiles and early Indian opening: the Indian government narrowed openness by promoting "calibrated globalization," whereas China reasserted the central state's role in automobile production.

In the mid-1980s, as JVs stumbled, the national government tried to take more control over the sector's development. Premier Zhao Ziyang announced in 1984 that if China was going to double production volume of passenger vehicles and reach global standards by 1990, the industry should "center around large-scale factories based on modern technology" and the national government should "promote and lead" economic collaborations among SOEs (Thun 2006, 55).

The State Planning Commission separated automobiles from other machinery industries and placed it in the category of heavy central planning. Beijing's planners deemed decentralization of the auto industry harmful to the sector's growth. In 1987, they issued Document No. 5, which downgraded the China National Automobile Industry Corporation (CNAIC) and further strengthened executive powers. The State Planning Commission then selected three auto producers for supervision and promotion: Jiefang, Dongfeng, and Heavy Automotive Factory. These companies reported directly to the Commission, enhancing these companies' access to the national government. Each of these SOEs supervised more than a dozen auto-related factories designed to supplement its core production. Each received support in the form of material provisions, fixed asset investments, technology transfers, and favorable terms of trade.[20]

Protection and subsidies to state companies were systematic. China's First Auto Works (FAW), for example, updated a new model – the CA15. The company succeeded in securing RMB 200 million in subsidies and asked the government to implement mandatory replacements of older models with the new model, thus promoting the sale of the CA15.[21] Local officials in the areas where important state automakers were located provided financial and political support to them. Lacking new development based on external linkages, SOEs were important sources of jobs and revenues for these local governments.[22] Protection had a negative effect on FDI liberalization in the industry. On the one hand, SOEs were disinclined to form foreign partnerships that might

[19] Wang Fengying, "Zizhu pingpai bianyuanhua," *Shidai qiche* [*Auto Times*], no. 4, 2009.

[20] *Diyi qichechang nianjian [The First Auto Works Yearbook]*, 1987. Beijing.

[21] Ibid, p. 70.

[22] For a discussion of the nested problem and mutual capture in SOE–local government relations, see Steinfeld (2000).

restrain their control of their firms, and on the other, economic bureaucrats were vigilantly wary of infringement by foreigners. Such policies became indefensible in the 1990s, when foreign automakers arrived in large numbers and domestic pressure for openness mounted.

The 1990s: Influx of MNCs, Domestic Pressure, and Moderate FDI Liberalization

Despite 220 percent tariffs, passenger car imports skyrocketed in China during the 1990s. Vehicles in China cost two or three times more than comparable ones in the global market. Consumers were dissatisfied with price gouging – particularly new private consumers who purchased their sedans with their own money. In 1993, the widely circulated magazine *Liao Wang* [*Outlook*] conducted an extensive survey on China's passenger vehicle production and produced a report conveying immense criticism. Consumers demanded a reduction of tariffs on vehicle imports. Calls for liberalization of the auto sector were strong.

The 1990s also witnessed the arrival of more foreign automakers; indeed, almost all major global players were "knocking [on] the door of China," according to industry watchers.[23] Western MNCs proactively and directly lobbied policy makers, industrial ministries, and SOEs in the auto sector. In the parts and components subsector, Taiwanese investors soon arrived. Interpersonal relations between Taiwanese investors and Chinese policy makers were extensive, most notably between President Jiang Zemin and Zhonghua Auto chairman Wu Shunwen – both natives of Jiangsu Province.

In 1993 alone, there were sixty-five high-profile meetings and visits to China by major Western automakers. In the same year, eighteen technology licenses were signed and forty-seven pieces of automobile production equipment were transferred. Western MNCs pursued direct contact with top leaders, high-ranking officials, and major SOEs involved in the sector, seeking to form elite-level external networks. On July 8, 1994, the CEO of General Motors (GM), Jack Smith, met with Jiang Zemin to present the company's newest electric sedan to the Science Commission of the State Council. Although it entered China later than Germany's Volkswagen, GM was more active (and successful) in establishing JVs in Beijing and Shanghai.[24]

Behind this flurry of MNC-led external networks was the painful recognition by the Chinese government that industrial policy in the auto sector had failed.[25]

[23] Author's interviews conducted at the China Automobile Association headquarters [Qiche xiehui zong gonghui] and China's Ministry of Science and Technology, Beijing, July 2004 and November 2005.

[24] *Zhongguo qiche gongye tongji nianjian* [*PRC Automobile Industry Yearbook*], 1994 edition.

[25] "Zhongguo qiche gongye chanye zhengce de yanbian" [Evolution of Industrial Policies in China's Automobile Industry], *Shangwu zhoukan* [*Business Weekly*], April 6, 2004.

As one auto minister complained to a visiting Taiwanese industrial delegation, "Chinese medicine has been tried to no avail, Western medicine has been tried to no avail, and [a] magical potion has also been tried. Nothing seems to work" [*zhongyao chiguole, xiyao chiguole, pianfang yeyongguole, mei zhaoer*].[26] In 1994, as calls for change mounted, the national government passed a new auto policy. Tariffs on sedans were reduced from 220 percent to 150 percent, and tariffs on mini-cars were reduced from 180 percent to 110 percent.[27] The 1994 policy also loosened the conditions for establishing and managing JVs. Although large JVs remained under the purview of the central government, the majority of JV projects were decentralized and overseen by local governments. Technology imports were also made easier: in 1995 alone, China signed 313 technology transfer contracts with foreign automakers, including whole car projects, engines, parts, and components.[28]

Although diaspora entrepreneurs helped to build export-oriented electronics production in China, the auto sector was conversely domestic market-oriented. Western automakers came to China seeking a share of what was becoming the world's largest passenger vehicle market. Existing state automakers welcomed JVs' expansion (or maintenance) of their domestic market shares. The 1994 Automobile Industrial Policy Guidelines reiterated and formalized the guidelines created in 1986. The objective was the same: "to build China's automobile industry into a pillar industry of the nation." Tariffs remained as high as 150 percent, and the government stressed the importance of localization in all negotiated JVs.

Chinese SOEs monitored new entrants while using external collaboration. The government industrial policy discouraged the formation of new auto companies and stipulated that central licensing was needed to manufacture vehicles in China. Private firms had difficulty obtaining such authorization. Western automakers needed to form partnerships with the big SOEs if they wanted to come to China. This situation was very different from that in the electronics industry, where private companies emerged and grew by drawing on diaspora networks operating in South China.

To be sure, auto manufacturing had higher capital and technology thresholds for entry. The gap between FDI liberalization in automotives and electronics, however, cannot be sufficiently explained by sectoral differences. Even in electronics manufacturing, nondiaspora investors did not invest much in the early stage. For example, when Japanese electronics makers came to SEZs in the 1980s, they reported a poor investment environment and only began to set up manufacturing plants in the 1990s, at the same time as auto sector investors. On the other hand, automaking is not as daunting as it appears: a rural entrepreneur, Li Shufu, learned to make cars and founded Geely in 1998, and

[26] *Liao Wang*, 1994, no.12, p. 15.
[27] *Zhongguo qiche chanye zhengce* [*China's Automobile Industrial Policies*], 1994.
[28] *Zhongguo qiche gongye tongji nianjian* [*China's Automobile Statistics Yearbook*], 2001 edition.

the company's performance rapidly surpassed that of SOEs. The lack of diaspora entrepreneurs to provide technology and capital in the early stage was clearly a factor that caused automaking liberalization to lag behind the electronics sector.

In the auto sector, private entrants were more inhibited than they were in the electronics sector. Were diaspora networks available, they would have identified the market potential in China sooner and overcome existing barriers by working with domestic producers earlier and more persistently, comparable to diaspora entrepreneurs in the electronics sector. Since the development of Taiwan's auto and parts manufacturers in the mid-1990s, diaspora firms have fashioned investment patterns different from those of Western automakers.

Foreign direct investment liberalization in the Chinese auto industry was analogous to India's, where indigenous players adopted a similar strategy: welcoming MNC partnerships to enhance their domestic advantage, but resisting FDI liberalization that would herald more external competitors. Table 7.3 includes all the auto sector JVs emerging in the 1990s. There were more than in the previous decade, and their sources were more diversified; yet all these companies, with the exception of Taiwan's Zhonghua and Korea's Daewoo, held minority or equal shares relative to their Chinese partners. Zhonghua was the only "foreign" automaker that had complete equity control of its subsidiary on the Mainland. Daewoo, a small operation in Guilin, had 60 percent equity control. Furthermore, foreign investors had to specify in JV contracts those segments that their manufacturing would focus on. The concentration of foreign investment followed the Chinese state automakers, as Map 3 indicates.

Foreign direct investment liberalization in automaking was import-substituting in nature. With the establishment of these JVs, imports of passenger cars quickly decreased. Such a pattern suggests that auto sector JVs were formed to circumvent high tariffs. Japan, once the largest source of China's passenger vehicle imports, established six JVs in China from 1993 to 1996. Chinese imports sharply declined from 162,227 units in 1994 to 2,963 in 1997. The figure recovered slightly in 1998. Similar patterns held for Germany, France, the United States, Italy, and Korea.

The biggest pressure for liberalization in the auto industry came from China's negotiations over WTO membership. Starting in 1997, PRC policy makers launched efforts to negotiate terms to join the WTO – a decision reflecting the general economic conditions in the country rather than in the auto sector. Yet the sector was heavily affected by these negotiations because Western countries considered entering the auto market crucial to their business interests in China (Lardy 2002). If China were to join the WTO, this sector needed to be open. Chinese policy makers conceded. In 1997, tariffs on autos were reduced from 150 to 100 percent and then to 80 percent within a year. External pressures, however, intensified domestic resistance. Facing global pressure, left-leaning intellectuals and technocrats called for the development of "Chinese"

TABLE 7.3. *China's Auto Sector Joint Ventures in the 1990s*

Foreign Company	Chinese Partner	Foreign Equity (%)	Year	Products
Japanese Toyota	Jinee	51	1992	Minivans
Japanese Toyota	Xiamen Kinlong	40	1992	Light buses
Japanese Isuzu		30	1993	Light trucks
Japanese Nissan	Zhengzhou	5	1993	Pickups
Japanese Suzuki	Changan	50	1993	Mini cars
Japanese Suzuki	Chongqing	49	1993	Sedans
Japanese Daihatsu	Tianjin	50	1995	Mini cars, light trucks
Japanese Honda		50	1998	Passenger cars
American Flexible		50	1992	Large and medium buses
American GM	Jinbei	30	1992	Mini trucks
American GM	Shanghai	50	1997	Sedans
French Citroen	Shenlong	30	1990	Passenger cars
French Citroen	Dongfeng	30	1992	Sedans
French Renault	Sanjiang	45	1993	Minivans
French Renault	Sanjiang	45	1993	Light buses
German VW	FAW	40	1990	Cars
German Benz	Nanfang	45	1995	Vans
German Benz	Yaxing	50	1996	Light and medium buses
Italian IVESCO SPA	Nanjing	50	1996	Light buses
Korean Daewoo	Guilin	60	1993	Luxury buses
Swedish Volvo		50	1994	Buses
Taiwanese Yulong		50	1997	Passenger car
Taiwanese Zhonghua		100	1998	Passenger car

Source: *Zhongguo qiche gongye* [*Automotive Industry of China*], Tianjin: China Automotive Technology and Research Center, 1999.

automakers and connected indigenous automobile production with technological nationalism.[29]

The 1990s as a whole confirms that although external pressure, helped by domestic consensus for change, led to the initiation of FDI liberalization, strong internal networks continued to prevent consolidation – as seen in remaining restrictions on foreign investors. The disjuncture between initiation and consolidation seen in the auto sector was uncommon in China, where diffusion of FDI liberalization was generally rapid, and yet similar to India's, where such

[29] *Gaige neican* [*Internal Reports on Reform*], no. 21, 1999.

disjunctures have prevailed. Despite very different political regimes in the two countries, the story of the auto industry in China can be retold in India. The social networks – a lack of entrepreneurial diasporas, the dominance of Western MNCs, and domestic interests in protection – apply to China's auto sector and India in general, with the exception of India's software industry, as the next chapter explains.

Diaspora Involvement: Although Limited, Helped FDI Liberalization

Diaspora entrepreneurs, central to electronics development, had limited strength and involvement in the auto sector. As diaspora auto companies emerged in Taiwan and Hong Kong, they were immediately and deeply involved in Mainland auto manufacturing. In 1997, Taiwan's Yulon Motors invested $200 million to build a massive Southeast Auto City in Fujian and brought a large number of Taiwanese parts and components manufacturers to southern China, earlier than the arrival of Western parts manufacturers.[30] In 1998, Taiwan's whole car manufacturers Taiwan Ford, He Tai, and San Yang set up factories on the Mainland, bringing dozens of suppliers and their component investments along with them. By June 1998, a Fujian–Taiwan auto project was in full swing, involving the first installment of investment of more than $300 million.[31] Although China resisted wholly foreign-owned companies in auto manufacturing, Taiwan's China Motor (*Zhonghua*) held sole ownership of its subsidiary to produce passenger cars on the Mainland.[32]

Hong Kong's own auto sector was small, but served as a key testing ground for Chinese automakers seeking to export to advanced markets. FAW, for example, after achieving success in domestic markets, envisioned itself selling a range of both luxury and low-end passenger cars to developed countries. In 2007, it launched an ambitious plan to use Hong Kong as a bridge to other advanced markets.[33] Hong Kong's auto market is considerably different from that of the United States, but FAW reasoned that Hong Kong, as an advanced capitalist market with institutions different from those on the Mainland, would enhance FAW's brand recognition and help it to build sales channels to global markets.

China's Chief Automakers and FDI Liberalization

Automobile companies constitute important social networks that shape FDI liberalization in China. Analysis of these automakers demonstrates the change

30 Taiwan, *jingji shibao*, April 4, 1997.

31 Taiwan, *jingji shibao*, June 27, 1998.

32 Taiwan, *jingji shibao*, April 7, 1998.

33 Although Hong Kong reverted to China in 1997, its economic system remained separate from the Mainland. Isabella Chan, "FAW Group Corporation: Launching the First Chinese-made Car in Hong Kong," the University of Hong Kong, case Ref. 08/400C, 2008.

and continuity in the interests and interactions of key players in the sector. The selected companies and their FDI liberalization support the general findings described here. One, the dominant external networks were Western automakers (including Japanese), and their investment was slow coming. Two, their early collaborations with foreigners was somewhat mistrustful and competitive. When Western investors came in a big way in the more recent period, they generated intense nationalist backlashes in the country. Individual auto companies, to be sure, showed significant variations. Yet, as a sector, FDI liberalization in the auto industry was much harder to achieve than in the electronics sector.

SOE Joint Ventures with Western MNCs

State-owned enterprises dominated China's automaking, and SOEs' collaboration with Western automakers constituted the primary mode of FDI liberalization in the auto sector. The SOEs' internal structures and relationships with governments have affected their external collaborations, as revealed in their specific corporate histories. Thun (2006) provides an extensive account of the reasonably successful development of the Shanghai-Volkswagen venture. Here, I present Beijing, Guangzhou, and FAW, which experienced more difficulty in opening to FDI.

The Beijing Internal Combustion Engine Factory – the core division of Beijing Auto – began manufacturing engines in the 1950s with technology imported from the Soviet Union. For decades, the factory was under the purview of the Ministry of Agriculture, and its product line was tied to suppliers and end-users within the Ministry. In the 1970s, the Factory was transferred to the Ministry of Machinery Industry and then again to Beijing Auto in the 1980s. Despite administrative changes, however, it remained largely independent because its production line involved firms outside the company. Unwilling to channel its profits into Beijing Auto, the Internal Combustion Factory essentially transformed its parent company into an empty shell without core units of manufacturing or investment.

Beijing Auto's weakness in the 1980s and the 1990s, however, strengthened its later collaboration with South Korean Hyundai – a newcomer to China. In May 2002, Beijing Auto signed a contract with Hyundai, and by October the Chinese government had approved the JV, leading to the establishment of "Beijing Hyundai." Four months later, Beijing Hyundai rolled out its first mid-sized sedan, the EF Sonata. Due to Beijing Auto's weak position among state automakers and Hyundai's low profile compared to that of Western MNCs, industry watchers were skeptical of Beijing Hyundai's prospects for success in the Chinese market. The company, however, grew rapidly, outperforming other major SOE-MNC alliances. In 2005, Beijing Hyundai sold 234,000 Elantras in China, making it the leading compact model of the year.[34] In that year, all new

[34] Jae-Gu Kim and Mooweon Rhee, "Hyundai Motor Company in China," Case IB-91, Stanford University, 2008.

taxis in the capital were Elantras, due to the government's preference for using local cars [*Beijing che*].

Beijing Hyundai's success reveals three things: first, the perception of failure at Beijing Auto made the automaker eager for external partnership; second, Beijing's local government played an important role by designating the Elantra (assembled at Beijing Hyundai) as the new taxi model in the lead up to the 2008 Olympics; and third, Hyundai's success also lies in its efforts to work through local social networks and build public relations. Although Beijing Hyundai primarily assembled parts and components directly imported from South Korea, its Elantra model was widely viewed in Beijing as a local car. This perception was important for its broad acceptance in the capital.

As with Beijing Hyundai, Guangzhou Auto had a complicated development history and fragmented internal interests that rendered external collaboration difficult. Yangcheng, the principal manufacturer of Guangzhou Auto, was created in 1958 under the control of the Transportation Bureau of the municipal government. It had little to do with Junda, which was under the authority of the Ministry of Machinery and Electronics. Subsidiaries of Guangzhou Auto were spread across six different ministries and bureaus. When the company formed a JV with Peugeot in 1985, internal division continued. Despite calls for unified government oversight, the heads of each respective ministry were concerned that their power would be diminished if they let the large firms slip away. The interests of individual ministries prevailed. The JV was ultimately viewed as unsuccessful by both the Chinese and the French, and before long Peugeot withdrew. Guangzhou (the capital city of Guangdong), a pioneer in electronics, lagged in automobile production and only became competitive in domestic markets in the new century when it partnered with Honda and Toyota.

The FAW, located in northeastern China, was a prioritized, national-level SOE. In 1966, it produced the first and only Chinese indigenous passenger vehicle, the *hongqi*. It was not only Chairman Mao's favorite car, but also a symbol of Chinese industrial self-reliance. Unlike other SOEs, FAW remained largely unscathed by the Cultural Revolution, but during reform it experienced significant difficulties. It was the slowest among major automakers to form external collaborations. Only in 1990 did FAW sign its first JV contract with German Volkswagen, and even then its main motive was to unload employee burden on its foreign partner. This led to scores of complaints by Volkswagen. The lack of trust, typical of SOE-MNC JVs, slowed the growth of FAW in the 1990s.

Since the late 1990s, China has become one of the world's largest auto markets and has attracted inflows of technology, expertise, and capital from Western automakers. It is presently the largest auto producer in the world. Not only have state automakers grown substantially, but indigenous players have also emerged in the recent decade. Compared to electronics, this sector's liberalization has taken much longer, and its effects have differed. Contrary to the electronics industry, which became a major export juggernaut, automobile manufacturing in China has primarily served the domestic market.

New Indigenous Players in Chinese Automobiles

The aforementioned SOE-MNC JVs monopolized China's passenger car market until the late 1990s, when a handful of newcomers emerged. These newcomers had humble and covert operations at their outset: the government discouraged new entrants, and foreign automakers seldom deemed them as worthy partners. As these new automakers gradually increased their market shares (and some even began exporting), they became embroiled in intellectual property lawsuits filed by foreign companies. Paradoxically, however, they gained national fame and support from such lawsuits. To illustrate such interactions among state-owned, domestic, and international automakers, I examine Geely and Chery. The first case demonstrates acquired government and public support after growth, whereas the second reveals complicated interactions between the government and foreign MNCs in the intertwined process of nationalism and globalization.

Geely (*Jili*), located roughly a four-hour drive south of Shanghai, was the largest (and perhaps the only) private automaker in China. It began to manufacture passenger cars in 1998, when its founder dissembled two Mercedes Benzes to learn the art of automobile manufacturing. By 2003, the company had already exported cars abroad and sold patents to other developing countries. Geely proved that small-scale manufacturing, prevalent in electronics, also worked for manufacturing automobiles. In fact, from 1998 to 2003, Geely accrued domestic market shares and exports without attracting much visibility. Then, in 2004, it made its initial public offering (IPO) in Hong Kong and became a media sensation on the Mainland. As a real "indigenous" automaker, Geely received cheers from national bureaucrats and the public alike. From 1998 to 2004, there were thirty-two articles written about the company.[35] From 2005 to 2009, there were 163 articles on the company.[36] And when Geely tendered acquisition of Volvo with Ford, media coverage of the company skyrocketed. Within four months, there were 241 articles on Geely published in major newspapers.[37] The Geely-Volvo deal was widely acclaimed as the "Lenovo-IBM deal of the auto sector" and became a symbol of industrial nationalism.[38]

Chery (*Qirui*) was a company based in Anhui that arose from the consolidation of five companies in the province. Unlike Geely, Chery had strong backing from the local government but was largely covert in operation from the national state. The company expanded its domestic sales aggressively in the 2000s (85,000 units in 2003, 189,000 units in 2005, and 381,000 units in 2007) and was ambitious in going abroad. In 2003, it set up a CKD assembly plant in Iran.

[35] See CNKI, China Core Newspaper Database.

[36] Ibid.

[37] Ibid.

[38] "Geely-Volvo: Creating Lenovo-IBM in the Automobile Sector," *Zhongguo lianhe shangbao [Joint Business Newspaper]*, December 28, 2009.

In the next two years, it built similar plants in Russia, Ukraine, Egypt, and Uruguay (Farmer 2007).

During Chery's ascent, its intellectual property lawsuit with GM gained it public support. Chery's most popular mini-car, QQ, was similar in design to GM's Spark. Yet, using its cost-saving manufacturing and management structure, Chery was able to sell QQ at just two-thirds of the price of Spark, quickly eroding Spark's market share in China. GM was not only concerned about sales of Spark in China; it also worried about Spark's sales abroad because Chery made plans to export QQ to other markets. The lawsuit became a rallying point for Chinese nationalism against MNCs. It was no longer a matter of whether Chery had violated GM's intellectual property rights; it had become an issue of Chinese companies fighting a Western giant. GM's main concern, however, was not with losing the lawsuit; rather, it focused on its relationship with the Chinese government. The Chinese media alleged that GM used lawsuits to emasculate an aspiring Chinese company. In May 2004, a Beijing-based business newspaper ran a story entitled, "Why Do MNCs Hate Chinese Enterprises with Their Own Intellectual Property Rights?"[39]

Differences in legal provisions in China and America further complicated GM's lawsuit. In the United States, copyright law protects elements of the design of individual vehicles without explicitly requiring registration of those elements. In China, the design itself is required to be patented. Thus, Chery registered many parts and elements of QQ which were similar to those of Spark, as required under Chinese patent law. Based on this legal difference, the Chinese court ruled in favor of Chery and found that a similar appearance did not necessarily represent a violation of intellectual property rights. Given the intense nationalist atmosphere in China, GM did not pursue the issue further. After all, GM had a considerable interest in China that required it to maintain good relations with the host government and public.

The social network analysis demonstrates that the internal and external networks of Chinese automakers were different from those of electronics producers. In electronics, the most successful manufacturers were firms with strong connections to diaspora entrepreneurs in Hong Kong and Taiwan, whereas state electronics producers were outcompeted. In automobile production, state manufacturers dominated and fashioned strategic collaborations with Western MNCs. Such external ties were difficult to maintain and resulted in strong nationalism in the auto sector. However, the analysis of key automakers does show that industries with limited diaspora networks and strong domestic interests can be liberalized, although the diffusion process is more difficult, and the scope of liberalism is more constrained. These two sectors in China, electronics

[39] See Liu He, "Qirui hefa caishang juren jianbang" [Chery Built its QQ Legally], *Zhongguo zhishi chanquan bao [China IPR Newspaper]*, September 21, 2004; Ge Zhiyu, "Waiguan xiangsi ye youcuo?" [Is Anything Wrong with Similarities in Appearance?], *Guoji shangbao [International Business]*, September 22, 2004.

and automobiles, indeed epitomize the two pathways of FDI liberalization hypothesized in Chapter 2.

FDI IN OTHER SECTORS

Diaspora networks and domestic resistance influence cross-sector variation in FDI liberalization. A large division in China occurred between light manufacturing and heavy industries. One may argue that nationalism embodied in heavy industries (often called "strategic" industries) is sufficient to prevent FDI liberalization, with or without diaspora networks. The cases of infrastructure, transportation, and property development are indicative of just the opposite. Core to national autonomy, these sectors deeply involved diaspora entrepreneurs during reform (see Chapters 3 and 5). Further, intrasector variations are considerable. Within individual sectors, the segments with diaspora networks and those without experienced different forms of FDI liberalization.

When China's reform began, light manufacturing was decentralized to local authorities. Except for diaspora-invested manufacturers in SEZs, the national government required new entrants to have state licenses and ownership. Decentralization allowed local governments in South China to support nascent private firms and diaspora entrepreneurs, whereas local officials elsewhere sponsored SOEs. The performance of new entrants and state manufacturers diverged. Shanghai's SOEs had historically dominated light manufacturing industries, but by the mid-1980s, their advantage had diminished compared to firms in Guangdong. It was easy to draw the conclusion that FDI (actually diaspora investment) was superior to SOEs. In addition to the electronics manufacturing sector, the toys, textiles, shoes, leather goods, and sporting products sectors, among others, experienced the same transition from socialism to FDI based on the early success of liberalization in these sectors. In these sectors, diaspora entrepreneurs played a significant role in production, exports, and domestic sales. Also, in places with substantial diaspora networks, private indigenous producers emerged and would go on to become global players in these industries.

By contrast, heavy industries experienced a generally different pattern of FDI liberalization – a pattern (represented by the auto sector) a lot like India's. Foreign direct investment liberalization in heavy industries started late, was restricted, and proceeded slowly. Similar sectors included steel and energy, where Western MNCs entered into SOE-MNC cooperation, but with unsatisfactory results. Indigenous players opposed FDI liberalization while allowing technology input from abroad.

Steel manufacturers were privileged during the socialist period. The government was their main investor and producer, spinning off major SOEs such as Beijing's Capital Iron and Steel and Anshan Iron and Steel in Liaoning province. When reform began in 1979, steel companies transferred technology from advanced countries, yet no FDI liberalization was attempted. Steel producers continued to enjoy direct connections to top planners and influenced self-serving policies (Kennedy 2005). Steel companies' monopolies over China's protected markets have recently harmed their prospects for globalization. Basking in domestic dominance, large steel makers generally lack the tenacity to persist in overseas markets.

The petroleum industry was another heavy sector in which the state played a leading role. When reform began, foreign MNCs were interested in accessing China's petroleum production. Bureaucrats in this industry (dubbed "the petroleum clique") were also interested in foreign technological and financial collaborations. The "petroleum clique," which included some of the most powerful officials in the government,[40] established high-ranking SOEs such as the China National Offshore Oil Corporation to broker the country's relations with foreigners in the area of energy. Foreign collaboration was difficult, however. Different agencies fought for the authority to handle external transactions, and each wanted to maximize its relative gains and maintain independence in its dealings with foreigners (Lieberthal and Lampton 1992, 208).

The unique role of diaspora investors can also be seen in sectors such as infrastructure, transportation, and property development. These sectors embodied strong socialist ideologies and nationalist sentiments in China. Although the government generally discouraged FDI in these sectors, diaspora entrepreneurs have played an important part by contributing capital and technology to develop China's infrastructure suitable for manufacturing sectors.[41] Their role in China's infrastructure development stems from two factors: first, diaspora investors had gained significant experience and resources from developing Hong Kong, Macao, and Southeast Asia prior to China's opening; and second, they developed trusting interpersonal ties to individuals in the central government, as well as to local officials. By working through social networks at both the top and local levels, diaspora investors were able to help transform China's infrastructure and property development.

CONCLUSION

Cross-sector analysis refines what we found regarding China's FDI liberalization at the national level. Although China is a case demonstrating speedy diffusion of FDI liberalization, industries that lacked strong diaspora connections had difficulty opening to FDI and continued to oppose whole-scale liberalization. Speedy diffusion was demonstrated in electronics, where strong diaspora networks and

[40] Representatives included State Capital Construction Commission and Foreign Investment Control Commission Chairman Gu Mu; Minister of Coal Gao Yangwen; Minister of Metallurgy Tang Ke; Minister of Petroleum Song Zhenming; Minister of Chemical Industries Sun Jingwen; Minister of the Fifth Ministry of Machine Building Zhang Zhen; and Beijing Mayor Lin Hujia.

[41] *Jingji yanjiu cankao* [*Report on Economic Research*], December 30, 1981, pp. 27–31.

weak domestic resistance interactively shaped the process of FDI liberalization. Foreign direct investment has played a central part in the industry's growth and globalization. The auto sector, by contrast, had weak diaspora networks and strong internal networks that resulted in limited external collaboration. Western MNCs came to China, but they were unable to play as effective a role in policy as diaspora entrepreneurs had in electronics. When the industry was forced open by China's WTO negotiation near the end of the 1990s, technology transfers from Western automakers helped Chinese auto companies to become sizable producers within the country. Their ambition to export to the world remains elusive.

The social network theory underscores the importance of diaspora networks, but it does not negate the roles of government agencies, domestic companies, and Western MNCs. Supportive governments at the national and local levels were instrumental to diaspora investors in textiles, electronics, and other industries where FDI liberalization experienced rapid diffusion. Indigenous entrepreneurs that drew on diasporas' managerial, financial, and technical strength further hastened China's industrialization and globalization. Western MNCs were the end users of textiles and electronics produced by diaspora-invested and indigenous companies. Diaspora entrepreneurs relied on Western MNCs for more advanced technology.

This electronics–auto comparison shows that, other things being equal, diasporas had an easier time interacting with domestic actors to shift socialist economic ideas and were more willing to transfer their funds and technology to help homeland development than were Western investors. The fact that Western electronics makers did not invest in large measure until the 1990s, a similar entry point as automakers, and the fact that a rural entrepreneur became the only private automaker and main auto exporter in China, although much later, prove that sectoral differences in technology and capital intensity are not sufficient explanations for the divergence between China's electronics and automobiles. Diaspora networks have to be brought in to account for the two pathways of FDI liberalization across sectors.

These general findings from China's cross-sector analysis also apply to India. With propitious mixtures of strong diaspora networks and comparably weak domestic resistance, specific sectors in India have had successful diffusion of FDI liberalization, as the next chapter investigates.

8

FDI Liberalization in India's Informatics and Autos

India's informatics and auto sectors correspond to China's electronics and auto sectors. As in China, foreign direct investment (FDI) liberalization has been clearly different in these two sectors in India. The informatics sector has had strong diaspora networks and weak domestic resistance. The diffusion of FDI liberalization was reasonably smooth, intrasector variations notwithstanding. The auto sector, by contrast, inherited a long history and well-knit domestic industry interests. Foreign direct investment liberalization in autos was difficult, and changes were more modest. Indian immigrants in informatics, however, differed from China's diaspora entrepreneurs in electronics and acted most clearly as bridges between homeland and international markets and helped indigenous companies to find global commerce, finance, and technology. In China, on the contrary, diaspora entrepreneurs were mainly investors. Another contrast between the two countries' immigrants is that whereas Chinese entrepreneurial diasporas had sectoral strength in electronics hardwarc manufacturing, India's had more success in software services, and a clear intrasector divergence ensued between the two countries' electronics development.

INDIA'S DIASPORA AND INFORMATICS

The Chinese experience demonstrates the importance of diaspora networks to FDI liberalization (see Chapters 3, 5, and 7). India has a large number of emigrants, spread primarily across South Asia, the Gulf, Britain, and the United States. Indian emigrants to the United States were more recent, and many worked at American companies or were entrepreneurs in Silicon Valley. These U.S.-based Indian diasporas most closely resemble the Chinese diaspora in East Asia and have strong presence in global markets. When India began its economic reform, these diasporas circulated back their experiences and capital and connected India's production with global markets. Directly and indirectly, they helped to generate growth and facilitate globalization in informatics.

India's informatics sector includes software, computer hardware, electronics, and R&D. The speedy diffusion model examined here is based on the software services industry. It is in this fairly new and human-capital intensive industry that India has achieved remarkable growth rarely seen in other sectors or in other developing nations. The similarity between FDI liberalization in India's software services and China in general was robust: moderate openness led to impressive growth, and visible success led to rapid diffusion of openness. India's electronics hardware industry, on the other hand, featured different FDI liberalization. It began with "dislodging multinationals" to a modest and contested opening in the 1990s and gained momentum after strong success in the software industry. Such diffusion from software to hardware subsectors made FDI liberalization in informatics as a whole more profound than in other sectors, such as automobiles.

Compared to other sectors, it is *not* that domestic interest groups were weak or nonexistent in informatics; rather, these indigenous players' ideas and incentives were different from protectionism in other sectors. At the top, policy makers in informatics were educated abroad and had ties to foreign companies. At one point they were "dislodging multinationals," but once they recognized the need for external collaborations, their external ties revived quickly. Companies in this sector grew during reform and drew capital, technology, and market access from abroad. Information technology (IT) workers particularly sought jobs at foreign companies and embraced their arrival. And local governments, which were criticized as obstructionist in many sectors, likewise embraced FDI in informatics. Again, the perception that India could succeed in the IT sector, as well as the idea that incoming FDI benefits domestic industry and the national economy, are factors not present in other industrial sectors.

External networks that participated in the development of India's informatics sector included both diasporas and Western multinational corporations (MNCs). In informatics, Indian diasporas' impacts were similar to those of overseas Chinese. Like Chinese immigrants, Indian diasporas connected their homeland with the world market and acted as conduits of technology and capital into India. Also as in China (although on a smaller scale), immigrants led the beginning of many infrastructural developments in the informatics sector. Sam Pitroda, for example, received a doctoral degree and founded a company in the United States before his return to India in 1984. Thanks to Rajiv Gandhi's support, Pitroda laid the foundation for India's telecom infrastructure, vital to the subsequent growth of the software industry.

The Early History: Dislodging MNCs in Hardware Manufacturing

India produced its first minicomputer in 1978, three years ahead of IBM's comparable model. Three decades later, however, India's computer hardware consumption and manufacturing lagged behind the world, and Indian consumers

TABLE 8.1. *Policy Developments in India's Informatics Sector*

Period	
Pre-reform	Emergence of new technocrats; "dislodging multinationals"
1980s	Rise of external networks: diaspora, multinational corporations, and the growth of domestic private companies
1990s	Intensified diaspora networks; domestic firms orienting toward the U.S. market
2000s	Software industry took off; intensified networks of domestic firms, American companies, and Indian diasporas

used outdated models.[1] All the while, India was becoming the world's major destination for software services outsourcing. Why were hardware and software developments in India so different? The answers to this question also speak to differences between the informatics and auto sectors in general. Table 8.1 presents the three development periods in informatics.

The development of India's informatics sector has its origins in state structures. In the 1960s, the government formulated goals for developing indigenous informatics. The driving force was the Bhabha Committee, which comprised leading bureaucrats Vikram Sarabhai, M. G. K. Menon, A. Parthasarathi, N. Seshagiri, and A. S. Rao – all experts with impressive scientific credentials. Possessing technological expertise on par with their fellow graduates from elite Western universities, members of the Bhabha Committee saw no reason why India could not produce computers on its own.

Strong technocracy and yet slow liberalization of hardware manufacturing suggest that bureaucratic strength may prevent policy makers from pursuing FDI. Well trained at elite universities in the West, such bureaucrats saw no reason to yield India's market to foreign companies and sought to produce India's own brands. As they gained influence within the national government, technocrats questioned the value of having foreign companies in India. The government implemented a set of industrial policies known as "dislodging multinationals" (Encarnation 1989). IBM, for example, had been manufacturing in India since 1963, but in 1978, it was pressured by the Bhabha Committee to either dilute its stake or leave the country. Faced with this ultimatum, IBM decided to withdraw from the Indian market and move its production to Australia and Singapore to serve its remaining Indian customers. Coca-Cola met the same fate in the dislodging multinational wave and left India.

After IBM was expelled, the government assigned the responsibility for developing indigenous informatics to a few state agencies. The Department of Electronics (DOE) and a corresponding Electronics Commission were formed in 1970–71 and remained organizationally intact throughout the next two decades.

[1] The author's own observation and experience in India.

The DOE's leading officials came largely from the Bhabha Committee, which was closely associated with the Electronic Corporation of India (ECI) – the company later chartered to manufacture computers. To preserve ECI's monopoly status, the government discouraged private capital from entering computer manufacturing. In 1972, for example, DOE and the Electronics Commission ignored a dozen applications by private companies looking to manufacture minicomputers. The only exception was made to the Tata Group, which had tight connections to leading members of the Bhabha Committee, DOE, and ECI. In 1968, Tata launched Tata Consultancy Services (TCS), which would go on to become the leading player in the industry.

The state monopoly in the informatics sector was diluted in the late 1970s when private entrants began to emerge, thanks to the growing influence of private businessmen. In 1976, for example, a few managers of the Delhi Cloth Mills (owned by one of India's major business families) established Hindustan Computers Ltd. (HCL). HCL produced the first Indian-made microcomputers in 1978, the same year as Apple and three years before IBM's PC. In 1980, WIPRO came into being as a direct offspring of an established business house specialized in cooking oil. It became the second largest hardware manufacturer in India in the 1980s. In 1981, seven entrepreneurs started Infosys, which later became the leading software services exporter in India. These private companies benefited from economic liberalization in the 1980s. Foreign players, including diaspora professionals, also came to play a bigger role in this decade.

Rajiv's Passion for Technology and the Growth of Informatics in India

Rajiv Gandhi played an important role in the development of India's IT industries. He had a penchant for modern technology and was frustrated with India's technological backwardness. In 1984, upon assuming premiership, he was ready to implement policies that would enhance India's technological edge – either via private companies or by inviting Western investors.

Under Rajiv's influence, members of the DOE backed liberalization. N. Seshagiri, founder of the Indian Informatics Center, authored directives liberalizing the rules for investment and imports in 1984 and 1986, respectively. Other DOE members greeted this change with support rather than opposition. The growing influence of private producers changed the power base of DOE and shifted its attitude toward liberalization. When asked what he thought were appropriate criteria for judging the department's performance, one DOE official replied, "Industry reaction is the best gauge of the DOE's success. If you want to know if I am doing a good job, ask WIPRO, HCL, or TCS" (Evans 1995, 115). Domestic companies, however, were interested in technological collaboration with advanced companies in the West, not in sharing domestic markets with them. The number of Westerners entering India was small.

India's software services exports, initially "IT body shopping," started in the 1970s, when TCS sent twelve employees to deliver a software project to the company's first American customer in 1974. Five years later, TCS founded its first software services office in New York. IT body shopping grew in the 1980s, followed by another major increase in the 1990s thanks to U.S. visa relaxation for skilled workers. The visa restriction – limiting each worker to a maximum of six years – helped to circulate diaspora connections and American experience back to India, paving the way for the software industrial takeoff in the country. Throughout reform, America was the most important partner for India's software industry, and the rise of diaspora networks between these two countries intensified this connection further.

The role of diaspora professionals was clear in TCS. The company was India's biggest and grew rapidly in the 1970s and 1980s, possessing an absolute advantage in exports among Indian companies by 1980. In its early history, TCS hired Indian diasporas in the United States to help grow its services business in America. L. S. Kanodia, an MIT PhD, led TCS in the 1970s. Then, Kanodia quit TCS and founded his own company, Datamatics; by the end of the 1980s, Datamatics had become the fifth largest software company in India. Diaspora entrepreneurs would become even more prominent after the 1991 liberalization.

Among Western MNCs, the first to operate in India was Texas Instruments, which arrived in 1985 with its own satellite communications equipment. The company allowed the Indian government to use its satellite equipment for international communications and encouraged the government to relax restrictions on the import of foreign software. It also demonstrated to Indians that IT professionals could earn export revenue while working for a foreign company and provided a model of external networks that persisted (CASI 2005). Other multinational corporations also came to India. Microsoft set up a subsidiary in 1987, which quickly grew into a major part of the company's global operation chain. Today, Microsoft's India Development Center constitutes its biggest unit outside its headquarters in Redmond, Washington. Another IT giant, Hewlett-Packard, which sold computers in India during the 1970s, set up an office in Bangalore in 1989 with a staff of ten. By 2005, it employed more than 1,000 people in its Bangalore office. Nortel came to India in 1989 via ties to large Indian companies, such as Infosys, Wipro, TCS, and Silicom Automation Systems (CASI 2005).

Software Took Off in India

India's informatics sector as a whole had grown steadily, but the software segment accomplished stellar successes in export markets. In the 1990s alone, India's informatics sector expanded twenty-five times and became a $10 billion industry – with two-thirds of these gains attributed to software. In 1991–1992, Indian software production amounted to only $150 million, but by 2000 it was a staggering $5.7 billion.[2] The software industry's performance in the global market truly differentiated it from other industries. Of the

[2] "India Information Technology Superpower," *The Korea Herald*, January 26, 2001.

$5.7 billion generated in 2000, $4 billion was from exports. More than a third of the *Fortune* 500 companies outsourced their software needs to India that year.[3]

The importance of software exports to India's national economy has risen rapidly since 2001. In 2000/01, software exports constituted 1.2 percent of gross domestic product (GDP). In 2007/08, India's software exports were 3.2 percent of GDP, reaching $37 billion. In 2011, India's IT revenues were $100 billion, accounting for 7.5 percent of GDP and 26 percent of merchandise exports. Growing economic clout offered the software industry a strong voice in national policy making and influenced public perception of liberalization – although this was confined to the well-to-do segments of society.[4]

Due to compelling gains from and high dependence on the global market, FDI liberalization progressed stridently in this sector. The software industry began exploring external collaboration in the 1980s, and these collaborations evolved into influential external networks. When India launched its industrial policy in July 1991, which allowed foreign investors to hold 51 percent of equity in joint ventures (JVs), informatics was part of this liberalization. As a new industry, software had no qualitative restriction (QR) system that capped imports in many sectors, and the 1991 opening to FDI had an immediate impact. Other sectors continued to be protected by QR, which was to phase out only at the turn of the century. Furthermore, the government, with strong input from industrial representatives, implemented two additional schemes of FDI liberalization – software technology parks (STPs) and electronics hardware technology parks (EHTPs) – tailored to the development of informatics.

In these parks, the equity cap for foreign investors was raised to 100 percent, imports were duty-free, and foreign banks were allowed to operate.[5] The parks also offered tax incentives to foreign investors. Foreign-invested firms could enjoy a five-year tax holiday upon their establishment. To make these technology parks even more attractive, ministries and local governments pledged to increase administrative efficiency and improve infrastructure. In early 1992, Minister of State for Science and Technology P. R. Kumaramangalam announced that, in addition to preferential tax, import, and equity policies, any foreign company wishing to set up an EHTP unit would be able to obtain all required clearances (including land use) within two weeks.[6] Infrastructure, in terms of roads, office buildings,

[3] Ibid.

[4] The leaders of Infosys, for example, were often consulted on national events in India's leading newspapers.

[5] "Mini Hong Kong Concept Proposed by Indian Electronics Department," *Xinhua Overseas News Service*, October 6, 1991; "India Allows 100 Percent Equity in Electronics," *Xinhua Overseas News Service*, August 4, 1992.

[6] "India Keen on Luring Computer Hardware Makers," *The Nikkei Weekly* (Japan), September 26, 1992.

electricity, and water supplies, was better supplied in these parks than in other places in India.[7]

In the mid-1990s, the liberalization of many industries (including the auto industry) experienced intensified domestic opposition, which stymied FDI liberalization. In the informatics sector, domestic opposition was relatively weak; FDI liberalization deepened in this decade. The government reduced import duties on electronics products and simplified the approval process for foreign investment. Tariffs were reduced from 85 percent to 45 percent on the items found on the "negative list" for imports.[8] More importantly, the national government delegated more authority to the directors of the STPs and EHTPs, who gained power to permit additional imports of capital goods valued up to Rs10 crores (around $3 million). Restrictions on the approval of capital goods imports were also removed.[9]

To sum up the developments of the 1990s, FDI liberalization in informatics conformed to a diffusion model: significant inflows of diaspora actors (and foreign companies) met eager domestic producers. Although India's FDI liberalization lagged behind China's at the national level, the country's liberalization of informatics resembled that of China's, offering free entry, tax incentives, better infrastructure, and streamlined administration to foreign investors. Also similar to China, local governments and diasporas played more important roles in informatics than in other industrial sectors. The following pages analyze the roles of diasporas, indigenous companies, and local governments, which together constitute the more positive mix of social networks for India's informatics development.

Diasporas in Informatics

A key difference between India's informatics and auto sectors was the strong presence of diaspora networks in the former. Indian diasporas were not dominant investors; rather, they were professionals working at Western companies who helped to connect the Indian market with global demand. Diaspora networks channeled capital and technology into India and facilitated the entry of Western MNCs. In the recent decade, Indian entrepreneurs in Silicon Valley returned and invested in their homeland. Together, diaspora networks gave advantages to India's software sector and expedited FDI liberalization. Domestic producers gained strong incentives to incorporate diaspora networks into their operations.

According to AnnaLee Saxenian (1999), between 1995 and 1998, Indians were running 9 percent of Silicon Valley start-ups – almost 70 percent of which were in the software sector. Diasporas' knowledge of the needs and strengths of both American and Indian firms made them useful intermediaries in the search for business partners on both sides. Working between the two worlds,

7 "Electronics Hardware Projects Approved in India," *Xinhua Overseas News Service*, May 24, 1993.
8 "India to Cut Some Import Duties," *Xinhua Overseas News Service*, July 2, 1993.
9 "India More Powers for STP Directors," *Business Line*, July 11, 1997.

diasporas helped Western and Indian companies to deal with complex transaction problems inherent in transitional economies. Furthermore, diasporas accomplished success in Silicon Valley and shaped Westerners' perceptions of Indian technology firms. Diasporas' reputational effect thus facilitated India's software exports to the United States.

In Chapter 6, New York-based Warburg Pincus drove the growth of Bharti, but two Indian diasporas working there initiated Warburg's investment and provided support for Bharti's globalization. India's business process outsourcing (BPO) industry drew on diaspora networks, although Western MNCs were the end users of the sector in India. GE was the first investor in India's BPO and remains the largest investor and employer. Indian diasporas working there led GE's involvement in India. In 1995, Pramod Bhasin and Nigel Andrews of GE made a case for captive back-office operations in India. They helped GE to establish GE Capital International Services (GEcis) in Gurgaon in 1997. To manage the division in India, GE hired Raman Roy to be the CEO of GEcis and outsourced services to Indian indigenous companies such as TCS and WIPRO.[10] WIPRO alone earned almost 50 percent of its revenue from its dealings with GE. By outsourcing to India, GE cut significant costs, and its success brought other major American companies such as Citibank, Bank of America, and American International Group to India as well.[11] Motorola began operations in Bangalore in 1991 with a staff of fifty; in 2005, its headquarters in Gurgaon employed more than 1,500 people (CASI 2005).

Thanks to diaspora connections, the United States is the majority export market for Indian software production. In 1999–2000, more than 60 percent of Indian software exports went to the United States (Kumar 2001). Table 8.2

TABLE 8.2. *Indian Software Exports in Global Markets, 1999–2000*

Region	Share of India's exports	Share of global software market	Relative performance*
America	62.0	45.1	16.9
Europe	24.0	27.6	-3.6
Japan	4.0	16.9	-12.9
SE Asia	3.5	2.8	0.7
Australia & NZ	1.5	2.1	-0.6
West Asia	1.5	1.8	-0.3
Rest of the World	3.5	3.7	-0.2

* India's relative performance in the respective markets was measured by dividing each market's share of India's exports by its share of global exports.
Source: Original raw data from Kumar (2001).

[10] See the self reflection by GE's CEO Jack Welch (2001).
[11] Interviews with Kiran Karnik, President, NASSCOM; and also see, Businessworld, *BPO Industry Report 2006*.

assesses India's relative performance in the world's software export markets. America topped the world in software imports at 45 percent, followed by Europe at 27.6 percent, and Japan at 16.9 percent. Yet the American market accounted for 62 percent of India's software exports, followed by Europe, which imported 24 percent of India's software, and Japan, which imported merely 4 percent. These numbers suggest that India was overperforming by almost 17 percent in the United States and underperforming by 13 percent in Japan. Language differences may partly explain India's underperformance in Japan, but diaspora connections clearly have facilitated India's exports to the United States.[12]

Nonresident Indians (NRIs) with work experience in the United States have served as investors and information providers for India's informatics industries. According to a survey of Silicon Valley's Indian population conducted by AnnaLee Saxenian in 2002, 38 percent of Indian diasporas reported working in the software industry. Of these, 46 percent claimed to have been a contact for domestic Indian business, 23 percent said they had invested their own money in an Indian start-up, and 10 percent had invested more than once. Furthermore, 77 percent of those interviewed replied that one or more friends had returned to India to start a company, 52 percent traveled to India on business at least once a year, 27 percent regularly exchanged information about jobs or business opportunities with those back home, and 33 percent regularly exchanged technological insights with someone in India. Finally, when asked about the possibility of bringing their much-improved skills home, 45 percent of those surveyed reported this to be a moderate to strong possibility (Saxenian 2002).

Diasporas' most prominent role, however, was as an intermediary for foreign companies investing in India. American companies like Yahoo, Hewlett Packard, and GE commenced their initial operations in India largely because of the confidence generated by the presence of many Indians working in their U.S. operations (Kapur 2002, 101). Furthermore, once they made their initial investments, Western MNCs relied on Indian immigrants to supervise their subsidiaries and deal with relations with local governments and indigenous entrepreneurs.[13] According to one estimate, seventy-one of the seventy-five multinationals in Bangalore's STP were headed by Indians who had lived and worked overseas, mostly in the United States (Ghemawat 2000).

Confirming Saxenian's survey in Silicon Valley, America-based Indian entrepreneurs founded software companies such as Mastech, CBS Inc., and IRM, among others. They invested heavily in India, which provided services primarily for their U.S. operations. These immigrant entrepreneurs operated between two worlds and took advantage of both. Reliant on Indian production, they benefited commercially and helped to compete in the American market. The return rate of

[12] Also confirmed by Lateef (1997) and Arora et al. (2001).

[13] Examples included Pramod Bhasin and Nigel Andrews of GE and Raman Roy of American Express. All of these individuals were critical to MNCs' decisions to invest in India and the management of their investment projects. See *BPO Industry Report 2006*.

U.S.-based Indian immigrants was increasing rapidly, from merely 2 percent in 1991 to 10 percent in the late 1990s. Senior software professionals also returned to India to set up their own companies. In Hyderabad of Andhra Pradesh (AP) alone, about 100 companies had been established by returning software professionals by 2000.[14]

Many of these diaspora investors drew financing from the West. Sanjeev Agarwal, driven by the internet boom in 1999, secured $3 million in venture funding from UK-based CDC Capital Partners to set up Daksh eServices, an email support company in Gurgaon. Raman Roy, who led GE's operations in India since 1988, quit GE in 2000 and established Spectramind in Gurgaon. With the help of Western venture capital, Indian diasporas established CustomerAsset and 24/7 Customer in Bangalore. These diaspora entrepreneurs designed their business models around e-mail support services and led to the birth of India's third-party industry.[15]

FDI-Prone Industrial Interests

In India, industrial interests are important forces shaping FDI liberalization. But the dominant interests in informatics differ from those in other sectors such as automobiles. India's indigenous industries primarily resisted FDI, but the informatics sector (particularly the software segment) has embraced foreign influence since the 1980s. The two schemes – STP and EHTP – were both pushed by industrial associations.[16]

The National Association of Software and Services Companies (NASSCOM) appealed directly to economic bureaucrats and politicians in Delhi and to the local chiefs of various states for the establishment of STPs and EHTPs. NASSCOM and its foreign collaborators also lobbied for free imports of computer hardware, which were indispensable to the growth in software outsourcing from the United States to India (Parthasarathy 2000; Forbes 2002; Saxenian 2002). The growth of NASSCOM indicates the astronomical gains in the software industry. In 1988, NASSCOM had only thirty-eight members. In 2001, it had 850, one-fourth of which were foreign companies. Domestic members of NASSCOM typically had connections with foreign investors and markets. The industrial association explicitly brands itself as a pro-liberalization organization and has been organizing conferences to argue for IT-enabled services as an engine for economic growth in India.[17]

Policy stances of industry associations typically reflect the interests of their members. The leading association, the Confederation of Indian Industry (CII),

14 "IT Industry May Face Shortage of Manpower," *Express India*, March 2000. www.expressindia.com/infotech/00300051.htm. Accessed on August 1, 2006.

15 "Third-party industry" refers to one-stop shopping for outsourced services.

16 From interviews conducted at NASSCOM in New Delhi, summer, 2005.

17 "IT-Enabled Services to Get $200mi FDI in Two Years," *Economic Times*, May 31, 2001.

represents many industries, and, as we shall see later, has helped to resist FDI liberalization in the auto sector in the recent decade. Regarding informatics, however, CII has been an advocate for liberalism. In 2002, it urged the Indian government to adopt the global patent regime and provide patents for all inventions, including computer software, so as to make the informatics sector more attractive to FDI.[18] Like NASSCOM, CII draws substantial numbers of its foreign members from software services and domestic software producers that rely on global markets.

As a whole, dominant interests of indigenous informatics players differ considerably from producers of automobiles, and their stances on FDI liberalization have been largely positive. The largest companies – TCS, WIPRO, and Infosys – all provide services to foreign MNCs and rely heavily on foreign markets. The corporate histories of these companies suggest that their personnel draw significantly on diaspora entrepreneurs and that IT technicians are eager to study abroad or gain overseas work experience (Xiang 2006). It is hard to imagine that these companies would oppose FDI. In fact, during times of domestic resistance in related sectors, software companies are lobbyists *for* FDI liberalization.

Local Governments: More Active in Informatics

In India, Lloyd Rudolph and Susanne Rudolph (2001) argue that economic liberalization since 1991 has resulted in "ionization of [Indian] states," in which local governments became increasingly important to economic development. Aseema Sinha (2003) demonstrates that across India's local states, developmental proclivity varied and caused divergent growth trajectories in the country. Compared to China, however, there were fewer entrepreneurial diasporas in India, and diaspora networks at the local level were evidently weaker. Local governments have been less persistent in pursuing FDI liberalization than the national government, as Chapters 4 and 6 have explained.

The informatics sector is exceptional in that local governments are quite proactive. The STP and EHTP schemes were decentralized, and local governments had higher stakes in their construction. Visible success in informatics, such as high-paying jobs, revenues from exporting industries, and tax-paying foreign investors, energized local governments that hosted some of these parks. Politicians in other areas competed to construct these parks, invite foreign companies, and achieve these gains associated with the informatics industry, criticism notwithstanding.

In Punjab, local governments provided the informatics sector with the best available infrastructure. The Rajasthan government set up an EHTP at Kukas electronics city. Even in West Bengal, the government encouraged the establishment of large IT complexes to ensure that the electronics industry occupies

[18] "Indian Chamber Body Supports Patent Liberalization," *Asia Pulse*, December 28, 2000.

a prominent place in the economy.[19] Gujarat and Tamil Nadu have been aggressive in pursuing pro-business policies and attracting private entrepreneurs (Sinha 2003). Maharashtra and Karnataka, where Mumbai and Bangalore are located, have attracted substantial numbers of foreign investors. The AP case below demonstrates how diasporas networks have helped.

Andhra Pradesh, with significant diaspora networks in IT services, is one of the fastest growing states in India. Under Chief Minister N. Chandrababu Naidu, AP made persistent efforts to brand itself as a destination for investment in software services in the late 1990s. In 1999, the state trailed the nation in many key indicators of human development, but by 2001, it had made compelling progress in promoting its capital city, Hyderabad, as a new destination for MNCs seeking good infrastructure and low-cost labor for outsourcing "backroom" operations in information technology and related service industries. In 2000, Hyderabad – now nicknamed Cyberabad – was the fourth largest recipient of foreign-invested companies in the software industry (in terms of the number of companies), behind only Mumbai, Bangalore, and Delhi.[20]

Going beyond ordinary STP and EHTP incentives, AP bestowed ten-year tax holidays and other economic incentives on foreign companies in Hyderabad. In contrast to infrastructure bottlenecks in the rest of the nation, Hyderabad assured a reliable supply of power so that "multinational companies would not have interrupted power five minutes in a year" (Frankel 2005, 619). By 2001, when construction began on Phase II of Hitec City in Hyderabad, the complex had attracted about $500 million in FDI and employed about 60,000 people. Efforts to attract investment in informatics propelled AP to become the top state in the economic freedom score in 2009, surpassing Gujarat and Maharashtra (Debroy, Bhandari, and Aiyar 2011).

In sum, the informatics sector as a whole experienced faster FDI liberalization than other sectors – but the diffusion model described earlier covers only the software industry. It is in the software industry that the auspicious mix of diaspora networks and domestic resistance was clearly present. Private companies were new and internationalized, local governments were active participants, Western companies offered markets and financing, and diaspora networks served as intermediaries connecting India with the world market and made India's experience with FDI liberalization in software much better than other sectors. Although only one industry, software services' resemblance to China's FDI liberalization strengthens the case for social network theory (SNT) and sheds light on the interaction of social networks and democratic institutions. In this case, they worked in one direction: vibrant associations, policy advocacy, and ease of transnational communications in a democracy enhanced liberalization toward FDI.

[19] "Opportunities for SSIs in Electronics Industry," *Financial Express*, October 12, 1998.

[20] Nasscom. *The IT Software and Services Industry in India: Strategic Review, 2000*.

A Different Pattern in the Hardware Subsector

In China, hardware manufacturing experienced speedy FDI liberalization, whereas in India this subsector was slower to open than the software sector. In the early 1990s, Indian policy governing hardware and software production was similar (in STP and EHTP schemes); yet by 2000, hardware liberalization lagged behind.

India's hardware division had a longer development history and stronger state roles than its software division. When reform began, internal networks opposing FDI were clearly stronger. A perhaps more important factor, however, was the lack of meaningful diaspora networks in hardware manufacturing, contrasting to the software division, where diaspora networks helped India to capture a global notch. In the world marketplace, Chinese entrepreneurs in East Asia occupied electronics/computing production. As the People's Republic of China (PRC) opened, diaspora entrepreneurs relocated their manufacturing facilities and global commerce to the Mainland. Although the Indian government announced the EHTP and STP schemes in 1989 (rather timely for the relocation of hardware manufacturing in East Asia), overseas Chinese-controlled hardware production moved to the PRC and bypassed opportunities in India. In India's hardware division, inflows of external technology, capital, and commerce were slow and did not help the growth of the industry. Indian indigenous producers that enjoyed protection did not try to capture the opportunity and feared the possible threats from the EHTP scheme. Collaboratively, indigenous producers opposed external opening. From 1991 to 2000, FDI liberalization in India's computer hardware sector was a faltering experience, contrary to the speedy diffusion of China's hardware and India's software.

The call for FDI and freeing of imports in the hardware subsector heightened in the new millennium thanks to the success in software development. Figure 8.1

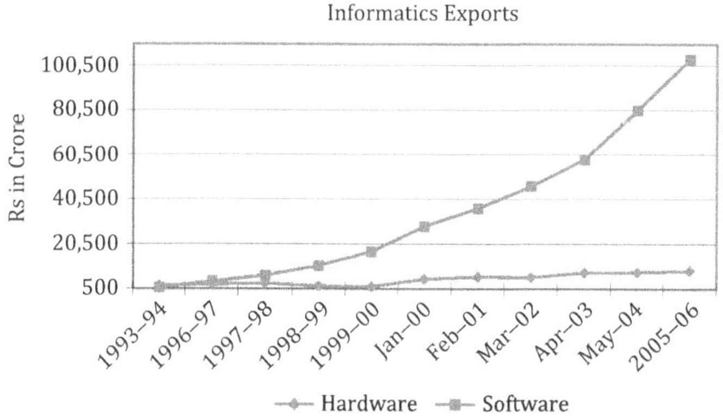

FIGURE 8.1. Differential Performance of India's Hardware and Software Exports
Source: Raw data are from Ministry of Communication and Technology, Government of India

draws the relative performance of hardware and software sectors in India after 1991. The two subsectors both benefited from the 1991 industrial policy and opened to foreign trade and investment under similar terms. In 1993, when the new industrial policy was more or less implemented, hardware exports, including consumer electronics, industrial electronics, computers, and components, were not significant but amounted to twice the value of software exports. Within three years, software exports had greatly surpassed hardware exports, at $822 million versus $575 million. The gap rose rapidly in the following decade. In 2005, software exports were worth more than twelve times hardware exports, reaching $22.9 billion.

Hardware's comparatively lackluster export growth slowed FDI liberalization in this subsector. Throughout the 1990s, the government consistently vetoed proposals to speed up opening to FDI and imports of electronics hardware.[21] The 2001–2002 export-import (exim) policy continued this practice.[22] The situation improved as indigenous software companies became critical of the restriction and requested more liberal policy frameworks for hardware manufacturing and imports. As the software industry grew, the government began to listen more closely to the voices clamoring for liberalization in hardware. Local governments, eager to develop software services, became advocates of liberalization in the hardware division, believing that, without development in hardware, software growth would suffer. In 2004, for example, Karnataka Chief Minister N. Dharam Singh announced plans to implement a new hardware policy to encourage hardware manufacturing in the state. In the same year, Orissa IT and Energy Minister Suryanarayan Mahapatra openly echoed these remarks.[23]

As a result of the corporate and local government push, the national government modified the EHTP scheme in 2002 and removed export obligations on foreign investors in the parks, which were viewed as a key hurdle to FDI in the electronics sector.[24] The 2002 exim policy incorporated important measures to facilitate FDI and modified the "net foreign exchange positive" requirement in favor of foreign investors.[25] Policies were further liberalized in 2003, with a new exim policy passed to boost hardware exports through the free movement of laptops, computers, and other office equipment and to provide flexibility to software professionals.[26] Both the hardware and software industries welcomed these changes. FDI liberalization in the hardware industry moved forward.

[21] "India: MAIT Seeks SEZs for Hardware Sector," *Business Line*, March 15, 2001.

[22] "India: Ministry Turns a Deaf Ear to Hardware Parks' Plea," *Business Line*, April 17, 2001.

[23] "Software is Passe, Feels Karnataka CM," *Financial Express*, November 1, 2004.

[24] "Hardware Tech Park Scheme Modified," *India Business Insight*, April 1, 2002.

[25] "Hardware Sector Upbeat," *Financial Express*, April 1, 2002.

[26] "Policy Soft on Hardware," *Financial Express*, March 31, 2003.

INDIGENOUS INDUSTRY AND AUTO SECTOR LIBERALIZATION

India's auto sector had much in common with China's auto sector: both lacked diaspora entrepreneurs, and domestic interests called the shots. The difference was that state-owned enterprises (SOEs) dominated China's automaking, whereas private automakers were the chief players in India's auto sector. Sanjay Gandhi founded the state automaker Maruti, but managed it as his private operation, and via Sanjay, private automakers became more influential in the country's economic policies, as shown in Chapter 4. Although opposing unfettered FDI liberalization, private automakers entered many JVs in the 1990s, but problems quickly arose. Indigenous players were able to narrow liberalization in India during that decade.

In the new millennium, private companies took upon themselves active self-restructuring and built global competitiveness. The leading members succeeded in global acquisition and exports. Their stances on liberalization have since somewhat shifted. In India's auto sector, there are small-scale industries that make ancillary components. These firms have faced more competition since 1991 and remain generally opposed to FDI. The investigation of auto liberalization here focuses on major auto producers in India, not subsectors, and companies constitute key social networks of policy making in the sector.

Table 8.3 provides the industrial history of India's auto sector. The first period was marked by a strict licensing system. A few business families controlled the industry, and imports were discouraged. The 1980s witnessed dilution of licensing due to deregulation. Liberalization in the early 1990s attracted international automakers, and their entry created pressure on domestic auto companies, intensifying domestic resistance. Only in the new millennium did resistance decline, thanks to new partnerships between domestic companies and foreign multinationals in both domestic and international markets. Taking the

TABLE 8.3. *India's Policy Frameworks in the Auto Sector*

Periods	Policy frameworks
Pre-1980	Strict license-raj; few imports; domination by well-defined domestic automakers
1980s	Diluted license-raj; continued protection; Maruti (state-owned)–Suzuki (Japan) joint venture
1990s	Slow liberalization: The early 1990s: private production delicensed and imports of capital goods deregulated The mid-1990s: domestic resistance rises The late 1990s: partial and moderate liberalization
2000s	Domestic players go abroad

three decades together, FDI has indeed entered India's auto sector but its pace was gradual and concentrated in areas with vibrant domestic auto markets, as illustrated in Map 3.

Pre-Reform Producer Networks

Indian auto manufacturing has a long history, starting under British rule and expanding after independence. Before 1980, the government's policy toward this sector was based on import substitution. It forbade imports of fully built vehicles and applied "progressive manufacture" conditions to foreign automakers in India, asking them to localize parts manufacturing within a set period or leave (Singh 2004). Domestic companies were the main beneficiaries of protectionism. Prominent business families firmly controlled the sector, and little competition existed. The passenger vehicle market was divided between Tata and Hindustan, the two leading automakers. Another five companies, all belonging to traditional business houses, were selected by the government to produce four-wheelers and engines, while small-scale manufacturers reserved the right to make ancillary parts and components.

The government put into place an elaborate system of support for the auto sector. The Ministry of Commerce launched the Engineering Export Promotion Council (EEPC) in 1955 to manage international trade in engineering goods and services. In 1959, the government created the Development Council for Automobiles and Allied Industries to promote automobile production as a selective industry reserved for public enterprises. Existing auto companies set up industrial associations to enhance their capacity to bargain with the government. In 1959 and 1960, respectively, the Automotive Component Manufacturers Association of India (ACMA) and the Society of Indian Automobile Manufacturers (SIAM) were established. In 1966, the Automotive Research Association of India was launched in Mumbai, the center of auto manufacturing. Both industrial bureaucracies and associations aimed to promote Indian auto companies and to protect domestic producers from foreign competition.

Today, these institutions remain tightly connected and serve to strengthen domestic interests in this sector. The EEPC, comprised of large business houses, trading houses, and small- and medium-scale enterprises, is committed to promoting the "made in India" trademark both domestically and internationally. The ACMA is the central agency of the automobile components industry. It represents more than 498 companies whose aggregate production accounts for more than half of auto components output in the organized sector. The SIAM serves as the main advocate for Indian auto manufacturers. Its policy preferences changed gradually under reform as the number of foreign members expanded. Yet it remains a voice of indigenous automaking.

Table 8.4 lists all Indian automobile companies in operation before 1980. The product differentiation and concentration demonstrate symbiotic networks in this sector, with leading business houses dominating the large-scale production

TABLE 8.4. *India's Auto Manufacturers before Reform*

Companies	Founding Year	Location	Products
Greaves Cotton	1922	Chennai	Engines
Simpson & Co.	1925	Chennai	Engines
Hindustan*	1942	Chennai	Passenger cars, LCVs
Ashok Leyland	1948	Chennai	MCVs, LCVs, engines
Royal Enfield	1955	Chennai	Motorcycles
Premier Ltd	1944	Mumbai	Passenger vehicles
Bajaj Auto	1945	Mumbai	2-wheelers, 3-wheelers
Tata Motors	1945	Mumbai	M&H&LCV, suvs
Mahindra & Mahindra	1945	Mumbai	LCVs, 3-wheelers, engines, tractors
Force Motors	1958	Mumbai	LCVs, 3-wheelers, tractors, engines
Cumins (Tata)	1962	Mumbai	Engines
Kinetic Engineering	1970	Mumbai	2-wheelers
Eicher	1959	Delhi	LCVs, CVs
LML	1972	Kapur	2-wheelers
Majestic Auto	1973	Ludhiana	2-wheelers
Scooters India	1972	UP	3-wheelers
Yamaha Motor India	1963	UP	Motorcycles

* Hindustan also had sizable production in Calcutta, West Bengal.
CVs refer to commercial vehicles, and LCVs, MCVs, HCVs refer to light, medium-size, and heavy commercial vehicles, respectively.
Source: Compiled from the membership information of the SIAM, available at www.siamindia.com, supplemented with other sources.

of two-wheelers, three-wheelers, scooters, commercial vehicles, and passenger cars. Several small- and medium-sized enterprises supplied engines and engaged in small-vehicle production. Mumbai and Chennai, both in South India, were the two centers of auto-related manufacturing. The companies and organizations located in these two cities were well connected. A few companies, less prominent than those in Mumbai and Chennai, also existed near New Delhi, including Eicher, LML, and Majestic Autos.

Table 8.4 also indicates that competition hardly existed among the auto manufacturers. Hindustan and Premier were the main producers of passenger cars, but their production was located in two different cities: Premier operated in Mumbai and Hindustan in Chennai. Bajaj Auto, located in Mumbai, dominated scooter production, whereas the few much smaller manufacturers located near Delhi – LML, Scooters India, and Majestic Autos – also made scooters but presented no competition. In the commercial vehicle market, Tata, Hindustan, and Mahindra and Mahindra (M&M) divided production and sales. In addition, only a few small manufacturers produced engines, parts, and components.

This system insulated leading automakers from competition until 1980, when the sector was slightly opened to new players.

The 1980s Deregulation

The auto sector was among those industries that benefited from Indira Gandhi's deregulation. Although no serious liberalization was pursued, the government loosened controls over private automakers and allowed existing automakers to expand more freely. New players began to emerge in the production of two- and three-wheelers in the 1980s. In passenger car manufacturing, Sanjay Gandhi founded Maruti Udyog. A state company in name, Maruti operated as Sanjay's private equity and was successful in building business partnerships. Hindustan Motor's owner K. K. Birla facilitated Maruti's collaboration with Suzuki, with the Japanese partner holding 20 percent of the company's shares. When the JV began manufacturing in 1984, it quickly became the largest supplier of passenger cars in India.[27]

Triggered by the Maruti–Suzuki success, the auto sector became most attractive to prominent Japanese investors. Honda established a JV to produce motorcycles in 1984. Indian auto manufacturers such as Hindustan, PAL, and Tata Motors adopted technology upgrades and expanded production during this decade, primarily in concert with Japanese automakers. Meanwhile, Indian policy makers and industrialists, attracted by Japan's technology and management structure, were eager to collaborate with Japanese automakers. Liberalization policies such as delicensing and deregulation advanced considerably. In 1985, the government no longer required commercial vehicle makers to be licensed, nor were licenses required for non-MRTP (Monopolistic and Restrictive Trade Practices Act) and non-FERA (Foreign Exchange Regulations Act) ventures. After thirty years of stagnation in the auto sector, new car, scooter, and truck models, mainly of Japanese origin, began to appear on the roads. Car production rose from 91,000 units in 1985 to 200,000 in 1989.[28]

However, India remained stringent when it came to foreign ownership and imports. Foreign investors were required, on a case-by-case basis, to obtain approval from national bureaucracies and partner with domestic firms upon entering the market. Tariffs and import quotas were extensive and expensive. Except for the few major Indian automakers, it was practically impossible for other players to overcome these restrictions and make inroads into India's auto market.

Moderate liberalization did not increase competition. Because the demand for scooters and cars rose rapidly in the 1980s while imports remained prohibited, existing automakers benefited handsomely. The average wait-time to purchase a passenger vehicle, for example, was reportedly eight to ten years, and for a scooter, ten to twelve years. As Madhur Bajaj of Bajaj Auto later

[27] "Japanese Business in India," *Japan Economic Journal*, October 9, 1984.
[28] "Rapid Progress in Modernization Plans," *Financial Times*, May 12, 1986.

recalled of this period, the job of marketing was one of allocation, not selling (Forbes 2002). The Maruti–Suzuki venture started to produce vehicles in 1984, but it did not increase pressure for economic liberalization in India. Instead, like other indigenous producers, this state–Japanese automaker partnership profited from market protection and continued to increase its private gains. Indeed, in this decade, excise duties on the price of imported cars increased, rather than decreased.

FDI Liberalization in the 1990s

There were significant policy changes in the 1990s. In July 1991, within the framework of the new industrial policy, the auto sector applied automatic approval to foreign technology and investment agreements below the foreign equity cap of 51 percent. In 1993, the government further deregulated the passenger car division, permitting foreign equity shares larger than 51 percent. These foreign investment projects, however, had to navigate within the case-by-case approval system, judged mainly by projected exports, sophistication of technology, and other parameters. After the mid-1990s, wholly foreign-owned investments were also permitted in individual cases.

With liberalization and the emergence of new domestic and international players in India, competition in the auto sector intensified, and Indian auto manufacturers' domestic market dominance was no longer protected. They had to upgrade their technology, improve their product design, and compete with each other and with foreign producers. Domestic companies faced pressure to change.[29] In this context, the reaction from existing producers was to wage large-scale opposition against FDI and to demand a "level playing field" for domestic companies while holding off openness to foreign investors. The influential "Bombay Club," discussed in Chapter 6, developed rapidly.

In the meantime, however, the entry of Western automakers led to the development of more external networks between foreigners and Indian policy makers, as well as ties between foreign automakers and domestic players. Thus, there emerged two trends in India during the 1990s: while fear of competition intensified domestic opposition to liberalization, indigenous producers saw more opportunities to form external ties. External networks helped to co-opt members of domestic resistance to support FDI liberalization.

Even as the "Bombay Club" campaigned strongly for protection from 1993 to 1996, foreign entrants into the auto sector multiplied. In 1994, Daimler Chrysler established a subsidiary in Mumbai. Honda Siel Cars was formed in Uttar Pradesh (UP) in 1995. In an extraordinary move by the Korean automaker Hyundai, the company set up the largest wholly owned company in Chennai in 1996. Overall,

[29] Real changes were modest. In the 1990s, the waiting list for a Baja-produced scooter was still five to eight years, and the 1960 Ambassador, manufactured by Hindustan, continued to turn a profit.

TABLE 8.5. *India's New Automakers in the 1990s*

Companies	Date of Establishment	Location	Products
French Peugeot	1993	Mumbai	Medium-size sedans
Daimler Chrysler	1994	Mumbai	Passenger cars
Fiat India Pvt	1997	Mumbai	Passenger cars
Piaggio Vehicles Pvt	1998	Mumbai	3-wheelers
Skoda Auto	1999	Mumbai	Passenger cars
Hyundai Motors	1996	Chennai	Passenger cars
Tatra Vectra Motors	1998	Chennai	M&HCVs
Ford India Pvt	1999	Chennai	Passenger cars
Toyota Kirloskar Motor	1997	Bangalore	UVs, passenger cars
Volvo India Pvt.	1997	Bangalore	M&HCVs
General Motors	1994	Calcutta	Medium-size passenger cars
General Motors	1994	Gurgaon	Passenger cars
Honda Siel Cars	1995	UP	Passenger cars
Honda Motors	1999	New Delhi	Motorcycles & scooters

Source: Compiled from the membership information of the SIAM, with supplementary materials.

whereas FDI was practically nonexistent in the 1980s, JVs emerged as important players in India's auto sector in this decade, as indicated in Table 8.5.

Table 8.5 demonstrates the importance of domestic automakers as well. The two places with the most foreign-invested firms were Chennai and Mumbai, the two traditional auto manufacturing sites in India (see Map 3). The industry has become more diverse than it was in the past. Bangalore, although lacking strong domestic automakers, hosted two important foreign automakers, Toyota and Volvo. General Motors and Honda set up facilities in and around Delhi in 1994 and 1999, respectively, in addition to Honda's Siel plant in UP founded in 1995. Most JVs were formed with traditional automakers. French Peugeot, for example, teamed with M&M and PAL. General Motors partnered with Hindustan Motors, Mercedes Benz AG with Tata, and Rover Group with Sipani Automobiles.[30]

Before reform, private automakers cherished their arms-length relationship with policy makers by virtue of their location in South India. Liberalization from the 1980s on brought about three changes. First, private companies intensified their connections to the national government. Second, more private companies came into being. And finally, JVs helped to develop MNC-indigenous company networks in the auto sector. In this decade, domestic automakers also began to compete in the world market for the first time. Their expansion and experience

[30] "Foreign Relations Forged to Combat Import Push," *The Nikkei Weekly*, Japan, October 31, 1994.

abroad changed the ideas and interests of Indian automakers and in turn shifted their stance on FDI liberalization.

Rahul Bajaj, owner of Bajaj Motors and the leader of the antiliberalization "Bombay Club," dropped his opposition to FDI liberalization in the late 1990s when his company found "new worlds to conquer."[31] While maintaining strong market shares within India, Bajaj took on the MNCs on their own turf and exported two-wheelers to Europe, Latin America, Africa, and Asia.[32] Chapter 6 has also examined Tata Motor's transformation since the late 1990s. When the government pressured MNCs to find indigenous partners, preeminent business houses found themselves in an enviable position. Within India, they were coveted by MNCs as local partners, and in the world, they could capitalize on newly acquired external networks. Indigenous business interest in controlling domestic market, however, limited their support for FDI liberalization. As the following pages show, when their access to domestic markets was threatened, indigenous business concerted to oppose opening and narrowed liberalization.

Policy Debates Intensify in Autos

Multinational corporation–indigenous business cooperation began to crumble in the late 1990s when both parties were concerned with their relative gains in JVs. Furthermore, as disagreements between domestic and foreign automakers erupted around 1997, it became difficult to pursue openness to FDI in the auto sector, and India's liberalization in general was slowed. That year, Suzuki waged a tug of war with the government for control of Maruti.[33] Joint ventures between Premier Auto and Peugeot and between Tata and Mercedes Benz, as well as many others, demonstrated clear frictions.[34] French Peugeot announced its decision to get out of India and took its local partner, PAL, to a Mumbai court.[35] India's two premier auto manufacturing families – the Doshis and the Birlas – had a similarly bad year in their relations with foreign partners. The Doshis experienced difficulties in all their JVs. Birlas' Hindustan Motors reported poor sales. The relationship between Tata and Mercedes-Benz also worsened that year after Mercedes announced the company's desire for a majority stake.[36]

Industry's displeasure with foreign automakers was reflected in the new auto policy in 1997. The concerns of Indian players, including traditional business houses, trading companies, small-scale industry (SSI) units, and regulatory associations, were incorporated, and the policy stressed the need for a level

[31] "Bajaj Finds New Worlds to Conquer," *India Business Intelligence*, May 3, 1995.

[32] Ibid.

[33] "Suzuki on the Reverse Gear," *The Hindu*, September 7, 1997; "India: Needed a Clean-Cut Government Agenda on Maruti," *Business Line*, September 24, 1997.

[34] "Indian Auto Industry Drives in Lower Gear in 1997," *AAP Newsfeed*, December 29, 1997.

[35] Ibid.

[36] Ibid.

playing field before FDI liberalization. The policy did not address foreign investors' concerns but laid out explicit conditions for foreign firms' operations in India, including entry, exports, and indigenization. The policy stipulated that majority foreign-owned companies should invest at least $50 million in equity. Furthermore, it forced them to take on export obligations to fund their auto-parts imports and required them to submit a schedule for increasing the percentage of locally made parts used in their cars. Mere car assembling operations were not welcomed. Permission for foreign entry also applied only to car projects and not to the production of other four-wheeled vehicles. Foreign automakers were additionally asked to meet at least half of their requirements for using locally made parts by the third year of operation in India and at least 70 percent by the fifth year (Singh 2004).

Following the 1997 auto policy, domestic companies continued to complain about foreign investors in their JVs and to lobby against additional FDI in the auto sector.[37] One of their chief complaints was that foreign partners failed to provide advanced technology to their Indian production units.[38] Domestic players reasoned that, because foreign investors were unreliable sources of technology, the government should therefore support the strengthening of indigenous industry. In 1999, A. Sivasailam, chairman of the Amalgamations Group, emphasized the need for an integrated automobile policy to resolve the "conflict between the interests of multinational corporations in the industry and India's national goals" and to strengthen *Indians*' "contribution to the established component manufacturing base."[39]

Domestic automakers shaped industrial associations' stance on FDI liberalization as well. In December 1999, SIAM submitted its recommendations for developing a new auto sector policy to the government.[40] In its recommendations, SIAM expressed its domestic members' main concerns – the fear of market uncertainties and what the withdrawal of qualitative restrictions on imports would do to existing companies. V. M. Raval, executive director of Telco, argued that these factors threatened the survival of the industry.[41] SIAM represented the interests of domestic industry and asked for government support. Representatives of the organization argued that the government policy of granting unrestricted entry to foreign investors would only worsen existing conditions in the industry. "No government can afford to ignore the interest of the domestic industry," the recommendation stated.[42]

SIAM's recommendation, however, suggests that domestic automakers did not oppose foreign influence; instead, they requested protections exclusively

[37] "Monopolies Are Out of Place," *Business Line*, February 11, 1999.

[38] "Strategy: Has Honda Stepped Out of the Two-Wheeler Race?," *Business Today*, October 7, 1998.

[39] "India Call for Strengthening Indigenous Industry," *The Hindu*, June 27, 1999.

[40] "Automobiles: Driving in the Reverse Gear," *Indian Express*, October 11, 1999.

[41] SIAM, President's Message, "The WTO Regime and its Implications for the Indian Automobile Industry," 1999.

[42] Ibid.

from *unwanted* investors. Awasthi, an industrial representative, argued, "The country has to be open for technology and markets.... But it cannot be allowed to become a dumping yard or a testing ground for global players without any contribution to the country's growth."[43] SIAM's recommendation represented the interests of Indian players and suggested that these companies had competing concerns with foreign MNCs. Although SIAM had a number of foreign members, the industrial representatives who signed the recommendation were all Indian, including Seshasayee of Ashok Leyland, Madhur Bajaj of Bajaj Auto, Abhay Firodia of Bajaj Tempo, Sunil Kant Munjal of Hero Honda, Ravi Santhanam of Hindustan Motors, Alan Durante of M&M, Jagdish Khattar of Maruti, V. M. Raval of Telco, Venu Srinivasan of TVS-Suzuki, and Indian representatives from the components industry.[44]

Rahul Bajaj, the leader of the "Bombay Club" in the mid-1990s, became the president of CII in 1999–2000. He was generally less critical of FDI, but on the import of used cars he was entirely in concert with other indigenous producers. Facing pressure from India's World Trade Organization (WTO) obligations, Bajaj argued, "[n]ow, it is a matter of life and death."[45] When it was announced that 715 items in the qualitative restriction (QR) system were to be phased out in 2001, industry representatives fretted over the possibility that foreign consumer products and automobile components would flood the domestic market.[46]

In a report entitled "How Can India Avoid the Pitfalls of Globalization?" Rahul Bajaj and Sanjiv Goenka, vice-chairman of RPG Enterprises, argued that foreign companies were gaining control of the domestic market at a relatively low cost without developing significant stakes in the economy.[47] Painting a fairly grim picture of the economy, the group, led by Bajaj and Goenka, claimed that the country's economic health was highly vulnerable to the forces of globalization.[48] The report stated that the basic objective behind FDI liberalization (namely, to access the latest technologies, management skills, and exports) had not been achieved in many sectors. Rather, they claimed, liberalization had served to destabilize indigenous enterprises. Hence the group asked the government to restrain the entry and monitor the activities of MNCs in India.

Politicians and bureaucrats in Delhi paid careful attention to the concerns of industry. Narasimha Rao, the former prime minister and a chief champion of economic liberalization between 1991 and 1996, called for "an intensive look-back" at the first decade of the liberalization program and its overall

43 "Automobiles: Driving in Reverse Gears," *The India Express*, October 11, 1999.
44 Ibid.
45 "India: Auto Expo Opens Today," *Business Line*, January 12, 2000; "Powered by the Passion for Perfection," *The Hindu*, January 19, 2000.
46 "Rahul Bajaj Is Back with Some More Classic Bombay Club-speak. This Time to Caution Against Growing MNC Power," *Economic Times*, May 12, 2000.
47 Ibid.
48 The Indian automobile sector was doing very well in 2000. "Cars: Luxury Segment Booming," *Economic Times*, September 5, 2000.

effects on the people.[49] As the government prepared to unveil a comprehensive new auto policy in early 2000, politicians held meetings with bureaucrats and industry representatives to discuss industry concerns and India's global obligations.[50] At those meetings, the government consulted the industry's views on second-hand vehicle imports, auto emission norms, incentives for research and development, rules for FDI, and general issues related to the globalization of the industry.[51] SIAM and its leading members asked the government not to allow second-hand auto imports.

Industry advocates were especially concerned about the phasing out of the QR system in 2001 because it would open the door to more imported vehicles. In 2000, an interministerial committee was established to assess the impact of the QR phase-out. It met twice with bureaucrats and industry representatives to identify the specific products and subsectors of concern. The committee produced a report in which it recognized the strategic importance of the auto sector to India's national economy and argued that the government would "not allow the auto industry to be destroyed by second-hand imports."[52] The new auto policy addressed those specific concerns and minimized negative effects on domestic players.

In line with its WTO membership obligations, India had to phase out QRs in auto trade in 2001 and remove export obligations imposed on CKD (completely knocked-down)/SKD (semi knocked-down) imports. To reduce the possible negative impacts on domestic companies after these measures, the government implemented a new exim policy that took into account the demands of local carmakers.[53] The exim policy set stricter regulations for the import of second-hand cars and specified the types of new foreign cars that would be allowed into the Indian market. Both terms aimed to make sure that imported cars would not pose threats to local producers.

Regarding the import of second-hand cars, the policy banned vehicles older than three years, fixed the residual life of second-hand cars at five years, required mandatory conformation to the Motor Vehicles Act, and adopted provisions relating to the supply of spare parts for older vehicles that helped to stop the unchecked import of second-hand cars. The government also required pre- and postshipment certifications that capped the number of vehicles entering domestic market. On new car imports, the exim policy employed a twin strategy of allowing the import of new cars with engine capacities of below 1,000 cc and above 2,500 cc. Cars above 2,500 cc were allowed because the technology in this division was not available in India, and the volume of sales in

49 "Reform Introduced to Transform Society," *The Hindu*, November 2, 1999.

50 "The Government to Prepare a Comprehensive New Auto Policy," *Economic Times*, April 11, 2000.

51 These refer to the European emission standards for new vehicles in the European market.

52 "Imports No Threat to Industry," *Economic Times*, October 14, 2000.

53 "India: Local Car Makers Happy," *The Hindu*, April 1, 2001.

this premium division was negligible. The easing of importing cars below 1000 cc was simply a token gesture because domestic players dominated production of such cars whereas foreign automakers had long ceased manufacturing them. Furthermore, the Indian government abided by the wishes of domestic companies and rejected the granting of "automatic" trading rights to foreign automakers, arguing that this was not required under WTO's General Agreement on Trade in Services.[54]

Thus, some observed that after April 1, 2001, when the QR system was removed in the auto sector, foreign trade of automobiles actually became more restrictive in India than it was before. After removing the QR, heavy customs duties and stringent conditions spelled out in the new policies were imposed on the import of new and old vehicles, representing setbacks for foreign automakers since the 1997 auto policy. According to the 1997 policy, imports of SKD and CKD kits and components were evaluated on a case-by-case basis. Foreign companies could enter into a memorandum of understanding (MOU) with the Ministry of Commerce's director-general of foreign trade. Of course, foreign investors were required to increase their use of parts produced by indigenous manufacturers within a specified timetable and were subject to export obligations to achieve broad neutralization of foreign exchange over the entire period of the MOU. These conditions were not daunting. From 1997 to 2000, foreign investors entered into JVs with Indian partners either by fulfilling these conditions or individually negotiating favorable MOUs. Many argued that the 2002 auto policy institutionalized the protection of Indian companies and the restriction of foreign competition.[55]

Domestic Industry and Strategic Protectionism

Since 2000, domestic companies' ideas and interests regarding FDI have shifted. Indian companies have expanded globally, and opposition to FDI has currently lessened. Initially concerned about competition, they adjusted rather successfully and produced better products for the Indian market and even succeeded overseas. The 2002 policy provided more systematic and transparent regulations on FDI and allowed 100 percent foreign equity shares in vehicles and components.[56] The national government has persisted in welcoming foreign investors,[57] and local governments have also been more engaged in liberalization in the auto sector. Haryana, for example, applied schedules to promote auto manufacturing: improving infrastructure development, curtailing labor activism, and building special economic zones (SEZs). Tamil Nadu and Uttarakhand simplified the

[54] "New Delhi against Automatic Trading Rights for Foreign Auto Majors," *Financial Express*, March 25, 2002.

[55] "Will It Remain a Cozy Club?," *Business Line*, November 17, 2002.

[56] "Indian Cabinet Approves Comprehensive Auto Policy," *The Press Trust of India*, March 5, 2002.

[57] "Foreign Funds Have Helped Automobile Units," *The Hindu*, October 22, 2004.

approval process for FDI projects in this sector (Narayanan and Vashisht 2008). Indigenous industry's confidence in the auto sector was clear – a major improvement from the past decade – and such confidence has softened resistance to FDI.[58]

Starting in 2005, the Indian auto industry has become less concerned about the threat by foreigners than it is about India's labor policies. Because the auto sector employed only organized labor, labor activism had the potential to disrupt production. In late 2005, the Karnataka High Court declared the auto industry a Public Utility Service and banned employee strikes. The Court justified the ruling by citing the changed industrial situation brought on by globalization and liberalization, which required that the wheels of the auto industry keep moving.[59] Maharashtra also passed a "pro-industry dispute act" that strengthened auto companies' power versus labor.

However, India's automobile market remains one of the most protected in the world, with tariffs grossly surpassing those in other countries: In 2006, India's nominal tariff rates of passenger vehicles were twice China's, eight times South Korea's, and almost twenty-five times more than the United States' (Narayanan and Vashisht 2008). Using effective protection rates, calculated using the differences in prices of the same products in the open market, India's auto sector is not only protectionist: it has actually increased the level of protection since 2001. As Figure 8.2 suggests, after liberalization in 1991, the effective rate of protection in the auto sector did drop below 100 percent. Since 2001, however, effective protection in the sector has increased significantly, climbing to more than 200 percent by 2004–2005. The most recent data, from 2006–2007, suggest that the effective rate of protection in passenger vehicle production was still above 180 percent.

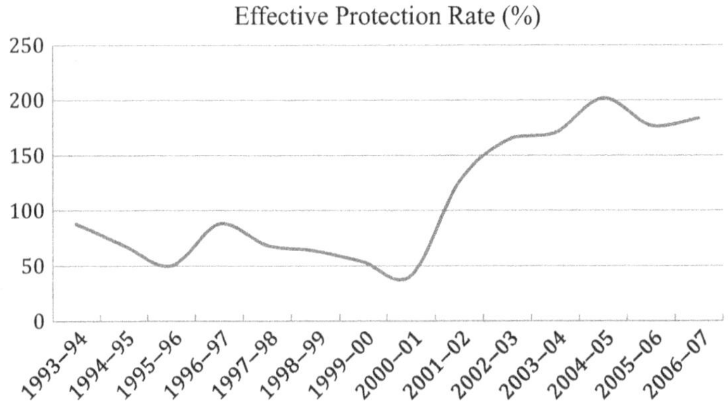

FIGURE 8.2. The Protection of Passenger Vehicles in India, 1993–2007

[58] "Automobiles: Running High on Confidence," *Business Line*, August 11, 2005.
[59] "Gov't Empowered to Ban Automobile Industry Strike," *Hindustan Times*, October 26, 2005.

Based on this analysis, we see that the social network structure in the auto sector was representative of India in general. The internal networks were very strong, with long existing, well-connected automakers, influential industrial associations, and embedded economic bureaucrats. The industry concentrated in three hubs: Mumbai, Chennai, and New Delhi, making them connected among themselves and influential in national policy making. External networks were weak in the 1980s: there were no diaspora connections, and Western automakers were generally few.

India's opening, combined with shrinking markets in advanced countries, resulted in substantial numbers of foreign automakers coming to India after 1991. Their arrival, meanwhile, created pressure on domestic industry and intensified resistance. External networks with Western automakers existed at bureaucratic and major corporate levels, yet mutual trust and commitment were lacking. Additionally, such nonethnic external networks excluded smaller political and economic actors. Despite progress, FDI liberalization in the auto sector had clear limits: prerequisite domestic partnership, localization requirement, and high protection of domestic market.

OTHER SECTORS: CONTINUITY OR CHANGE

In the range of sectors in India, continuity ruled over change, and FDI liberalization was lengthy and limited. In the industries briefly covered here, diaspora networks had little presence and indigenous interests were strong. Liberalization, if it happened at all, relied on the formation of partnerships between Western MNCs and domestic businesses. As a whole, these sectors support that, absent diaspora networks, Western players should also enter the market, albeit later, and that Western capital can change the incentives of domestic industries, but the process tends to be more difficult and protracted, depending on gradual cross-industry diffusion.

In the machine tools industry, for example, Indian firms enjoyed protection beginning in the 1940s. Despite low efficiency and poor quality, the 50 large, 100 medium, and 3,000 small companies in machinery tools continued to divide and control domestic markets well into the 1990s. When FDI liberalization encompassed other sectors, pressures for liberalization in the machine tools sector mounted. Large manufacturers in other industries began to set up their own machine tools operations, thanks to delicensing. Small- and medium-sized manufacturers in other related industries began to import second-hand machine tools from Southeast Asia. The current state of FDI liberalization in machine tools remains uncertain as pressure for change meets powerful resistance.

India's insurance sector was long dominated by two government companies: the Life Insurance Corporation (LIC) and General Insurance Corporation (GIC). These companies possessed extensive distribution networks and established ties to their supervising bureaucracies. In the late 1980s, Western insurance providers became interested in entering India's insurance market and had their home governments exert pressure on India. Because the Indian government needed foreign capital in the insurance sector, it carefully engaged foreign investors' concerns. Nevertheless, actual FDI liberalization was modest. Controls largely remained in place, and foreign participation in the sector was heavily regulated. In the mid-1990s, foreign investors were only allowed to enter joint ventures as minority shareholders.[60]

Meanwhile, foreign companies solicited the cooperation of Indian partners. By 1996, some fourteen agreements had been reached between Western insurers and Indian companies to set up JVs, anticipating the passage of an insurance regulatory authority bill that would liberalize the sector for FDI.[61] The bill, however, was rejected in 1997 due to opposition parties resisting any potential opening of the insurance sector to foreign participation.[62] Although Indian insurance companies remained interested in expanding partnership with influential foreign capital, smaller players in the sector – the distributors and the unions – rejected FDI in the sector. These small actors had few external networks with foreign MNCs, and their protectionist ideas and interests were largely unaltered by liberalization in the country.

CONCLUSION

Cross-sector FDI liberalization provides a deeper understanding of government–business interactions in India. The political regime is the important context for these interactions, but the varied outcomes of these interactions demonstrate three points that complement political analyses. First, diaspora networks are crucial to policy liberalization. With entrepreneurial diasporas, policy makers are more likely to implement liberal policies, and domestic industries are more prone to support them as well. The singular opening of India's software services was based on diaspora entrepreneurs providing ideas, technology, and connections to American markets. Second, Western MNCs can be influential as well. But they are slower to arrive and their cooperation with domestic partners is challenged from time to time. Third, in India, indigenous business has generally shaped industrial liberalization. Their interests are not static, however. When they form important external alliances, their stances on FDI change. However, such transformation takes time and remains incomplete, as many small economic actors are excluded from external alliances with Western MNCs. Foreign direct investment liberalization in India thus conforms to the slower, narrower pathway predicted in Chapter 2.

60 Even today, the existing regulatory authority retains the final say over which policy changes are feasible. "Insurance Sector Restructure High on India Gov't Agenda," *Asia Pulse*, August 6, 1996.
61 "Foreign Insurers Target New Market," *Business and Industry*, April 1996.
62 "India: Insurance Liberalization Plans Hit Fresh Setback," *Life Insurance International*, August 1997.

9

Conclusion: The State, Diasporas, and Development

China and India are presently undergoing historic economic transformations, yet with enormous complexities and divergence. The foremost divergence is their policy liberalization concerning foreign direct investment (FDI). The People's Republic of China (PRC) opened to FDI quickly when it initiated reform and built an export economy based on FDI; India, on the other hand, delayed FDI until more than a decade after its domestic deregulation, and even then the process has been tenuous.

Previous comparative studies have highlighted these countries' very different political systems and placed heavy emphasis on the institutions and political forces within each country. Conversely, globalization literature has underscored multinational corporations (MNCs), international organizations (IOs), and the United States as central to economic transformations in China and India. The social network theory (SNT) builds on politics and sociology and investigates the contrasting effects of diaspora and domestic business on FDI liberalization, via their interactions with policy makers. In China, entrepreneurial diasporas influenced the rapid diffusion of FDI liberalization. In India, where indigenous business was influential, policy makers eschewed speedy opening to FDI while simultaneously drawing upon accomplished diaspora professionals in the West.

This book arrives at two broad conclusions. First, China's and India's political institutions may have less bearing on liberalization than previously argued. The Chinese reform was not autocratic; rather, it drew on entrepreneurial diasporas that helped the government pursue new policies and rendered liberalization successful. Political actors within the country – national leaders, local governments, and indigenous entrepreneurs – formed strong ties to diasporas and amplified their influence. With diasporas' and domestic groups' ideas and incentives in alignment, China's authoritarian institutions served to expedite the diffusion of liberalization. Conversely, in India, democratic institutions did not prevent policy change; yet, due to the presence of relatively weak external networks, indigenous industry played a more central role during reform. These domestic businesses were able to successfully express and promote their policy interests via democratic venues. When pro-FDI ideas and incentives emerged in specific sectors (such as software services) and subregions (such as Andhra Pradesh) in the recent decade, FDI liberalization in these sectors and regions was, in fact, rather rapid. In such cases, the democratic elements of India – such as vibrant associations, free business media, and ease in information exchange with abroad – have facilitated liberal policy diffusion.

Second, diaspora networks operating across national boundaries (as opposed to Western MNCs and IOs) have fueled globalization in China and in India. Entrepreneurial diasporas contributed significantly to the establishment of infrastructure and market institutions in the early stages of reform and helped to generate export successes in China. Although a large proportion of Chinese exports ultimately went to the global market, Western MNCs came to invest much later and in smaller numbers. When they invested, they targeted domestic markets and encountered frictions with indigenous producers and antiglobalization backlashes in China. As China completes its capitalist transition, Western MNCs that harbor the world's top technology and business models become critical to China's industry and globalization. In this stage, Chinese diaspora professionals working at Western companies often orchestrate collaboration and partnerships with Western MNCs.

In India, diaspora professionals with education and experiences in the West have provided crucial help in policy making and the growth of domestic businesses. At the policy level, those diasporas with expertise and connections to industrially advanced countries influenced economic liberalization in the 1980s and beyond. At the corporate level, diaspora entrepreneurs in the United States facilitated the integration of Indian business into the global market, especially in information technology and software services. Yet India lacked the entrepreneurial diasporas that could help with infrastructure and market development on a broader scale, and patterns of FDI liberalization in the country have thus been decidedly different from China.

Several analytical and empirical questions remain. First, to what extent have history and geography conditioned social networks and therefore the development trajectories described here? Second, how do social networks relate to political institutions and state capacity – the two central explanations found in comparative development literature? Third, how do diasporas offer a new field of development study? In addition, I address more practical concerns: the differences between diaspora investment and nonethnic FDI, the differences between China's and India's diasporas, and future changes in the two countries' reforms.

HISTORY AND GEOGRAPHY, NETWORKS, AND POLICIES

Chalmers Johnson famously noted in 1982 that, "developmental states are historically contingent." Peter Katzenstein (1978) also maintained that "geography and history" molded foreign economic policies. Both China and India have unique histories and geographic circumstances and although the SNT emphasizes the importance of internal and external networks, such networks are products of history and geography. Therefore, history and geography constitute critical background variables for the analysis here. This does not mean, however, that the two conditions are so deterministic that political agents have no choices – in fact, the choices agents make influence development for years to come. The diffusion model particularly supports that external ideas and resources that facilitate new policy innovation and change can overcome historical and geographical determinism in developing countries and that such ideas and resources are transferred via ties between external and internal actors (state and society included).

Part II (Chapters 3 and 4) contrasts China's and India's liberalization in the 1980s and finds that diaspora entrepreneurs influenced the PRC toward embracing foreign investment and that indigenous capitalists in India shaped domestic deregulation. Together, these two chapters demonstrate divergent capitalist networks underpinning the states' policy choices. The different compositions of these networks were historically contingent, however.

In China, private enterprises were eliminated under Mao, and the Cultural Revolution from 1966 to 1976 further weakened the state apparatus. When reform began in 1978, internal conditions for industrialization were extremely weak: the country was deprived of funds, technology, and expertise, and there was an absence of private entrepreneurs. These conditions were so dire that any return on reform would be a net gain for the country. State-owned enterprises (SOEs), for example, were active in their attempts to attract foreign technology and loans. Local governments were also eager to receive diaspora visitors and investors who could provide revenues. Entrepreneurial individuals in particular welcomed the economic possibilities created by reform. Overall, the internal opposition to opening was weak, although ideology-led campaigns were fairly salient in 1982–84.

Equally important, however, was the way in which the Chinese geo-economy differed from India's. After breaking away from the Soviet Union, the PRC improved diplomacy with America, Europe, and Japan, and embraced immigrant ties to capitalist regions near China (Hong Kong, Southeast Asia, and Taiwan). Geography enhanced the circulation of financially influential diasporas: South China, with its dense immigrant ties to diaspora entrepreneurs, was proximate to the world's fastest growing economies after World War II. As production costs rose and business opportunities declined in their settled lands, diaspora business was propelled to relocate elsewhere. Special economic zones (SEZs) and open coastal cities (OCCs) in the 1980s, and zone fever in the 1990s were expansions of the economy of "Greater China" in East Asia.

Postindependence India implemented socialist economic policies as China did, but it allowed for the continual existence of private capital. Although disadvantaged by the license-raj system, large business houses continued to grow and maintained their stronghold over many manufacturing industries.

When political elites became more growth-oriented, these already influential private businessmen gained even more influence; at the same time, external openness had not yet been initiated. Private business networks shaped specific policies adopted in the 1980s.

Historically, Indian immigrants went to Burma, the Gulf, and Great Britain. Although some in Britain rose to become weighty entrepreneurs, most Indian immigrants were laborers who struggled at the bottom of those societies. When reform began in the 1980s, India had much weaker entrepreneurial immigrants than China. Due to historical ties between India and Britain, many Indian elites went to study in the United Kingdom and gained work experiences at IOs. These professional diasporas did return to join the government in the period, but external openness to foreign imports and investment (attempted by Rajiv Gandhi) was forestalled by more powerful indigenous business.

Part III (Chapters 5 and 6) compares China's and India's globalization since the 1990s. India experienced impressive liberalization in the early 1990s, bolstered by diaspora professionals serving in the national government and a financial crisis that weakened domestic opposition. On the spectrum of FDI liberalization, India was inching closer to China. Two factors influenced by geography set China and India apart in this decade. First, Chinese diaspora entrepreneurs were in the vicinity of their homeland and were engaged in manufacturing and property development. As the need for and possibility of production relocation and outsourcing from the diaspora regions to the Mainland increased in the 1990s, business incentives between the two sides further intensified and deepened liberalization. The geographic proximity clearly helped the return of diaspora entrepreneurs to China.

Second, within China, local governments supported and led the diffusion of FDI liberalization. Local cadres were quick to discard unhelpful ideologies and were more concerned with practical matters such as revenues and employment. Regardless of national policy debates, local governments continued to privilege FDI. During times of encouraging national policy, local governments implemented more aggressive incentives to attract FDI. When the national government took a more cautious approach toward FDI, local governments interpreted policies flexibly to encourage diaspora investment. The distance between Beijing and China's economically most vibrant areas in the south strengthens local governments' autonomy from the national government.

In contrast, Indian entrepreneurial diasporas in the United States that emerged in the 1990s were important, but their influence was mostly limited to software services. The long distance between India and the United States (as opposed to the distance between the PRC and Southeast Asia) inevitably hindered the circularity between diasporas and homeland. Geographic distance was an even bigger barrier to Western visitors and investors. Lacking smaller and dialect-speaking diaspora entrepreneurs in India, a central–local disjuncture also developed in India's FDI liberalization – but its effect was opposite from that in China. In India, local politicians were less enthusiastic champions of FDI than national bureaucrats (with the exception of Andhra Pradesh, Gujarat, and areas surrounding Bangalore and Mumbai). And even in development-inclined regions, indigenous business is more often dominant in corporate networks than diaspora entrepreneurs – a pattern mirroring the national dynamic.

Post-2002 trends demonstrate some convergence between China's and India's FDI liberalization. In China, the influence of diaspora entrepreneurs has lessened as China's domestic capital, technology, and markets have grown. Furthermore, the increasing professionalism and bureaucratization of the state has made the Chinese state stronger, paradoxically limiting the access of diaspora networks to it. In contrast, Indian private business has experienced globalization in financing, technology, markets, and human resources, allowing external actors to increasingly influence their ideas and interests. Yet such a transformation has mainly occurred to large business houses and rising new entrepreneurs (Infosys and Bharti, for example). A large number of small economic actors and local politicians remain excluded.

History and geography also influence the network structures in different industrial sectors, as demonstrated in Part IV. As seen in Chapter 7, China's electronics and auto sectors had different socialist histories: consumer electronics were neglected before reform, whereas automobiles enjoyed protection. Upon reform, the new government implemented similar industrial policies, but local governments and local SOEs were the main actors in consumer electronics, whereas national bureaucracies and large SOEs were key players in autos. More importantly, diaspora networks varied significantly between the two sectors. Diaspora entrepreneurs near the Mainland were globally consequential players in electronics. Upon China's opening, they provided ideas, capital, and markets to facilitate FDI liberalization and created early success in this sector, which helped to override the state-led industrial policy. No such diffusion took place in automobiles. Although state automakers and supervising agencies were similarly eager to embrace foreign technology and resources, their early experiences with MNC-invested joint ventures (JVs) were quite different from those of diaspora-involved collaborators in electronics. The perceived failure in automobiles slowed liberalization and intensified nationalism in the sector.

As seen in Chapter 8, India's informatics sector experienced different industrial development and liberalization than the country's auto sector. To develop the informatics sector, the government established software technology parks and electronics hardware technology parks in order to solicit foreign investment without imposing explicit controls on equity, imports, and management. The sector as a whole has lowered barriers to foreign imports and capital. A propitious mix of external and internal networks helped these developments. In this sector, India had strong American-based diaspora networks that had been influencing industrial policies since the 1970s. When India's reform began, diaspora linkages resulted in pro-openness ideas and interests on the part of indigenous players. Reliant on diaspora connections, Western MNCs, and global markets for technology, financing, and sales, Indian information technology (IT) companies were influential in policy making, but their dominant interests were aligned with FDI liberalization. Lacking such diaspora networks, FDI liberalization in India's auto sector was slower – typical of other industries in India. Thus, as a whole, Indian indigenous business resisted FDI liberalization, and the government dodged measures that would undercut such internal interests. The development history of Indian industry and diasporas has clearly shaped the varied social networks across Indian sectors.

REGIME, STATE AUTONOMY, AND EMBEDDEDNESS

Political studies of China's and India's economic reforms have emphasized state capacity, state autonomy from society, and political regimes that shape state capacity. The literature generally viewed that autocracies enjoy autonomy from society, and thus authoritarian regimes have stronger state capacity. Samuel Huntington (1968) and Barrington Moore (1969), for example, praised authoritarian systems. In discussing economic reforms and development, Atul Kohli (1987) and Adam Przeworski (1991) theorized how democracies restrain states from implementing lasting change. In East Asia, the developmental state literature highlighted the authoritarian structure in such states and explained how well-trained, professional bureaucrats – or technocracy – have devised and implemented industrial policies to spur economic development in Japan, South Korea, and Taiwan (Johnson 1982; Amsden 1989; Haggard 1990; Wade 1990).

The SNT and the empirical evidence presented in this book elaborate on the ways that regimes shape economic policy making and reveal whether technocracy is a precondition for economic development. Indeed, FDI liberalization in China was accomplished without well-trained bureaucrats. The Maoist era purged Chinese technocrats, and Yasheng Huang (1995) found that China's reform success was in fact due to the weakness of national bureaucracies. Of course, in the recent decade, thanks to economic success, the government has recruited well-trained individuals, and meritocracy – measured by personnel training and skills – has greatly improved.

The SNT demonstrates that embeddedness, rather than autonomy alone, can help a government to pursue new and more effective economic policies. Peter Katzenstein (1985, 228) previously argued that "the linkage between the state and society ... affects state capacity in unexpected ways." And John Ikenberry pointed out that the "irony of state strength" was that past policy commitments bound both strong and weak states. "Where the state is strongest is likely where it is weakest," he said (Ikenberry 1986, 133). Furthermore, the process analysis shows that states are fragmented, rather than coherent. The state has different political coalitions, just as society is "a web of mélange" composed of diverse interest groups (Migdal 2001). In fragmented state–society interactions, external actors can play decisive policy roles at critical moments by supplying new ideas and resources to boost one group at the expense of the others. Influential diasporas, being more willing to convey ideas and resources through more trusting ties to domestic elites, thus facilitate policy innovation in the homeland.

In China, FDI liberalization shows that despite the presence of authoritarianism, economic policy making was highly fragmented, and local governments had substantial freedom to pursue and experiment with various policy options. Transnational diaspora networks stimulated local initiatives in parts of China to engage diaspora entrepreneurs and spurred successful industrialization based on diaspora investment. By drawing on such new, externally oriented social groups, the reformist coalitions of the national and local governments were strengthened and reinforced the trend of FDI liberalization in the country. Clearly, embeddedness in diaspora networks enhanced the reformist state.

In India, the relationship between democracy and state capacity is complex. Historically, industrial associations have offered venues for the industrial lobby to express itself, and the left-leaning press in the country constrained economic liberalization. The recent experience also demonstrates that democratic institutions helped the rise of new policy elites and social interests. For example, growth-minded leaders easily recruited returnee diaspora professionals to serve as high-level advisors and policy makers. When some domestic companies developed transnational businesses and succeeded overseas, they used industrial associations and the free press to lobby and advocate for economic liberalization in the country. India's judicial independence has helped foreigners to gain confidence in investing in India. Democratic institutions thus can be beneficial to FDI liberalization in India. Yet as the country's pro-liberalization groups are competitive with foreign investors in domestic markets, liberalization remains narrower there than in China.

The SNT places policy makers at the center of analysis but investigates social relations that transfer external ideas and resources critical to new economic policies. Diasporas, as channels of ideas and resources, are important to China's and India's economic reforms. In China, Deng Xiaoping's decision to approve SEZs was influenced by the diaspora's input and local cadres' lobbying. Furthermore, local governments formed strong alliances with diaspora entrepreneurs, and they developed their localities with diaspora's help. In India, Indira Gandhi formed new ties to private businessmen and launched deregulation. Rajiv Gandhi invited diaspora professionals to develop liberalization policies. The leaders in 1990s India continuously drew on diaspora professionals while establishing an alliance with indigenous industry undergoing globalization. In both countries, the state was embedded in social groups with ideas and resources facilitating reforms. The Indian government's alliance with leading indigenous industries, however, also narrowed its openness to FDI.

FDI AND DIASPORA INVESTMENT: A MISSING DISTINCTION

In addition to the comparative literature, SNT builds on ideas concerning globalization. The findings stress the importance of diaspora networks and the critical differences between FDI and diaspora investment – a subject missing in globalization literature, which generally assumes that the ethnicity of foreign investors does not matter. The empirical analysis in this book separates diaspora investment from nonethnic FDI and informs the literature on FDI. Indeed, although the process of globalization was crucial to late development in China and India, it was the diaspora networks connecting homeland to global markets that shaped the globalization unfolding in the two countries. Diaspora entrepreneurs dominated pro-FDI economic liberalization in China, and in India, diaspora professionals helped develop new economic policies and facilitated indigenous companies to "go global."

With regard to FDI, SNT finds that ethnicity of investors matters. First, the timing and scale of arrival are different between diasporas and nonethnic foreigners. China offered an array of opportunities for foreign and diaspora investments, but diaspora investors came sooner and in more substantial numbers. Diasporas' relations with domestic actors also appeared more extensive. The cases of diaspora investment include those by Henry Fok, Gordon Wu, Stanley Ho, Y. K. Pao, Tang Xiangqian, Lee Ka-shing, and Tang Junnian. Nonethnic FDI includes investment projects by Japanese Nippon Steel and Isuzu, French Peugeot, and American Motor Corp. and Occidental. Yasheng Huang's recent research finds that over the course of reform, the profit returns on investment for diaspora and nondiaspora investors have been quite similar in China – yet diaspora entrepreneurs have accounted for the lion's share of FDI in China (Huang 2012).

Second, it seems that at the outset of opening, technology from diaspora investors may be a better fit in the receiving country despite the fact that Western MNCs possess superior technology. In 1979, China's local technology and expertise were decades behind global standards. Yet in forming collaborations with foreigners, Chinese negotiators wanted to get the upper hand while Western firms tried to preserve their core technology, resulting in frictions in nascent JVs. Such frictions did not exist with diaspora investors, who brought intermediate technology and were absorbed efficiently into the national economy. Because diaspora investors also engaged with local officials and indigenous companies, knowledge transfer occurred more frequently via diaspora investment than FDI. Mainland Chinese picked up ideas and technology from diaspora entrepreneurs. The experiences of Chinese indigenous entrepreneurs demonstrated that shared ethnicity enhanced emulation and that they rapidly copied successful practices by diaspora entrepreneurs in the region.

Finally, diaspora investment, compared to FDI, is less likely to cause nationalist backlashes. In both China and India, JVs with MNCs encountered contention between domestic and foreign partners. Joint ventures involving diaspora investors, by contrast, were implemented without rousing much critical nationalism. In many nondiaspora JVs in India, indigenous partners accused foreigners of withholding advanced technology, unfair revenue sharing, and having contemptuous attitudes. Meanwhile, foreign partners criticized India's market for being irregular and restrictive regarding their entry and operations. In China, thanks to predominant diaspora investment, FDI has not caused widespread nationalist backlashes – despite the fact that similar frictions existed in China's JVs with foreign MNCs.

In conclusion, diaspora entrepreneurs are more likely to invest in their homelands and build better interpersonal ties with domestic actors than other investors might be. Such networks, however, are not substitutes for the technology and innovation that are typically led by advanced Western MNCs. The intermediary technology transferred via diaspora networks has worked well for China and India in the past three decades but as these economies move to the next stage of industrialization, global companies that harbor sophisticated technology, top-notch innovation, and world-class business models are highly coveted, and collaboration with such innovators would undoubtedly help posttransition economies to leapfrog into advanced economies.

The importance of diasporas will remain critical in this stage because substantial numbers of diaspora Chinese and Indians are working at these companies and are carriers of innovative knowledge and business practices. Home governments in both countries have rightfully made efforts to attract the return of such human talents. To what extent such diaspora talents return to their homelands and how they introduce policy innovations in various technology sectors after return remain critically uncertain at this point.

DIASPORA DIFFERENCES AND CONSEQUENCES ACROSS CHINA AND INDIA

The key arguments in this book are that diaspora networks have had significant, yet previously underappreciated, impacts on China's and India's policy change and that the differences between the two diaspora bodies account for the divergence in their FDI liberalization. Factors that influence diaspora effects come from both the supply and demand sides. The following pages summarize the findings in the book and synthesize main differences between the two diaspora bodies, their ties to homelands, and domestic conditions that have constrained or enhanced diaspora effects.

During my research, some interlocutors suggested that Chinese diasporas were culturally more devoted to their homeland than were Indian diasporas. No evidence supports such a view in this book. Instead, the two countries' diaspora bodies both exhibit remarkable dedication to their homelands' development. With much smaller investable funds than Chinese diasporas, Indian diaspora investment accounted for 24–29 percent in homeland FDI inflows during the first half of the 1990s; in 2011, diaspora remittances amounted to $23 billion in India, almost the same amount as FDI the country received. The sum of diaspora deposits in Indian banks was also greater than the sum of all external funds in the country.

As the book reveals, there are at least four differences between China's and India's émigrés, which account for the varied diaspora impacts on homeland liberalization captured here: geography, economic strength, homeland ties, and homeland policies. Each of the variations has been captured by the conceptualization and measurement of network strength in Chapter 2.

First, geographic concentration. The largest number of Indian emigrants are in Burma, with which India has historical and geographic proximity. But it is a place where development and liberalization are not pursued. Outside South Asia, Indian diasporas can be divided into three groups: contractual labor in the Gulf, earlier immigrants to the United Kingdom, and more recent immigrants to the United States. China's overseas population was different. The 1949 Communist revolution resulted in substantial exoduses to Hong Kong, Macao, and Taiwan, following earlier emigrants in Southeast Asia. These diasporas in China's vicinity were most important to the country's FDI liberalization. As noted previously, geographic proximity amplified the roles of such diaspora groups. The more recent Chinese elite emigrants to Japan, America, and Europe (after the country's opening) have begun to return to their home country to play critical roles in policy areas such as financial liberalization (Wang 2012).

Diasporas' professions and accomplishments in their host societies also matter. The SNT emphasizes ideational superiority and resources that shape diasporas' engagement in homeland reform, but ideational influence is often enhanced by material attraction. Successful diasporas thus have more ideational appeal among domestic elites and more resources to help homeland development than do unsuccessful or nonprestigious ones. Among FDI investors, the Chinese diasporas had more resources and more experiences in capitalism than their Indian counterparts as a whole. Chinese diasporas were the main players in East Asia's high growth after World War II and were globally consequential manufacturers, financiers, and developers.[1] When China's economic transition began, Chinese entrepreneurial diasporas had investable capital, manufacturing technology, and extensive ties to global markets to strategically exploit business opportunities in the Mainland. China's economic rise was, then, indeed inseparable from the previous East Asian miracles.

India's diasporas were primarily professionals and laborers – although there were also some important entrepreneurs in Great Britain who had complicated relationships with their homeland. The reincorporation of professional diasporas

[1] Katzenstein and Shiraishi (1997) argue that two business networks were driving East Asian development: Japanese Keiretsu and Chinese family businesses.

into home government and the emergence of entrepreneurial immigrants in the services sectors in America, as this book explains, have indeed shaped the country's economic liberalization and globalization. However, the effects on specific policies and industrialization in India have differed from China.

The third major difference between China's and India's diasporas lies in their homeland access. The Chinese diaspora networks as a whole included top-level, local–state, and societal connections, and they were mostly entrepreneurial. Together they drove the PRC in a more liberal economic direction. Conversely, in India, diasporas with education and experience in the United States and Britain had connections at the national-elite level but lacked effective ties to local governments. Such Indian émigrés connected Indian elites with Western MNCs and IOs and played important policy roles. Yet ties limited to the national level are insufficient to sustain nationwide economic change, which typically involves actors outside policy-making circles. Recently, Indian states like Andhra Pradesh, Maharashtra, and Gujarat have attracted diaspora business and pursued FDI liberalization more persistently. Their relative economic success began to influence politicians in other states. Such internal diffusion resembles China's post-1980 FDI liberalization, although more diaspora entrepreneurs will be needed in India to expedite the process. In many sectors, Indian diaspora entrepreneurs are still lacking.

Last but not the least, there are differences between China's and India's policies toward diasporas. Diasporas' domestic access, critical to their impacts on homeland development, is reliant on the perception and reception of diasporas in their home country. For example, diaspora networks' strength is partly derived from their ideational superiority. Indian diasporas, however, have historically faced social obstacles that have limited their connections to domestic elites due to the legacy of independence movement and anticolonial history. In the 1960s and 1970s, domestic elites' perception of diasporas worsened because of migration studies that stressed "brain drain," the idea that the out-migration of the country's educated population permanently undermined the homeland's development. Only since the 1980s has India's public opinion of émigrés improved. Yet traditional hostility restrained diasporas' influence, and time is needed to repair relations between diasporas and their homeland. By contrast, the Chinese diasporas have long enjoyed ideational appeal in Chinese society. The fact that Chinese diasporas were significantly wealthier than domestic Chinese when China opened its door in 1978 dramatically intensified the ideational superiority of diaspora entrepreneurs.

On the other hand, states are critical to the formation of diaspora networks and the roles diasporas can play in their homelands. When Deng Xiaoping took over China after Mao, government personnel and priorities changed. The Chinese state invited back those who had been exiled in the 1940s, from top leaders to local officials, providing sentimental and material incentives for their return. Motivated by such hospitality and engagement, overseas Chinese gradually returned, set aside their previous political differences, and invested heavily in the Mainland. The Indian government, even in the recent decade, has yet to provide real incentives for diaspora investment, other than rhetoric and symbolic gestures. Indian entrepreneurs abroad remain underutilized resources. Yet the government has claimed, "We do not want your investment; we want your ideas. We do not want your riches; we want the richness of your experiences."[2]

LESSONS AND TRENDS

How will the future trends affect diasporas' impacts on China and India? In India, antiglobalization nationalism runs deep, and a wide range of industries remain fearful of foreign competition. Diaspora investors could potentially play greater roles if they form trustworthy interpersonal relationships with local actors. In China, when the government initiated reform, diaspora investors arrived quickly and built ties to local actors with whom they formed business partnerships. The Indian government can indeed learn from China's experience by promoting diaspora networks at lower levels and by facilitating interactions between domestic actors and diaspora returnees. Building up pro-liberalization ideas and incentives can potentially strengthen liberalization in the country from below, in addition to top-down macroeconomic policy schemes helped by diaspora professionals.

Chinese diaspora networks have thus far played a more influential role in China's FDI liberalization than their counterparts have in India. Going beyond this stage, however, the future comparison between the two countries' diaspora bodies is uncertain. Some trends suggest that the situation may be reversed. China's domestic enterprises (private and public included) are growing, and it has less a need for diaspora capital. The ideational superiority that diasporas once held has diminished. Although Hong Kong's unique role remains, the general perception in the PRC is that Hong Kong businesses need Mainland support more than the Mainland needs them. The completion of the Closer Economic Partnership Agreements with Hong Kong and Macao in 2003, the Economic Comprehensive Framework Agreement with Taiwan in 2010, and a free trade agreement with the Association of Southeast Asian Nations (ASEAN) a decade earlier all demonstrate that the Chinese economy has gained an advantage in trade, investment, and market size over regions where Chinese diasporas dominate business. Chinese diasporas in advanced countries maintain relative strength over their domestic counterparts in various scientific and engineering fields. This advantage is also declining, because

[2] Prime Minister A. B. Vajpayee speech at the inaugural session of the First Pravasi Bharatiya Divas celebrations, January 9, 2003. Accessed http://www.rediff.com/money/2003/jan/09pbd4.htm.

of advances in domestic training and the assimilation of diaspora professionals into domestic networks.[3]

China's political conditions may inhibit the return of the most talented human capital or the full use of those returned, which in turn deters the very best from coming back. One such condition is the promotion system within the Chinese state. After twenty years of bureaucratic reforms, the possibility of "lateral entrants" – talented people entering the government ranks without going through a rigorous promotion system – has not increased. Instead, the study of elite politics recently shows that family connections and party work experiences, such as the Chinese Communist Youth League, are the two dominant criteria for political promotions.[4] Second, the bureaucratization of the state has paradoxically reduced the informal influence of diaspora actors. Informal influence on policy was prevalent in the 1980s and the early 1990s and was important to economic policy innovations in China. Now each policy-making agency develops its own trusted think tanks and expert groups that the agency relies on for policy advice. Diasporas in China's vicinity have more or less lost their ideational appeal, whereas those trained in the West can only play limited roles until they gain real trust from the government. Such bureaucratic compartmentalization may have reduced cross-agency consultation and coordination within the Chinese state.

India, on the other hand, has shifted from its earlier bias against immigrants. Top executives, the Prime Minister's Office, the Finance Ministry, the Reserve Bank of India, and other bureaus, now hire and consult diaspora advisors as a standard operating procedure. The return of Indian immigrants in America (as operators for Western MNCs, managers at aspiring indigenous companies, and entrepreneurs who aim to utilize business opportunities in the homeland) has induced a clear social change in India and enhanced the desire to go West. Such a growing trend reflects the changed social basis of the Indian government and is demonstrated in the prevalence of electoral victories of foreign-trained candidates in the national parliament. Those diasporas yet to return are also playing policy roles in India. Famous scholars of Indian origin, sometimes critical of the home government's inefficiency in policy making and implementation, carry influence within India's policy-making circles. At the societal level, Indians seek diaspora connections to industrially advanced countries. The number and accomplishments of Indian émigrés are growing. If the government embraces their influence and offers them incentives to return, diasporas' development effect will predictably increase and facilitate homeland industrialization and integration into the global market.

[3] As sociologists Alejandro Portes (2013) and Sidney Tarrow (2009) suggest, diasporas play more influence as external actors but rooted in domestic context. Reassimilation actually reduces diasporas' impact.

[4] For the recent findings on China's leadership succession, see Shih (2008) and Zheng (2013).

Overall, the two countries face challenges of different natures. China, on the one hand, has completed the transition from socialism to capitalism and dealt with its capital needs for industrialization. But critical institutional reforms lie ahead, and the political entity is currently too exclusive to accept stronger external impact. India, on the other hand, has unmet needs for investment in infrastructure, small industry, and local programs that may bring jobs, revenues, technology, and information that transform primordial ideologies and protectionist interests. In these areas, unfortunately, the government has not made progress and is yet to recognize the severity of the task. The government remains intent on supporting large companies' pursuit of globalization, without actively promoting external partnerships beyond the highest echelons of Indian business.

CONCLUSION

China's and India's FDI liberalization have differed in their respective starting points and progress. China opened to FDI in 1980; India did so in 1991. China's FDI liberalization followed the rapid diffusion model. The Indian experience can be described as "two steps forward, one step behind." Two different capitalist networks were behind this divergence. In China, strong diaspora networks helped to initiate and expand FDI liberalization rapidly. Conversely, in India, domestic business led policy liberalization from the 1980s to the present. Indigenous industry slowed FDI liberalization when FDI clashed with their economic interests.

The China and India comparison raises important theoretical questions regarding regime and reform, globalization, and the effects of diasporas. It finds, first, that the dominant social networks (diaspora in China and domestic business in India) were crucial to FDI liberalization in these countries. On globalization, we see that diaspora investment has a different development impact than does nonethnic FDI, which tends to be more reluctant to come to these countries and more contentious upon their arrival. Even when Western MNCs are dominant sources of FDI, diasporas play critical, although perhaps indirect, roles, such as proposing and executing such investments. The phenomenon is particularly prevalent in India, where diaspora professionals at American MNCs have led the massive services outsourcing from the United States to India.

The effects of diasporas, however, are dependent on open and permissive environments in their homelands. The Chinese reformist state and open-minded top leaders in the 1980s and 1990s were the preconditions for diasporas' return and contributions. Indian government's fundamental change starting in the mid-1980s was likewise important to the policy effect of returned diaspora professionals. For other countries keen on late industrialization, immigration policies are developmental. Instead of viewing out-migration as "brain drain," immigrants to advanced nations can become a brain (and capital) gain – if provided proper domestic conditions for their return in the future.

Bibliography

Abbas, K. A. (1985). *Indira Gandhi: The Last Post*. Bombay: Popular Prakashan Ltd.

Abdelal, Rawi, Mark Blyth, and Craig Parsons. (2010). *Constructing the International Economy*. Ithaca, NY: Cornell University Press.

Acharya, Shankar. (2008). "Macroeconomics Policy in India in the 2000s." *ICRIER Working paper*.

Ahlquist, John. (2006). "Economic Policy, Institutions, and Capital Flows." *International Studies Quarterly*, 50, 681–704.

Ahluwalia, M. (2002). "Economic Reforms in India Since 1991: Has Gradualism Worked?" *Journal of Economic Perspective*, 16(3), 67–88.

Alexander, P. C. (1991). *My Years with Indira Gandhi*, New Delhi: Vision Books.

Ampalavanar-Brown, R. (1998). "Overseas Chinese Investments in China – Patterns of Growth, Diversification and Finance: The case of Charoen Pakphand." *The China Quarterly*, 155, 610–636.

Amsden, Alice. (1989). *Asia's Next Giant: South Korea and Late Industrialization*. New York: Oxford University Press.

Amsden, Alice. (2003). *Rise of the Rest: Challenges to the West from Late-Industrializing Economies*. New York: Oxford University Press.

Andersen, Walter. (1982). "India in 1981: Stronger Political Authority and Social Tension." *Asian Survey*, 22(2), 119–135.

Andersen, Walter. (1983). "India in 1982: Domestic Challenges and Foreign Policy Successes." *Asian Survey*, 23(2), 111–122.

Andersen, Walter. (1995). "India in 1994: Economics to the Fore." *Asian Survey*, 35(2), 127–139.

Appleyard, Reginald (ed.). (1999). *Migration and Development*. Geneva: International Organization for Migration.

Arora, A., V. S. Arunachalam, Jai Asundi, and Ronald Fernandes. (2001). "The Indian Software Services Industry," *Research Policy*, 30 (8), 1267–1287.

Arora, Dolly. (1981). "Big Business, Influence-Generation, and Decision Making in India." *Economic and Political Weekly*, 16(9), February 28, M2–M14.

Bajpai, K. S. (1992). "India in 1991: New Beginnings." *Asian Survey*, 32(2), 207–216.

Bardhan, Pranab. (1984). *The Political Economy of Development in India*. New York: Basil Blackwell.

Bardhan, Pranab. (1993). "Democracy and Development." *Journal of Economic Perspectives*. 7(3), 45–49.

Bardhan, Pranab. (2010). *Awakening Giants: Feet of Clay*. Princeton, NJ: Princeton University Press.

Barnett, W.P., J. Kim, and M. Rhee. (2008). "Hyundai Motor Company in China." Stanford Graduate School of Business, Case IB-91, September 24.

Barnouw, Eric. (1989). *International Encyclopedia of Communications*. New York: Oxford University Press.

Baum, Richard. (1986). "China in 1985: The Greening of the Revolution." *Asian Survey*, 26(1), 30–53.

Bentley, Arthur. (1967). *The Process of Government*. Cambridge, MA: Harvard University Press.

Bergsten, Fred et al. (2006). *China: The Balance Sheet*. Washington, DC: Institute of International Economics.

Bhagwati, Jagdish. (1993). *India in Transition: Freeing the Economy*. Oxford, UK: Clarendon Press.

Bhagwati, Jagdish. (2002). *A Stream of Windows*. Cambridge, MA: MIT Press.

Bhusan, B. (1990). "PMO's Hidden Economic Agenda." *Times of India*, June 25, 1.

Binder, Leonard. (1971). *Crises and Sequences in Political Development*. Princeton, NJ: Princeton University Press.

Birla, K.K. (1987). *Indira Gandhi: Reminiscences*. New Delhi: Vikas Publication House.

Blanton, Shannon, and Robert Blanton. (2007). "What Attracts Foreign Investors? An Examination of Human Rights and Foreign Direct Investment." *Journal of Politics*, 69(1), 143–155.

Blyth, Mark. (2002). *Great Transformations: Economic Ideas and Institutional Change in the Twentieth Century*. New York: Cambridge University Press.

Cable, Vince. (1995). *China and India: Economic Reform and Global Integration*. London: Royal Institute of International Affairs.

Cai, Hongbin, and Daniel Treisman. (2005). "Does Competition for Capital Discipline Governments? Decentralization, Globalization, and Public Policy." *American Economic Review*, 95(3), 817–830.

Cai, Hongbin, and Daniel Treisman. (2006). "Did Government Decentralization Cause China's Economic Miracle?" *World Politics*, 58(4), 505–535.

Calder, Kent. (1988). *Crisis and Compensation: Public Policy and Political Stability in Japan, 1949–1986*. Princeton, NJ: Princeton University Press.

Calder, Kent. (1993). *Strategic Capitalism: Private Business and Public Purpose in Japanese Industrial Finance*. Princeton, NJ: Princeton University Press.

Calder, Kent, and Min Ye (2004). "Regionalism and Critical Junctures: Explaining the 'Organization Gap' in Northeast Asia." *Journal of East Asian Studies*, 4(2), 191–226.

Calder, Kent, and Min Ye. (2010). *The Making of Northeast Asia*. Stanford, CA: Stanford University Press.

Callon, Scott. (1995). "Different Paths: The Rise of Taiwan and Singapore in the Global Personal Computer Industry." Working Paper, Asia/Pacific Research Center, Stanford University.

Cardoso, Fernando. (1973). "Associated Dependent Development: Theoretical and Practical Implications," in A. Stepan (ed.), *Authoritarian Brazil: Origins, Policies and Future*. New Haven, CT: Yale University Press, 142–178.

Carrington, Peter, John Scott, and Stanley Wasserman (eds.). (2005). *Models and Methods in Social Network Analysis*. New York: Cambridge University Press.

CASI. (2004). *Ideology, Politics and Economic Reforms: The National Democratic Alliance in Indian Politics, 1999–2004*.. Philadelphia, PA: Center for the Advanced Study of India, University Pennsylvania.

CASI (2005). "India's Strategy of IT-Led Growth: Challenges of Asymmetric Dependence," Working Paper, CASI, University Pennsylvania. http://casi.ssc.upenn.edu/research/DBI/IIT_summer2005.pdf. Accessed August 2, 2005.

Centeno, Miguel. (2005). "Growing Knowledge about Globalization: Observing Trade, 1980–2001." Working Paper, Princeton University.

Chang, C. Y. (1980). "Overseas Chinese in China's Policy." *The China Quarterly*, 82, 281–303.

Chatterjee, Partha. (2011). "Democracy and Economic Transformation in India," in Sanjay Ruparelia, Sanjay Reddy, John Harriss, and Stuart Corbridge (eds.), *Understanding India's New Political Economy*. New York: Routledge, 17–34.

Chaudhuri, A. (1975). *Private Economic Power in India*. New Delhi: People's Publishing House.

Chaudhuri, A. (1980). "Conglomerate Big Business Groups in India: Some Traits of Tycoon Capitalism." *Social Scientist*, 8(7), 38–51.

Chen, D. (2005). *Jingji quanqiuhua yu Taishang dalu touzi: Celue, buju yu jijiao [Economic Globalization and Taiwan's Investment in the Mainland: The Strategy, Location, and Comparison*]. Taibei: Dianjin wenhua shiye zhubangshe.

Chen, Hamin, and Tai-Jy Chen. (1998). "Network Linkages and Location Choice in FDI." *Journal of International Business Studies*, 29(3), 445–467.

Chen, Jinhua. (2005). *Guo shi yi shu [Memoirs of the Past Major Events]*. Beijing: CCP History Publisher.

Chen, Q. (1984). "Gangzi, qiaozi, yu jingji tequ de jianshe" [Hong Kong Capital, Overseas Chinese Capital and SEZ Development]. *Shijie jingji yanjiu [World Economic Research]*, 06.

Chen, Yuan. (1991). "Woguo jingji de shenceng wenti he xuanze" [The Roots of Economic Problems in China]. *Jingji yanjiu [Economic Research]*, 4, 18–26.

Chen, Yun. (1986). *Chen Yun wenxuan [Selected Works of Chen Yun]*. Beijing: People's Publishing House.

Chen, Yun. (2005). "Yao ba dianzi gongye gao shang qu [Should Develop the Electronics Industry]," *Chen Yun wenxuan [Selected Works of Chen Yun]* Vol. III. Beijing: Zhongyang wenxian chubanshe.

Cheng, Li. (2000). "China in 1999: Seeking Common Ground at a Time of Tension and Conflict." *Asian Survey*, 40(1), 112–129.

Choi, Inbom. (2003). "Korean Diaspora in the Making: Its Current Status and Impact on the Korean Economy," in Fred Bergsten and Inbom Choi (eds.), *The Korean Diaspora in the World Economy: Special Report 15*. Washington, DC: Peterson Institute for International Economics, 10–27.

Choi, Seung-Whan. (2009). "Effect of Outliers on Regression Analysis: Regime Types and Foreign Direct Investment." *Quarterly Journal of Political Science*, 4, 153–165.

CMIE. (1983) *Public Sector in the Indian Economy*. Bombay: CMIE, 14–15.

Cohen, Robin. (2008). *Global Diasporas*. London: Routledge.

Cohen, Robin, and Steven Vertovec (eds.). (1999). *Migration, Diasporas, and Transnationalism*. Cheltenham, UK: Edward Elgar.

Collier, David, and F. H. Cardoso. (1979). *The New Authoritarianism in Latin America*. Princeton, NJ: Princeton University Press.

Collier, Ruth. (1992). *The Contradictory Alliance: State-Labor Relations and Regime Change in Mexico*. Berkeley: International and Area Studies, University of California at Berkeley.

Cui, Ziyuan, and Y. Deng. (1996). *Nanjie cun* [*Nanjie Village*]. Beijing: Dangdai Zhongguo Chubanshe.

Datta-Chaudhuri, M. (1985). "The New Policy." *Seminar*, December, 18–22.

Debroy, Bibek, Laveesh Bhandari, and Swaminathan Anklesaria. (2011). *Economic Freedom of the States of India: 2011*. New Delhi: Academic Foundation.

Deng, Liqu et al. (1979). *Fangri guilai de sisuo* [*Thoughts upon Returning from Japan*]. Beijing: Zhongguo shehui kexue chubanshe.

Domes, Jirgen. (1977). "China in 1976: Tremors of Transition." *Asian Survey*, 17(1), 1–17.

Domes, Jirgen. (1978). "China in 1977: Reversal of Verdicts." *Asian Survey*, 18(1), 1–16.

Dittmer, Lowell. (1981). "China in 1980: Modernization and Its Discontents." *Asian Survey*, 21(1), 31–50.

Dittmer, Lowell. (1982). "China in 1981: Reform, Readjustment, Rectification." *Asian Survey*, 22(1), 33–46.

Dittmer, Lowell. (1990). "China in 1989: The Crisis of Incomplete Reform." *Asian Survey*, 30(1), 25–41.

Donnithorne, Audrey. (1972). *The Budget and the Plan in China: Central-Local Economic Relations*. Canberra: Australian National University Press.

Eckstein, Susan. (2004). "Dollarization and Its Discontents: Remittances and the Remaking of Cuba in the Post-Soviet Era." *Comparative Politics*, 36(3): 313–330.

Eckstein, Susan (ed.). (2013). *How Immigrants Influence Homeland Development*. Durham, NC: Duke University Press.

Eichengreen, B., G. Poonam, and R. Kumar (eds.). (2010). *Emerging Giants: China and India in the World Economy*. New York: Oxford University Press.

Eliot. (1971). "Social Control of Private Business." *Economic and Political Weekly*, 6(30/32). 1697–1702.

Elkins, Zackary, Andrew Guzman, and Beth Simmons. (2006). "Competing for Capital: Diffusion of Bilateral Investment Treaties, 1960–2000." *International Organization*, 60(4), 811–846.

Encarnation, Dennis. (1979). "The Indian Central Bureaucracy: Responsive to Whom?" *Asian Survey*, 19(11), 1126–1145.

Encarnation, Dennis. (1989). *Dislodging Multinationals: India's Strategy in Comparative Perspective*. Ithaca, NY: Cornell University Press.

Evans, Peter. (1979). *Dependent Development: The Alliance of Multinational, State, and Local Capital in Brazil*. Princeton, NJ: Princeton University Press.

Evans, Peter. (1985). "Transnational Linkages and the Economic Role of the State," in P. B. Evans, D. Rueschemeyer, and T. Skocpol (eds.), *Bringing the State Back In*. Cambridge, UK: Cambridge University Press.

Evans, Peter. (1995). *Embedded Autonomy: States and Industrial Transformation*. Princeton, NJ: Princeton University Press.

Farmer, R. (2007). "Chery Automobile Company: Evolution of the Chinese Automotive Industry," Working Paper, HKU 676, University of Hong Kong.

Feinberg, Susan, and Sumit Majumdar. (2001). "Technology Spillovers from FDI in the Indian Pharmaceutical Industry." *Journal of International Business Studies*, 32(3), 421–438.

Fernandez, J. A., and L. Underwood. (2006). *China CEO: Voices of Experience from 20 International Business Leaders*. Singapore: John Wiley & Sons.

Fewsmith, Joseph. (1994). *Dilemmas of Reform in China: Political Conflict and Economic Debate*. Armonk, NY: M. E. Sharpe.

Fewsmith, Joseph. (2001). *China since Tiananmen: The Politics of Transition*. New York: Cambridge University Press.

Fewsmith, Joseph. (2008). *China since Tiananmen: From Deng Xiaoping to Hu Jintao*. New York: Cambridge University Press.

Fewsmith, Joseph. (2013). *The Logic and Limits of Political Reform in China*. New York: Cambridge University Press.

Forbes, N. (2002). "Doing Business in India: What has Liberalization Changed?" In A. O. Krueger (ed.), *Economic Policy Reforms and the Indian Economy*. Chicago: University of Chicago Press, 129–168.

Frank, Kathleen. (2001). *Indira: The Life of Indira Nehru Gandhi*. London: HarperCollins Publishers.

Frankel, Francine. (2005). *India's Political Economy, 1947–2004: The Gradual Revolution*. New Delhi: Oxford University Press.

Frieden, Jeffrey. (1988). "Classes, Sectors, and Foreign Debt in Latin America." *Comparative Politics*, 21(1), 1–20.

Frieden, Jeffrey. (1991). "Invested Interests: The Politics of National Economic Policies in a World of Global Finance." *International Organization*, 45(4), 425–451.

Frieden, Jeffrey, and Ronald Rogowski. (1996). "The Impact of International Economy on National Policies," in Helen Milner and Robert Keohane (eds.), *Internationalization and Domestic Politics*. Princeton, NJ: Princeton University Press, 26–47.

Friedman, Edward, and Bruce Gilley. (2005). *Asia's Giants: Comparing China and India*. New York: Palgrave Macmillan.

Friedman, Thomas. (2005). *The World Is Flat: A Brief History of the Twenty First Century*. New York: Farrar, Straus and Giroux.

Fu, Q. (1992). "Jiejian riben zonghe shangshe moshi, zou you zhongguo tese de qiye guojihua zhi lu" [Use Japan's Keiretsu Model, and Build Chinese Global Companies with Chinese Characteristics]. *Kuaguo jingying [International Business]*, 10.

Fu, Y. (2002). *Taishang zai dalu touzi de quyu yanjiu [Regional Studies on Taiwan's Investment in Mainland China]*. Beijing: Taishang chubanshe.

Gallagher, Mary. (2005). *Contagious Capitalism: Globalization and the Politics of Labor in China*. Princeton, NJ: Princeton University Press.

Ganguly, S. (1997). "India in 1996: A Year of Upheaval." *Asian Survey*, 37(2), 126–135.

Ganguly, S. (1998). "India in 1997: Another Year of Turmoil." *Asian Survey*, 38(2), 126–134.

Garnaut, R., L. Song, S. Tenev, and Y. Yao. (2005). *China's Ownership Transformation: Process, Outcomes, and Prospects*. New York: International Finance Corporation.

Ghemawat, P. (2000). *The Indian Software Industry at the Millennium*. Master's thesis, Harvard Business School.

Ghose, A. (1974), "Investment Behavior of Monopoly Houses: I. Structure of Fixed Investment Decisions." *Economic and Political Weekly*, 9(43), 1813–1824.

Gilpin, Robert. (1987). *The Political Economy of International Relations*. Princeton, NJ: Princeton University Press.

Gold, Thomas, and David Wank. (eds.). (2002). *Social Connections in China: Institutions, Culture, and the Changing Nature of Guanxi*. Cambridge, UK: Cambridge University Press.

Goldstein, Avery. (1998). "China in 1997: A Year of Transitions." *Asian Survey*, 38(1), 34–52.

Gourevitch, Peter. (1978). "The Second Image Reversed: The International Sources of Domestic Politics." *International Organization*, 32(4), 881–912.

Gourevitch, Peter. (1986). *Politics in Hard Times: Comparative Responses to International Economic Crises*. Ithaca, NY: Cornel University Press.

Gowan, P. (1999). *The Global Gamble*. London: Verso.

Granovetter, Mark. (1973). "The Strength of Weak Ties." *American Journal of Sociology*, 78(6), 1360–1380.

Granovetter, Mark. (1983). "The Strength of Weak Ties: A Network Theory Revisited." *Sociological Theory*, 1, 201–233.

Granovetter, Mark. (1985). "Economic Action and Social Structure: The Problem of Embeddedness." *American Journal of Sociology*, 91(3), 481–510.

Grieco, Joseph. (1984). *Between Dependency and Autonomy: India's Experience with the International Computer Industry*. Berkeley: University of California Press.

Gu, Mu. (1998). "Zhongguo duiwai kaifang de fengfeng yuyu" [Winds and Rains of China's Open-Door Policy], *Ban Yue Tang*. 15, 20–21.

Guowuyuan, qiaowu bangongshi. (2001). *Deng Xiaoping lun qiaowu [Deng Xiaoping on Overseas Chinese Affairs]*. Beijing: Zhongguo wenxian chubanshe.

Gupta, J.D. (1981). "India in 1980: Strong Center, Weak Authority." *Asian Survey* 21(2), 147–161.

Haas, Peter. (1992). "Introduction: Epistemic Communities and International Policy Coordination." *International Organization*, 46(1), 1–35.

Habib, Mohsin, and Leon Zurawicki. (2002). "Corruption and FDI." *Journal of International Business Studies*, 33(2), 291–308.

Hafner-Burton, E., K. Miles, and A. Montgomery. (2009). "Network Analysis for International Relations." *International Organization*, 63(3), 559–592.

Haggard, Stephan. (1990). *Pathways from the Periphery: The Politics of Growth in the Newly Industrializing Countries*. Ithaca, NY: Cornell University Press.

Haggard, Stephan, and Sylvia Maxfield. (1996). "The Political Economy of Financial Liberalization in the Developing World." *International Organization*, 50(1), 35–68.

Haggard, Stephan, and Sylvia Webb. (1993). "What Do We Know About the Political Economy of Economic Policy Reform?" *The World Bank Research Observer*, 8(2), 143–168.

Hall, Peter (ed.). (1989). *Political Power of Economic Ideas*. Princeton, NJ: Princeton University Press.

Hall, Peter. (1993). "Policy Paradigms, Social Learning, and the State: The Case of Economic Policy Making in Britain." *Comparative Politics*, 25(3), 275–296.

Hamilton, Gary. (1991). *Business Networks and Economic Development in East and Southeast Asia*. Hong Kong: University of Hong Kong Press.

Hardgrave, Robert. (1984). "India in 1983: New Challenges, Lost Opportunities." *Asian Survey*, 24(2), 209–218.

Hardgrave, Robert. (1985). "India in 1984: Confrontation, Assassination, and Succession." *Asian Survey*, 25(2), 131–144.
Hardgrave, Robert, and Stanley Kochanek. (eds.). (1993). *India: Government and Politics in a Developing Nation*. Orlando, FL: Harcourt Brace College Publishers.
Harding, Harry. (1987). *China's Second Revolution: Reform after Mao*. Washington, DC: Brookings Institution.
Harriss, John. (1987). "The State in Retreat: Why Has India Experienced Such Half-Hearted Liberalization in the 1980s?" *IDS Bulletin*, 18(4), 31–38.
He, B., et. al. (1996). *Zhongguo jishu zhuanyi he jishu jinbu [Technology Transfer and Progress in China]*. Beijing: Jingji guanli chubanshe.
Heilmann, Sebastian. (2008). "Policy Experimentation in China's Economic Rise." *Studies in Comparative International Development*, 43(1), 1–26.
Hill, Michael. (1993). *The Policy Process: A Reader*. New York: Harvester-Wheatsheaf.
Hirschman, Albert. (1981). *Essays in Trespassing: Economics to Politics and Beyond*. New York: Cambridge University Press.
Ho, S., and R. Huenemann. (1984). *China's Open Door Policy*. Vancouver: University of British Columbia Press.
Holslag, Jonathan. (2010). *China Plus India: Prospects for Peace*. New York: Columbia University Press.
Horowitz, Michael. (2010). "Nonstate Actors and the Diffusion of Innovations." *International Organization*, 64(1), 34–64.
Hsing, You-Tien. (1996). "Blood, Thicker than Water: Interpersonal Relations and Taiwanese Investment in Southern China." *Environment and Planning A*, 28, 2241–2261.
Hsing, You-Tien. (1998). *Making Capitalism in China: The Taiwan Connection*. New York: Oxford University Press.
Hu, Angang and Shaoguang Wang. (1995). *Zhongguo diqu chaju baogao [Report on Regional Inequalities in China]*. Shengyang: Liaoning renmin chubanshe.
Huang, E., and J. Lawrence. (1995). *Hong Kong: Portraits of Power*. London: Weidenfeld & Nicolson.
Huang, Y. (2005). "Chufang huodong yu gaige kaifang juece de yunniang" [Foreign Visits and Decisions to Reform and Open]. *Deng Xiaoping yu gaige kaifang [Deng Xiaoping and Reform and Openness]*. Beijing: CCP History Publisher.
Huang, Yasheng. (1995). "Administrative Monitoring in China." *The China Quarterly*, 143, 828–843.
Huang, Yasheng. (1998). *FDI in China: An Asian Perspective*. Singapore: Institute of Southeast Asian Studies.
Huang, Yasheng. (2003). *Selling China: Foreign Direct Investment during the Reform Era*. New York: Cambridge University Press.
Huang, Yasheng. (2008). *Capitalism with Chinese Characteristics*. New York: Cambridge University Press.
Huang, Yasheng. (2012). "Does Ethnicity Pay?" working paper, MIT.
Huang, Yasheng, and David Lane. (2003). "Kelon: China's Corporate Dragon." Harvard Business School, Case 9-701-053, March 27.
Huntington, Samuel. (1968). *Political Order in Changing Societies*. New Haven: Yale University Press.
Ikenberry, John. (1986). "The Irony of State Strength: Comparative Responses to the Oil Shocks in the 1970s." *International Organization*, 40(1), 105–137.

Jalan, B. (1991). *India's Economic Crisis: The Way Ahead.* Delhi: Oxford University Press.

Jenkins, Rob. (1999). *Democratic Politics and Economic Reform in India.* New York: Cambridge University Press.

Jenkins, Rob. (2011). "The Politics of India's Special Economic Zones," in S. Ruparelia et al., *Understanding India's New Political Economy.* New York: Routledge, 49–65.

Jensen, Nathan. (2004). "Democratic Governance and Multinational Corporations: Political Regimes and the Inflows of Foreign Direct Investment." *International Organization*, 57(3), 587–616.

Jensen, Nathan. (2008). *Nation-States and the Multinational Corporation: A Political Economy of Foreign Direct Investment.* Princeton, NJ: Princeton University Press.

Jessop, Bob. (1990). *State Theory: Putting the Capitalist State in its Place.* Cambridge, UK: Polity Press.

Jha, L.K. (1985). "In Search of a New Economic Order." *Illustrated Weekly of India*, April 6, 20–23.

Jiang, Zemin. (1991). "Speech at the Fourth Plenum of the Thirteenth Party Congress, June 24, 1989." CCP Central Compilation Office (ed.), *Shisanda yilai Zhongguo wenxian xuanbian [Major Documents Since the Thirteen Party Congress].* Beijing: People's Publisher.

Jin, D. (1984). "Congratulatory Speech at the Opening of the Symposium on Investment." Policy Research Department of the Ministry of Foreign Economic Relations and Trade (ed.), *Guide to China's Foreign Economic Relations and Trade.* Hong Kong: Economic Information Agency.

Johnson, Chalmers. (1982). *MITI and the Japanese Miracle: The Growth of Industrial Policy, 1925–1975.* Stanford, CA: Stanford University Press.

Kahler, Miles. (2009). *Networked Politics: Agency, Power, and Governance.* Ithaca, NY: Cornell University Press.

Kallgren, Joyce. (1979). "China in 1978: The New Long March." *Asian Survey*, 19(1), 1–19.

Kallgren, Joyce. (1980). "China in 1979: On Turning Thirty." *Asian Survey*, 20(1), 1–18.

Kallgren, Joyce. (1984). "China in 1983: The Turmoil of Modernization." *Asian Survey*, 24(1), 60–80.

Kao, John (1993). "The Worldwide Web of Chinese Business." *Harvard Business Review*, 71, March–April, 24–36.

Kapur, Devesh. (2002). "The Causes and Consequences of India's IT Boom." *India Review*, 1(2), 91–100.

Kapur, Devesh. (2004). "Ideas and Economic Reforms in India: The Role of International Migration and the Indian Diaspora." *India Review* 3(4), 364–384.

Kapur, Devesh. (2010). *Diasporas, Development, and Democracy.* Princeton, NJ: Princeton University Press.

Kapur, Devesh, and John McHale. (2005). *Give Us Your Best and Brightest: The Global Hunt for Talent and Its Impact on the Developing World.* Washington, DC: Center for Global Development.

Kapur, Devesh, and P.B. Mehta. (1999). "India in 1998: The Travails of Political Fragmentation." *Asian Survey* 39(1), 163–176.

Katzenstein, Peter. (1978). *Between Power and Plenty: Foreign Economic Policies of Advanced Industrial States.* Madison: University of Wisconsin Press.

Katzenstein, Peter. (1985). "Small Nations in an Open International Economy," in P. B. Evans, D. Rueschemeyer, and T. Skocpol (eds.), *Bringing the State Back In*. Cambridge, UK: Cambridge University Press.

Katzenstein, Peter, and Takashi Shiraishi (eds.). (1997). *Network Power: Japan and Asia*. Ithaca, NY: Cornell University Press.

Keck, Margaret, and Kathryn Sikkink. (1998). *Activists beyond Borders*, Ithaca, NY: Cornell University Press.

Keefer, Philip, and Stuti Khemani. (2009). "When Do Legislators Pass on Port?" *American Political Science Review*, 103(1), 99–112.

Kennedy, Scott. (2005). *The Business of Lobbying in China*. Cambridge, MA: Harvard University Press.

Keohane, R. (1980). "The Theory of Hegemonic Stability and Changes in International Economic Regimes, 1967–1977," in J. Holsti, R. Siverson, and A. George (eds.), *Change in International Systems*. Boulder, CO: Westview Press.

Khan, Rafi. (1999). *Government, Communities, Non-governmental Actors in Social Sector Delivery*. Farnham, UK: Ashgate Publication.

Khan, Rafi. (ed.) (2007), *Harnessing and Guiding Social Capital for Rural Development*, New York: Palgrave MacMillan.

Khanna, Tarun. (2007). *Billions of Entrepreneurs*. Cambridge, MA: Harvard Business School.

Khanna, Tarun, K. Palepu, and R. J. Bullock. (2009). "House of Tata: Acquiring a Global Footprint." Harvard Business School, Case 9-708-446, revised, June 30, 2009.

Kidwai, Anser. (1996). *Indira Gandhi: Charisma and Crisis*. New Delhi: Siddhi Books.

Kobrin, Stephen. (1979). "Political Risk: A Review and Reconsidered," *Journal of International Business Studies*, 10(1), 67–80.

Kobrin, Stephen. (1980). "Foreign Enterprises and Forced Divestment in LDCs." *International Organization*, 34(1), 65–88.

Kobrin, Stephen. (1984). "Expropriation as an Attempt to Control Foreign Firms in LDCs: Trends 1960–1979." *International Studies Quarterly*, 28(3), 329–348.

Kochanek, Stanley. (1986). "Regulation and Liberalization Theology in India." *Asian Survey*, 26(12), 1284–1308.

Kochanek, Stanley. (1987). "Briefcase Politics in India: The Congress Party and the Business Elite." *Asian Survey*, 27(12), 1278–1301.

Kochanek, Stanley. (1995). "The Transformation of Interest Politics in India." *Pacific Affairs*, 68(4), 529–550.

Kochanek, Stanley. (1996). "The Rise of Interest Politics in Bangladesh." *Asian Survey*, 36(7), 704–722.

Kohli, Atul. (1987). *The State and Poverty in India: The Politics of Reform*. New York: Cambridge University Press.

Kohli, Atul. (1989). "Politics of Economic Liberalization in India." *World Development*, 17(3), 305–328.

Kohli, Atul. (1990). "Economic Liberalization in Indian," in Ezra Suleiman and John Waterbury (eds.), *Political Economy of Public Sector Reform and Privatization*. Boulder, CO: Westview Press.

Kohli, Atul. (2004). *State-Directed Development: Political Power and Industrialization in the Global Periphery*. New York: Cambridge University Press.

Kohli, Atul. (2006a). "Politics of Economic Reform in India, 1980–2005: Part I." *Economic and Political Weekly*. 41(13), 1251–1259.

Kohli, Atul. (2006b). "Politics of Economic Reform in India, 1980–2005: Part II." *Economic and Political Weekly*, 41(14), 1361–1374.

Kohli, Atul. (2012). *Poverty Amid Plenty: Political Economy of the New India*. Cambridge, UK: Cambridge University Press.

Kowalski, P. (2008). "China and India: A Tale of Two Trade Integration Approaches." *ICIER Working Paper*, no. 221.

Krasner, Stephen. (2000). "State Power and the Structure of International Trade." In Jeffrey Frieden and David Lake (eds.), *International Political Economy: Perspectives on Global Power and Wealth*. New York: St. Martin's.

Krueger, Anne. (2002). *Economic Policy Reforms and the Indian Economy*. Chicago: University of Chicago Press.

Krugman, Paul. (1992). "Toward a Counter-Counterrevolution in Development Theory." MIT World Economy Laboratory Working Paper, 92 (5), MIT.

Kumar, Negish. (2001). *Indian Software Industry Development in International and National Development Perspective*. Delhi: Research and Information Systems for the Nonaligned and Other Developing Countries.

Kundra, Ashok. (2010). *China and India: A Comparative Analysis of FDI Policy and Performance*. New Delhi: Academic Foundation.

Lake, David. (2000). "British and American Hegemony Compared: Lessons for the Current Era of Decline," in Jeffrey Frieden and David Lake (eds.), *International Political Economy: Perspectives on Global Power and Wealth*. New York: Bedford/St. Martin's.

Lardy, Nicholas. (1992). *Foreign Trade and Economic Reform in China, 1978–1990*. New York: Cambridge University Press.

Lardy, Nicholas. (2002). *Integrating China into the Global Economy*. Washington, DC: Brookings Institution.

Lateef, A. (1997). *Linking up with the Global Economy: A Case Study of the Bangalore Software Industry*. Geneva: International Institute for Labour Studies.

Lau, H., and S. Green, "The Electronics Industry: Can Manufacturing Continue in Hong Kong?" *World Economy*, 24(8), 1075–1090

Leblang, David. (2003). "To Devalue or To Defend? Political Economy of Exchange Rate Policy." *International Studies Quarterly*, 47(4), 533–559.

Leblang, David. (2010). "Familiarity Breeds Investment." *American Political Science Review*, 104(3), 584–600.

Leblang, David, and Shanker Satyanath. (2006). "Institutions, Expectations, and Currency Crisis." *International Organization*, 60(1), 245–262.

Legro, Jeffrey. (2005). *Rethinking the World: Great Power Strategies and International Order*. Ithaca, NY: Cornell University Press.

Lehmbruch, Gerhard. (1984). "Concertation and the Structure of Neo-Corporatist Networks," in J.H. Goldthorpe (ed.), *Order and Conflict in Contemporary Capitalism*. Oxford, UK: Oxford University Press.

Lever-Tracy, C. et. al (1996). *The Chinese Diaspora and Mainland China: An Emerging Economic Synergy*. Basingstoke, HK: Macmillan Press.

Levitsky, Steven. (2006). "Linkage versus Leverage: Rethinking the International Dimension of Regime Change." *Comparative Politics*, 38(4), 379–400.

Li, Lanqing. (2008). *Tuwei* [*Breakout*]. Beijing: Zhongguo wenxian chubanshe.

Li, Quan. (2009). "Outliers, Measurement, and the Democracy-FDI Controversy," *Quarterly Journal of Political Science*, 4, 167–181.

Li, Quan, and Adam Resnick. (2003). "Reversal of Fortunes: Democratic Institutions and Foreign Direct Investment Flows into Developing Countries." *International Organization*, 57, 175–211.

Li, Quan, and Dale Smith (2002). "The Dilemma of Financial Liberalization: State Autonomy and Societal Demands." *Journal of Politics*, 64(3), 764–790.

Lieberthal, Kenneth. (1983). "China in 1982: A Middling Course for the Middle Kingdom." *Asian Survey*, 23(1), 26–37.

Lieberthal, Kenneth, and David Lampton. (1992). *Bureaucracy, Politics, and Decision Making in Post-Mao China*. Berkeley: University of California Press.

Lieberthal, K., and M. Oksenberg. (1988). *Policy-Making in China: Leaders, Structures, and Processes*. Princeton, NJ: Princeton University Press.

Lin Zi. (2000). "Dalu mou jing la Taishang" [The Mainland Tried to Attract Taiwan Investment]. *Gangao cankao [Reference Report on Hong Kong and Macao]*, December 15, 2000.

Lin, Zi. (2000). "Shanghai kai dian qule" [Open a Store in Shanghai]. *Gangao cankao [Reference Report on Hong Kong and Macao]*, December 15, 2000

Lindblom, Charles. (1959). "The Science of 'Muddling Through.'" *Public Administration Review*, 19(2), 79–88.

Ling, Z. (2005). *Lianxiang fengyun [The Legend of Lenovo]*. Beijing: CITIC Publisher.

Little, Ian. (1982). *Economic Development: Theory, Policy, and International Relations*. New York: Basic Books.

Liu, C. (1994). "Tianjinshi liyong waizi jiajie gaizao guoyou qiye de duice sikao" [FDI to Transform SOEs in Tianjin]. *Jingji cankao [Economic References]*, November 23.

Liu, Xiaming, C. Wang, and Y. Wei. (2009). "Do Local Manufacturing Firms Benefit from Transnational Linkages with Multinational Enterprises in China?" *Journal of International Business Studies*, 40, 1113–1130.

Liu, Z. (ed.). (1999). *dianji – xin zhongguo jinji 50 nian) [Foundation – New China's Economy in 50 Years]*. Beijing: Zhongguo caijing chubanshe.

Lu, D. (2005). "Guangdong de duiwai kaifang yu jingji tizhi gaige" [Guangdong's Openness and Economic Structural Reform]. *Deng xiaoping yu gaige kaifang [Deng Xiaoping and China's Reform and Openness]*. Beijing: CCP History Publisher.

Lu, F., and K. Feng. (2005). *Fazhan woguo zhishi chanquan: Qiche gongye de zhengce xuanze [Developing China's Indigenous Technology and Policy Choices for the Auto Sector]*. Beijing: Peking University Press.

Luo, Yuanzheng. (1980). "Chinese Economy and Foreign Experiences." *Australian Journal of Chinese Affairs*, 3, 67–77.

Luo, Yadong. (2000). *Strategy, Structure, and Performance of MNCs in China*. Westport, CT: Quarum Books.

Mahler, Sarah. (2001). "Suburban Transport Migrants," in Heltor R. Cordeoro-Guzman, Robert Smith, and Grosfoguel Raman (eds.), *Migration, Transnationalization, and Race in a Changing New York*. Philadelphia: Temple University Press, 258–278.

Malhotra, I. (1989). *Indira Gandhi: A Personal and Political Biography*. London: Hodder & Stoughton.

Mann, James. (1998). *About Face: A History of America's Curious Relationship with China, from Nixon to Clinton*. New York: Vintage.

Manor, James. (1987). "Tried, then Abandoned: Economic Liberalization in India." *IDS Bulletin*, 18(4), 39–44.

Manor, James. (2005). "India's Reform Strength," in Friedman and Gilley (eds.), *Asia's Giants*, New York: Palgrave MacMillan, 97–122.

Mansfield, Edward, Helen Milner, and Peter Rosendorff. (2000). "Free to Trade: Democracy, Autocracies, and International Trade." *American Political Science Review*, 94(2), 305–321.

Martinez-Jerez, F., R. Kaplan, and K. Miller. (2009). "Infosys's Relationship Scorecard: Measuring Transformational Partnerships." Harvard Business School, Case 9-109-006, revised, December 8.

McClurg, Scott, and Joseph Young. (2011). "Political Networks." *PS: Political Science & Politics*, 44(1), 39–43.

Mercer, John. (2010), "Emotional Beliefs." *International Organization*, 64(1), 1–31.

Merchant, M. (1991). *Rajiv Gandhi, the End of a Dream*. New Delhi: Viking.

Migdal, Joel. (2001). *State in Society: Studying How States and Societies Transform and Constitute One Another*. Cambridge, UK: Cambridge University Press.

Milner, Helen. (1988a). "Trading Places: Industries for Free Trade." *World Politics*, 40(3), 350–376.

Milner, Helen. (1988b). *Resisting Protectionism: Global Industries and the Politics of International Trade*. Princeton, NJ: Princeton University Press.

Milner, Helen, and Keiko Kubota. (2005). "Why the Move to Free Trade: Democracy and Trade Policy in the Developing Countries." *International Organization*, 59(1), 107–143.

Ministry of Foreign Economic Relations and Trade. (1984). *Guide to China's Foreign Economic Relations and Trade: Cities Newly Opened to Foreign Investors*. Beijing: Economic Information and Agency.

Moore, Barrington. (1969). *Social Origins of Dictatorship and Democracy*. New York: Beacon Press.

Nagaraj, R. (2003). "Foreign Direct Investment in India in the 1990s: Trends and Issues." *Economic and Political Weekly*, 38(17), 1701–1712.

Namboodiripad, E. M. S. (1991). "The Present Economic Situation: Policy Alternatives." JANATA, October 13.

Narain, I. (1986). "India in 1985: Triumph of Democracy." *Asian Survey* 26(2), 253–269.

Narain, I.,and N. Dutta. (1987). "India in 1986: The Continuing Struggle." *Asian Survey*, 27(2), 181–193.

Narayanan, B., and P. Vashisht. (2008). "Determinants of the Indian Automobile Competitiveness." *ICRIER Working Paper*, 201.

Naughton, Barry. (1996). *Growing Out of the Plan: China's Economic Reform, 1978–1993*. New York: Cambridge University Press.

Naughton, Barry. (1997). *The China Circle*. Washington, DC: Brookings Institution Press.

Naughton, Barry. (1998). "The Third Front: Defense Industrialization in the Chinese Interior." *The China Quarterly*, 115, 351–386.

Naughton, Barry. (2007). *The Chinese Economy: Transitions and Growth*. Cambridge, MA: MIT Press.

Nayar, B. R. (1989). *India's Mixed Economy: The Role of Ideology and Interest in Its Development*. Bombay: Popular Prakashan.

Nayar, B. R. (2001). *Globalization and Nationalism: The Changing Balance in India's Economic Policy, 1950–2000*. New Delhi: Sage Publications.

Nigh, Douglas. (1985). "The Effect of Political Events on US Manufacturing Direct Foreign Investment." *Journal of International Business Studies*, 16, 1–17.
Oatley, Thomas. (1999). "How Constraining Is Capital Mobility? Partisan Hypothesis in an Open Economy." *American Journal of Political Science*, 43(4), 1003–1027.
O'Donnell, Guillermo. (1978). "Reflections on the Patterns of Change in the Bureaucratic Authoritarian State." *Latin American Research Review*, 13(1), 3–38.
O'Donnell, Guillermo. (1988). *Bureaucratic Authoritarianism in Argentina, 1966–1973 in Comparative Perspective*. Berkeley: University of California Press.
Oi, Jean. (1992). "Fiscal Reform and the Economic Foundation of Local State Corporatism in China." *World Politics*, 45(1), 99–126.
Olson, Mancur. (1993). "Dictatorship, Democracy, and Development." *American Political Science Review*, 87(3), 567–576.
Oneal, John. (1994). "The Affinity of Foreign Investors for Authoritarian Regimes." *Political Research Quarterly*, 47(3), 565–588.
Orenstein, Mitchell, and Peter Schmitz. (2006). "The New Transnationalism and Comparative Politics." *Comparative Politics*, 38(4), 479–500.
Padgett, John, and Christopher Ansell. (1993). "Robust Action and the Rise of the Medici, 1400–1434." *American Journal of Sociology*, 98(6), 1259–1319.
Pan, H. (1995). "Yinzi jiajie hua deshi" [On Gains and Losses in Using FDI in the SOE Reform]. *Touzi lilun yu shijian [Investment Theory and Practice]*, 11.
Panagariya, Arvind. (2008). *India: The Emerging Giant*. New York: Oxford University Press.
Pande, B. N. (1989). *Indira Gandhi*. Delhi: Publication Division of Government of India.
Pandya, Sonal. (2007). *Trading Spaces: The Political Economy of Foreign Direct Investment Regulations*. Dissertation. Harvard University.
Parthasaradhi, A., and N. Y. Sharada Prasad. (1985). *Indira Gandhi: Statesman, Scholars, Scientists and Friends remember*. New Delhi: Vikas publication.
Parthasarathy, B. (2000). *Globalization and Agglomeration in Newly Industrializing Countries: The State and the Information Technology Industry in Bangalore, India*, PhD Dissertation, University of California at Berkeley.
Patel, I. G. (1997). "On Taking India into the Twenty-first Century." *Modern Asian Studies*, 21(2), 209–231.
Patel, I. G. (2002) *Glimpse of Indian Economic Policy: An Insider's View*. New Delhi: Oxford University Press.
Patterson, Rubin. (2006). "Transnationalism: Diaspora-Homeland Development." *Social Forces*, 84(4), 1891–1907.
Pearson, Margaret. (1992). *Joint Ventures in the People's Republic of China: The Control of Foreign Direct Investment under Socialism*. Princeton, NJ: Princeton University Press.
Pearson, Margaret. (2005). "The Business of Governing Business in China: Institutions and Norms of the Emerging Regulatory State." *World Politics*, 57(2), 296–322.
Pedersen, Jod. (2000). "Explaining Economic Liberalization in India: State and Society Perspectives." *World Development*, 28(2), 265–282.
Pei, Minxin. (2006). *China's Trapped Transition: The Limits of Developmental Autocracy*. Cambridge, MA: Harvard University Press.
Pfeffermann, Guy. (2002). "Business Environment and Surveys: China vs. India." IFC Conference, April, Washington DC.
Pfeffermann, Guy. (2003). "China's Staying Power." *Foreign Policy*, 139, 6–8.

Portes, Alejandro. (2013). "Theorizing Immigrants and Homeland Development," in Susan Eckstein (ed.), *Immigrants and Homeland Development*. Durham, NC: Duke University Press.

Przeworski, Adam. (1991). *Democracy and Markets: Political and Economic Reforms in East Europe and Latin America*, New York: Cambridge University Press.

Quinn, Dennis. (1997). "The Correlates of Change in International Financial Regulation." *American Political Science Review*, 91(3), 531–551.

Quinn, Dennis, and Carla Inclan. (1997). "The Origins of Financial Openness: A Study of Current and Capital Account Liberalization." *American Journal of Political Science*, 144(3), 771–813.

Ramos, Joshua. (2004). "The Beijing Consensus." Foreign Policy Center.

Ratha, Dilip, and William Shaw. (2007). "South-South Migration and Remittances." *World Bank Working Paper* 102.

Reardon, Lawrence. (2002). *Reluctant Dragon*. Hong Kong: Chinese University of Hong Kong Press.

Ren, G. (1999). *huaqiao huaren yu guogong guanxi [Overseas Chinese and the CCP and KMT]*. Wuhan, China: Wuhan Publisher.

Resnick, Adam. (2001). "Investors, Turbulence, and Transition: Democratic Transition and Foreign Direct Investment," *International Interaction*, 27(4), 381–398.

Riskin, Carl. (1987). *China's Political Economy: The Quest for Development since 1949*. New York: Oxford University Press.

Risse-Kappen, Thomas. (1994). "Ideas Do Not Float Freely: Transnational Coalitions, Domestic Structures, and the End of the Cold War." *International Organization*, 48(2), 185–214.

Rodrik, Dani, and Arvind Subramanian. (2004). "From Hindu Growth to Productivity Surge: The Mystery of the Indian Growth Transition," Working Paper, National Bureau of Economic Research, Cambridge, MA.

Rogers, Everett. (1995). *Diffusion of Innovations*. New York: Free Press.

Rogowski, Ronald. (1987). "Political Cleavages and Changing Exposure to Trade." *American Political Science Review*, 81(4), 1121–1137.

Rogowski, Ronald. (1990). *Commerce and Coalitions: How Trade Affects Domestic Political Alignment*. Princeton, NJ: Princeton University Press.

Rokkan, S. (1966). "Norway: Numerical Democracy and Corporate Pluralism," in Robert Dahl (ed.), *Political Oppositions in Western Democracies*. New Haven, CT: Yale University Press.

Rosen, George. (1992). *Contrasting Styles of Industrial Reform: China and India in the 1980s*. Chicago: University of Chicago Press.

Rosen, Stanley. (1987). "China in 1986: A Year of Consolidation." *Asian Survey*, 27(1), 35–55.

Rosen, Stanley. (1988). "China in 1987: The Year of the Thirteenth Party Congress." *Asian Survey*, 28(1), 35–51.

Roy, Ramshray. (1993). "India in 1992: Search for Safety." *Asian Survey*, 33(2), 119–128.

Roy, Ramshray. (1994). "India in 1993: The Struggles of Economic Reform." *Asian Survey*, 34(2), 200–208.

Rubin, Barnett. (1985). "Economic Liberalization and the Indian State." *Third World Quarterly*, 7(4), 924–941.

Rudolph, Lloyd, and Susanne Rudolph. (2001). "Iconization of Chandrababu: Sharing Sovereignty in India's Federal Market Economy." *Economic and Political Weekly*, 36 (18), 1541–1552.
Sabatier, Paul (ed.). (2007). *Theories of the Policy Process*. New York: Westview Press.
Safran, William. (1991). "Diasporas in Modern Societies: Myths of Homeland and Return." *Diaspora: A Journal of Transnational Studies*, 1, 83–99.
Saich, Tony. (2005). "Development and Choice," in Friedman and Gilley (eds.), *Asia's Giants: Comparing China and India*, New York: Palgrave MacMillan.
Saxenian, AnnaLee. (1999). *Silicon Valley's New Immigrant Entrepreneurs*. San Francisco: Public Policy Institute of California.
Saxenian, AnnaLee. (2002). *Bangalore: The Silicon Valley of Asia?* Delhi: Oxford University Press.
Schram, Stuart. (1984). "Economics in Command? Ideology and Policy since the Third Plenum, 1978–84." *The China Quarterly*, 99, 417–461.
Schulte, Bettina. (2008). "Second Generation Entrepreneurs of Turkish Origin in Germany: Diasporic Identity and Business Engagement." Centre on Migration, Citizenship and Development (COMCAD) Arbeitspapiere, Working Paper 56.
Schuttler, Kirsten. (2007). *The Moroccan Diaspora in Germany: Its Contribution to Development in Morocco*. Eschborn, Germany: Federal Ministry for Economic Cooperation and Development.
Scott, John. (1991). *Social Network Analysis: A Handbook*. London: Sage Publications.
Seagrave, Sterling. (1995). *Lords of the Rim: The Invisible Empire of the Overseas Chinese*. New York: G. P. Putnam Sons.
Segal, Adam. (2003). *Digital Dragon: High-Technology Enterprises in China*. Ithaca, NY: Cornell University Press
Sekhar, Uday. (2006) "Funding Corporate India: Opportunities in International Financial Markets." *Economist Intelligence Unit Briefing Paper*, 30.
Sengupta, A. (2001). *Reforms, Equity, and the IMF: An Economist's World*. New Delhi: Har Anand Publications.
Sengupta, M. (2004). *The Politics of Market Reform in India: The Fragile Basis of Paradigm Shift*. Unpublished PhD Thesis, Department of Political Science, University of Toronto.
Shambaugh, David. (1991). "China in 1990: The Year of Damage Control." *Asian Survey*, 31(1), 36–49.
Shambaugh, David. (1992). "China in 1991: Living Cautiously." *Asian Survey*, 32(1), 19 31.
Sharma, Shalendra. (2009). *China and India in the Age of Global Integration*. New York: Cambridge University Press.
Shastri, Vanita. (1997). "The Politics of Economic Liberalization in India." *Contemporary South Asia*, 6(1), 27–56.
Shih, Victor. (2008). *Factions and Finance: Elite Conflict and Inflation*. New York: Cambridge University Press
Shirk, Susan. (1994). *How China Opened Its Door: The Political Success of the PRC's Foreign Trade and Investment Reforms*. Washington, DC: Brookings Institution.
Shue, Vivienne. (1988). *The Reach of the State: Sketches of the Chinese Body Politic*. Stanford, CA: Stanford University Press.
Simmons, Beth, Frank Dobbin, and Geoffrey Garrett. (2006). "Introduction: The International Diffusion of Liberalism." *International Organization*, 60, 781–810.

Simmons, Beth, Frank Dobbin, and Geoffrey Garrett. (2009). *The Global Diffusion of Markets and Democracy*. New York: Cambridge University Press.

Simmons, Beth, and Zackary Elkins. (2004). "The Globalization of Liberalization: Policy Diffusion in the International Political Economy." *American Political Science Review*, 98(1), 171–187.

Simon, Herbert. (1973). "The Organization of Complex Systems," in Howard Pattee (ed.), *Hierarchy Theory: The Challenge of Complex Systems*. New York: George Braziller.

Singh, N. (2004). "A Strategic Approach to Strengthening the International Competitiveness in Knowledge-Based Industries: The Case of Indian Automobile Industry." *RIS Discussion Papers*, no. 82.

Sinha, Aseema. (2003). "Rethinking the Developmental State Model," *Comparative Politics*, 35(4), 459–476.

Sinha, Aseema. (2005a). "Political Foundations of Market-preserving Federalism: Theoretical Lessons from India and China." *Comparative Politics*, 37(3), 337–356.

Sinha, Aseema. (2005b). "Understanding the Rise and Transformation of Business Collective Action in India." *Business and Politics*, 7(2), 1–35.

Slaughter, Anne-Marie. (2005). *A New World Order*. Princeton, NJ: Princeton University Press.

Smith, Robert. (2000). "How Durable and New Is Transnational Life?" *Diaspora*, 9, 203–232.

Sobel, Andrew. (1994). *Domestic Choices, International Markets: Dismantling National Barriers and Liberalizing Securities Markets*. Ann Arbor: University of Michigan Press.

Sobel, Andrew. (1998). "Domestic Policy Choices, Political Institution Change, and Financial Globalization." *International Interactions*, 24(4), 345–377.

Sobel, Andrew. (1999). *State Institutions, Private Incentives, and Global Capital*. Ann Arbor: University of Michigan Press.

Srinivasan, T. N. (2002). "India's Fiscal Situation: Is a Crisis Ahead?" in Anne Krueger (ed.), *Economic Policy Reforms and the Indian Political Economy*. Delhi: Oxford University Press.

Srivastava, S. (2003). "What Is the True Level of FDI Flows to India." *Economic and Political Weekly*, 38 (7), 608–610.

Staats, Joseph, and Glen Biglaiser. (2011). "The Democratic Advantage and Sectoral Foreign Direct Investment: The Importance of Strong Courts and the Rule of Law." Presented at the American Political Science Association, Seattle, WA, August 31.

Steinfeld, Edward. (2000). *Forging Economic Reform in China*. New York: Cambridge University Press.

Steinfeld, Edward. (2010). *Playing Our Game*. New York: Oxford University Press.

Stolper, Wolfgang, and Paul Samuelson (1941). "Protection and Real Wages." *Review of Economic Studies*, 9(1), 58–73.

Suleiman, Ezra, and John Waterbury. (1990). *Political Economy of Public Sector Reform and Privatization*. Boulder, CO: Westview Press.

Sun, X. (1994). "Zhongce xianxiang qishilu" [Implications of the China Investment Strategy Company]. *Guoji jingji hezuo [International Economic Cooperation]*, 10.

Sung, Y.-W. (1991). *The China-Hong Kong Connection: The Key to China's Open Door Policy*. New York: Cambridge University Press.

Swamy, A. (2001). "India in 2000: A Respite from Instability." *Asian Survey*, 41(1), 91–103.

Tang, Y. (1998). *1978 nian yilai Zhongguo gaige de licheng [China's Economic Reform since 1978]*. Beijing: Economic Daily Publisher.

Tarrow, Sidney. (2009). *Transnational Activists*. New York: Cambridge University Press.

Thun, Eric. (2006). *Changing Lanes in China: Foreign Direct Investment, Local Government, and Auto Sector Development*. New York: Cambridge University Press.

Tilly, Charles. (2007). "Trust Networks in Transnational Migration." *Sociological Forum*, 22(1), 3–24.

Toye, John. (1988). "Political Economy and the Analysis of Indian Development." *Modern Asian Studies*, 22(1), 97–122.

Tsai, Kellee. (2004). *Back Alley Banking: Private Entrepreneurs in China*. Ithaca, NY: Cornell University Press.

Tsai, Kellee. (2007). *Capitalism without Democracy*. Ithaca, NY: Cornell University Press.

Tsai, Lily. (2007). *Accountability without Democracy*. New York: Cambridge University Press.

UNCTAD. (2006). *World Investment Report*. New York: United Nations Conference on Trade and Development Publications.

UNCTAD. (2012). *World Investment Report*. New York: United Nations Conference on Trade and Development Publications.

Uzzi, Brian. (1996). "The Sources and Consequences of Embeddedness for the Economic Performance of Organizations: The Network Effect." *American Sociological Review*, 61(4), 674–698.

Uzzi, Brian. (1997). "Social Structure and Competition in Interfirm Networks: The Paradox of Embeddedness." *Administrative Science Quarterly*, 42(1), 35–67.

Vaitsos, Constantine. (1974). *Intercountry Income Distribution and Transnational Enterprises*. Oxford: Clarendon Press.

van de Walle, Nicolas. (2001). *African Economics and the Politics of Permanent Crisis, 1979–1999*. New York: Cambridge University Press.

Varshney, A. (1996). "Mass Politics or Elite Politics? India's Economic Reforms in Comparative Perspective," presented at the conference, "India's Economic Reforms," Center for International Affairs/Harvard Institute for International Development, Harvard University, December 13–14.

Vernon, Raymond. (1971). *Sovereignty at Bay: The Multinational Spread of U.S. Enterprises*. New York: Basic Books.

Vogel, Ezra. (1989). *One Step Ahead in China: Guangdong under Reform*. Cambridge, MA: Harvard University Press.

Vogel, Ezra. (ed.). (2004). *Deng Xiaoping Shakes the World*. Norwalk, CT: EastBridge.

Vogel, Ezra. (2011). *Deng Xiaoping and the Transformation of China*. Cambridge, MA: Harvard University Press.

Wade, Robert. (1990). *Governing the Market: Economic Theory and the Role of Government in East Asian Industrialization*. Princeton, NJ: Princeton University Press.

Wade, Robert. (1998–1999). "The Coming Fight over Capital Flows." *Foreign Policy*, 113, 41–54.

Wade, Robert. (2004). "Is Globalization Reducing Poverty and Inequality?" *World Development*, 32(4), 567–589.

Walder, Andrew. (1995). "Local Governments as Industrial Firms: An Organizational Analysis of China's Transitional Economy." *American Journal of Sociology*, 101(2), 263–301.

Wallerstein, Immanuel. (1979). "Dependence in an Interdependent World: The Limited Possibility of Transformation within the Capitalist World-Economy," in I. Wallerstein (ed.), *The Capitalist World Economy*. New York: Cambridge University Press.

Wang, Gungwu. (2000). *The Overseas Chinese*. Cambridge, MA: Harvard University Press.

Wang, Gungwu. (2001). *Don't Leave Home: Migration and the Chinese*. Singapore: Times Academy Press

Wang, Gungwu. (2003). *China and the Chinese Overseas*, 7th edition. Singapore: Eastern University Press.

Wang, Hongying. (2001). *Weak State, Strong Networks: The Institutional Dynamics of Foreign Direct Investment in China*. New York: Oxford University Press.

Wang, Huiyao. (2012). *Globalizing China: The Influence, Strategies, and Success of Chinese Returnees*. Bingley, UK: Emerald Publisher.

Wang, Shengze. (2005). "Fahui qiaoxiang youshi, xianxing duiwai kaifang: Fujian" [Taking Advantage of Diaspora Communities, and Implementing Open Door Policy Earlier: Fujian]. *Deng xiaoping yu gaige kaifang [Deng Xiaoping and Reform and Openness]*. Beijing: CCP History Publisher.

Wang, Xu. (1999). "Mutual Empowerment of State and Society: Its Nature, Conditions, Mechanisms, and Limits." *Comparative Politics*, 31(2), 231–249.

Wang, Z., and S. Wei. (2008). "The Chinese Export Bundles." *ICIER Working Paper*, no. 226.

Wariavwalla, B. (1988). "India in 1987: Democracy on Trial." *Asian Survey*, 28(2), 119–125.

Wariavwalla, Bharat. (1989). "India in 1988: Drift, Disarray, or Pattern?" *Asian Survey*, 29(2), 189–198.

Weidenbaum, Murray, and Samuel Hughes. (1995). *The Bamboo Network: How Expatriate Chinese Entrepreneurs Are Creating a New Economic Superpower in Asia*. New York: Martin Kessler Books.

Weingast, Barry. (1995). "The Economic Role of Political Institutions: Market-Preserving Federalism and Economic Development." *Journal of Law, Economics, and Organization* 11, 1–31.

Welch, Jack. (2001). *Jack, Straight from the Gut*. New York: Warner Business Books.

Weyland, Kurt. (2009). "The Diffusion of Revolution: 1948 in Europe and in Latin America." *International Organization*, 63(3), 391–423.

White, Lynn. (1998). *Unstately Power*. Armonk, NY: M. E. Sharpe.

Williams, John. (1989). "What Washington Means by Policy Reform?" in John Williams (ed.), *Latin America Adjustment*, chapter 2. Washington: Institute for International Economics. http://www.iie.com/publications/papers/paper.cfm?researchid=486. Accessed August, 2006.

Williamson, John. (2002). *Delivering Debt Relief*. Washington, DC: Center for Global Development.

Williams, John. (2012). "Is 'Beijing Consensus' Now Dominant?" *Asian Policy*, 13, 1–16.

Woo-Cumings, Meredith. (1999). *The Developmental State*. Ithaca, NY: Cornell University Press.

Woods, Ngaire. (2006). *The Globalizers: The IMF, World Bank, and Their Borrowers*. Ithaca, NY: Cornell University Press.

World Bank. (2002). *Global Development Finance Report*. Washington, DC: World Bank.

Wu, Heng. (1999). "Tang Xiangqian: The First to Invest in China." *Chinese World*, 10, 58–61.

Xi, Wen, and L. Shan. (1996). "Guanyu quanzhou guoyou qiye yu Xianggang Zhongce gongsi de shizheng fenxi" [The Study of Quanzhou SOEs and China Strategy Joint Venture Project]. *Jingji cankao [Economic References]*, Jan 24, 17–29.

Xiang, Biao. (2006). *Global "Body Shopping": An Indian Labor System in International Information Technology Industry*. Princeton, NJ: Princeton University Press.

Xiao, C. E. (2006). *Zhonggong gaige guanjian renwu [Key Figures in China's Reform]*. Hong Kong: Xia Fei er Publisher.

Xiao, Donglian. (2005). "1978–1984 nian Zhongguo jingji tizhi gaige silu de yanjin" [Reformist Thinking of China's Economic System, 1978–1984]. *Deng xiaoping yu gaige kaifang [Deng Xiaoping and Reform and Openness]*. Beijing: CCP History Publisher.

Yamaguchi, Kazuo. (1996). "Power in Networks of Substitutable and Complementary Exchange Relations: A Rational-Choice Model and an Analysis of Power Centralization." *American Sociological Review*, 61(2), 308–332.

Yang, Dali. (1994). "Dui 'binweilun' de jidian fanbo" [Some Points in Refutation of the 'thesis of proximate crisis']. *Ershiyi shi ji [Twenty-First Century]*, 2, 15–18.

Yang, Dali. (1997). *Beyond Beijing: Liberalization and Regions in China*. London: Routledge

Yang, Dali. (2004). *Remaking the Chinese Leviathan: Market Transition and the Politics of Governance in China*. Stanford, CA: Stanford University Press.

Ye, Min. (2009). "Policy Learning or Diffusion: How China Opened to Foreign Direct Investment?" *Journal of East Asian Studies*, 9(3), 339–432.

Yeung, Henry. (1997). "Business Networks and Transnational Corporations." *Economic Geography*, 73(1), 1–25.

Yeung, Y., and X. Hu. (eds.). (1992). *China's Coastal Cities: Catalysts for Modernization*. Honolulu: University of Hawaii Press.

Yu, G. (2008). "Zhuiyi shiyi jie sanzhong quanhui qian de zhongyang gongzuo huiyi" [Remembering the Central Committee Work Conference before the Third Plenum of the Eleventh Party Congress], in Zheng Hui (ed.), *Zhongguo mingyun da jueze [The Fateful Turning Point of the PRC]*, China: Shenzhen baoye jitao chubanshe.

Yu, J., and Z. Yang. (eds.). (2004). *Deng Xiaoping jiaowang shilu [Records of Interacting with Deng Xiaoping]*. Chengdu: Sichuan People's Publisher.

Yu, X. (2000) *Deng Xiaoping yu Bao Yugang [Deng Xiaoping and Y. K. Pao]*. Beijing: Chinese Cultural Publisher.

Zhang, S. (2005). "Cong zhongyang gongzuo huiyi dao shiyi jie sanzhong quanhui" [From the Central Committee Meeting to the Third Plenum of Third NPC], in *Deng xiaoping yu gaige kaifang [Deng Xiaoping and China's Reform and Openness]*. Beijing: CCP History Publisher.

Zhang, X. (2000). *zhongguo gaoceng zhinang (I) [Chinese Top Level Advisors to Policy Making]*. Beijing: Jinghua chubanshe.

Zhao, Litao, and Jinjing Zhu. (2009). "China Attracting Global Talent: Central and Local Initiatives." *China: An International Journal*, 7(2), 323–336.

Zhao, Qizheng. (2008) *Pudong luoji [The Logic of Pudong New Area]*. Shanghai: Sanlian Publisher.

Zhao, Ziyang. (2009). *Prisoner of the State*. New York: Simon and Schuster.

Zheng, Y. (2006). *Duo chong wangluo de shentou yu kuozhang [Multiple Networks' Mutual Penetration and Expansion]*. Beijing: World Knowledge Publisher.

Zheng, Yongnian. (2004). *Globalization and State Transformation in China*. New York: Cambridge University Press.

Zheng, Yongnian. (2013). "China's Politics: New Leadership Emerge from a Tumultuous Environment." *East Asia Policy*, 5(1), 5–13.

Zheng, Yu. (2009) *Incentives and Commitment*. Paper presented at International Studies Association, Annual convention, February 28–March 3, 2009, New York.

Zhonggong zhongyang dangshi yanjiushi (ed.). (2005). *Deng Xiaoping yu gaige kaifang de qibu [Deng Xiaoping and the Start of Reform and Openness]*. Beijing: CCP History Publisher.

Zhonggong zhongyang wenxian yanjiushi (ed.). (2004). *Deng Xiaoping nianpu, 1975–1997* [*Deng Xiaoping Chronology, 1975–1997*]. Beijing: Zhongyang wenxian chubanshe.

Zhou, Bo. (2008). *Gan wei tianxia xian [To be the First]*. Shanghai: People's Publisher.

Zweig, David. (2002). *Internationalizing China: Domestic Interests and Global Linkages*. Ithaca, NY: Cornell University Press.

Zysman, John. (1983). *Governments, Markets, and Growth: Financial Systems and the Politics of Industrial Change*. Ithaca, NY: Cornell University Press.

Index